a reader's guide to
JOSEPH CONRAD

a reader's guide to

JOSEPH CONRAD

REVISED EDITION

by Frederick R. Karl

SYRACUSE UNIVERSITY PRESS

First Syracuse University Press Edition 1997

97 98 99 00 01 02   6 5 4 3 2 1

Originally published in 1960. Reprinted by arrangement with Farrar, Straus & Giroux.

The paper used in this publication meets the minimum requirements of American National Standard for Information Sciences—Permanence of Paper for Printed Library Materials, ANSI Z39.48-1984. ∞™

Library of Congress Cataloging-in-Publication Data

Karl, Frederick Robert, 1927–
    A reader's guide to Joseph Conrad / by Frederick R. Karl. — Rev.
  ed., 1st Syracuse University Press ed.
       p.   cm.
    Originally published : Rev. ed. New York : Farrar, Straus & Giroux,
  [1969]
    Includes bibliographical references (p.   ) and index.
    ISBN 0-8156-0489-0 (pbk. : alk. paper)
    1. Conrad, Joseph, 1857–1924—Handbooks, manuals, etc.
    2. Adventure stories, English—Handbooks, manuals, etc.
    3. Political fiction, English—Handbooks, manuals, etc.   I. Title.
PR6005. 04Z76   1997
823'.912—dc21   97-21260

For Dolores

Acknowledgments

The author gratefully acknowledges use of copyrighted material from the following publishers and publications:

From the Kent Edition of Joseph Conrad's works, and JOSEPH CONRAD: LIFE AND LETTERS by G. Jean-Aubry, to Doubleday & Company, J. M. Dent & Sons, Ltd., and the Trustees of the Joseph Conrad Estate.

From "The Rise and Fall of UNDER WESTERN EYES," reprinted from NINETEENTH-CENTURY FICTION, XIII, No. 4, to the University of California Press.

From "Conrad's Stein: The Destructive Element," reprinted from TWENTIETH CENTURY LITERATURE, III, No. 4, to Alan Swallow.

From "The Significance of the Revisions in the Early Versions of *Nostromo*," reprinted from MODERN FICTION STUDIES, V, No. 2, to the Purdue Research Foundation.

From "Joseph Conrad: A *fin de siècle* Novelist—A Study in Style and Method," reprinted from THE LITERARY REVIEW, II, No. 4, to Fairleigh Dickinson University.

Also, the author wishes to thank Mr. William McCarthy and the Rosenbach Company of Philadelphia for permission to quote from the manuscript of NOSTROMO.

Contents

a reader's guide to
JOSEPH CONRAD

Introduction

Now, the moral side of an industry, productive or unproductive, the redeeming and ideal aspect of this bread-winning, is the attainment and preservation of the highest possible skill on the part of the craftsman. Such skill, the skill of technique, is more than honesty; it is something wider, embracing honesty and grace and rule in an elevated and clear sentiment, not altogether utilitarian, which may be called the honour of labour. It is made up of accumulated tradition, kept alive by individual pride, rendered exact by professional opinion, and, like the higher arts, it is spurred on and sustained by discriminating praise.

Joseph Conrad,
The Mirror of the Sea

In answer to a query from the *Chicago Tribune*, F. Scott Fitzgerald compiled a list of what were in his estimate the ten most important novels of all time; in his remarks he pointed to Conrad's *Nostromo* as "the greatest novel since 'Vanity Fair' (possibly excluding 'Madame Bovary')." The same author, during a conversation with John Galsworthy, remarked that Joseph Conrad, along with Galsworthy himself and Anatole France, were the three living writers he admired most. In a like manner, Ernest Hemingway, writing in 1924, paid his tribute to Conrad: "If I knew that by grinding Mr. [T. S.] Eliot into a fine dry powder and sprinkling that powder over Mr. Conrad's grave Mr. Conrad would shortly appear, looking very annoyed at the forced return, and commence writing,

I would leave for London early tomorrow with a sausage grinder."

But despite this indiscriminate praise from Fitzgerald and Hemingway, as well as more temperate praise from many lesser authors, Conrad's reputation fell after his death in 1924. His work was pushed into the background by the appearance of a new generation of writers, by Joyce and Virginia Woolf, by the young Auden and Spender, by the Freudians and Jungians, and by literary innovators like the surrealists. Passing into partial oblivion along with Meredith and other late Victorians, Conrad was hardly considered a subject of discussion or a serious literary force with which to reckon; he was not controversial like Joyce and Yeats, nor a writer who gained violent partisans like Hemingway and Faulkner. For many years, *Lord Jim*—with possibly "Heart of Darkness" and "The Secret Sharer"—constituted the principal and almost sole extent of his fame. Comment, it is true, appeared from his admirers, but their observations, with the exception of Ford Madox Ford's, were often more idolatrous than constructive. The new sophisticated generation had effectively relegated Conrad's work to the world of the nineteenth century, as old-fashioned and obsolete as the novels of Thackeray, Meredith, and Trollope, and far removed indeed from the important issues of the day.

Beginning in the late 1930's, however, Conrad emerged from neglect, as essays by David Daiches, Morton Dauwen Zabel, and others pointed out the significance of his themes for twentieth-century literature; and lengthier works, especially by Albert Guerard, Jr. (in 1947) and Walter F. Wright (in 1949) analyzed Conrad's place in modern letters. In England itself, V. S. Pritchett (in *The Living Novel*, 1946) and F. R. Leavis (in *The Great Tradition*, 1948) discussed Conrad's work in a framework of twentieth-century ideas. Meanwhile in France, where André Gide had early readied the French literary world for Conrad's work, a steady stream of books, essays, and dissertations on his life and fiction continued to be published. In the 1950's, the centennial anniversary of his birth increased the flow of Conrad studies, until, next to Joyce and perhaps Faulkner, he is at present the most discussed modern author writing in English.

More recent criticism has split, seemingly, into two types: political interpretation and psychological analysis. Of the former, the most important has been Zdzisław Najder's *Conrad's Polish Background: Letters to and from Polish Friends* (1964); Eloise Knapp Hay's *The Political Novels of Joseph Conrad* (1963) and Avrom Fleishman's *Conrad's Politics: Community and Anarchy in the Fiction of Joseph Conrad* (1967), although less authoritative, are also valuable correctives to earlier criticism and interpretations. But it is clearly psychological analysis, drawing chiefly on Freudian techniques, which has provided the major excitement and principal direction. Albert Guerard's *Conrad the Novelist* (1958), Thomas Moser's *Conrad: Achievement and Decline* (1957), and Dr. Bernard Meyer's *Joseph Conrad: A Psychoanalytic Biography* (1967) see Conrad's work as darkly symbolistic, full of personal nightmare, and blended with his own psychological needs. The publication in the 1970's of the *Collected Letters*, edited by Frederick R. Karl and Zdzisław Najder, will reinforce this view.

This book is an extended effort to analyze Conrad's work and to relate it to twentieth-century fiction as it has been developed principally by Gide, Proust, Lawrence, Joyce, Virginia Woolf, and Faulkner. In discussing Conrad's literary ideas, I have especially emphasized his techniques as they work with these ideas, for Conrad was a persistent experimenter in the form of the novel, although not strictly an innovator. In common with many Victorians and post-Victorians, he drew his literary methods from writers as disparate as Sterne, Richardson, Dostoyevsky, Dickens, Flaubert, and James, among others. The devices Conrad resorted to—such as character doubles, thematic recurrences, parallel situations, shifts in narrative sequences, central narrators, recurring symbols—had all been used by his predecessors. But even James, who envisaged a new type of novel, and Flaubert, who fathered many modern ideas and attitudes, did not rework the material of the novel as Conrad did. Exacting workers, visionaries to some extent, but traditionalists nonetheless, Flaubert and James opened up areas that Conrad was to explore thoroughly, though perhaps not so felicitously.

Conrad, it must be granted, knew far more about literature than he is generally given credit for. His early years devoted to land and sea adventures left time for reading and meditation; he readily admitted in *A Personal Record,* however, that sea life was not the best training for a life of writing.[1] Nevertheless, he did not spring from a ship into the world of letters and then without further preparation establish himself as an accomplished novelist and an extraordinary technician. He was not a primitive. He apprenticed himself to writing as he had earlier to sailing before becoming a master seaman. Those, like F. R. Leavis, who suggest that Conrad's basic intentions and intuitions were simple—who say that ". . . for all his sophistication, [Conrad] exhibits a certain simplicity of outlook and attitude."—ignore the fact that his fiction at its best contains a complicated and varied view of the world. When he started to write *Almayer's Folly* in 1889, at the age of 32,

[1] Henceforth, all my references in Conrad's work will be to the Kent Edition, Doubleday, Page & Co., 1925.

Conrad knew the traditions of the novel and saw that late nineteenth-century fiction needed fresh ideas and a new approach.

It was Conrad's belief that not only authorship but every act of man can be performed skillfully; every act—whether the loading of a ship or the rigging of a shroud to the mast—if it is performed with love and care has in it potentialities for the craftsman. It is this love and care previously bestowed on sailing that Conrad transferred to writing. In a phrase from Boethius—". . . for this miracle or this wonder troubleth me gretly"—which stands at the head of the autobiographical *The Mirror of the Sea*, there is an evident equation of the miracle of the sea with the wonder of art. Still, Conrad's double devotion to the sea and to writing contained moments of doubt and soul-searching as well as moments of great love and confidence. As John Dozier Gordan wrote in his valuable study of the early Conrad:

> A slow growth from amateur to professional was character-istic of Conrad in both his careers. Until he was forced by misadventures to leave the Mediterranean, he was an ama-teur seaman. Until he was forced to accept his dependence on writing, he was an amateur writer. But once the neces-sary stimulus moved him, he had the power to achieve his highest aim, to become a master seaman and a master novel-ist.

I I

When Stein in *Lord Jim* spoke about the necessity of im-mersing oneself in the destructive element of life, he was not only pointing the way for the redemption of modern common man but also for that of the modern artist. To plunge into life while endeavoring to interpret it, is the ordeal every serious artist must face, an ordeal that Conrad fully recognized in the Preface to *The Nigger of the "Narcissus."* It is not unusual that Conrad should have taken literature seriously and conformed to exacting standards, for his entire life had been a preparation for serious trial. His personality was earnest and his nature dogmatic; as his letters testify, he could not tolerate any nonsense in art or life. His serious standards were acquired as a youth; the broad range of his career reflects a man who faced up to reality and immersed himself thoroughly in life.

Conrad's father, Apollo Korzeniowski, was a scholar, an intellectual, a man whose strong principles became translated into revolutionary action, a patriotic idealist whose beliefs forced him, along with his wife and young child, from Poland into exile in Russia. Aside from his political activities, Apollo Korzeniowski had a lively interest in French and English literature, ably translating Victor Hugo, Alfred de Vigny, Shakespeare, and Dickens into Polish. Less than four years after Conrad's birth on December 3, 1857,[2] Apollo (in May 1861) came to Warsaw to start a literary journal, to be called the *Fortnightly Review.* Ostensibly, Apollo's activities in Warsaw were literary, but his real interests were political, specifically to increase resistance to Russian oppression, with the final aim of winning back Polish independence. He helped organize the secret National Committee, which met frequently in his own home. But even before the famous 1863 insurrection in Warsaw against Russian rule, he was

---

[2] At Berdyczów or Berdichev in Podolia (the Ukraine), baptized Józef Teodor Konrad Korzeniowski (coat of arms Nałęcz). Józef, after his maternal grandfather; Teodor, after his paternal grandfather; Konrad, after two heroes in Adam Mickiewicz's poems, *Konrad Wallenstein* (1827) and *Dziady* (1832).

arrested and condemned to exile. Conrad's mother, the former Evelina (or Ewa) Bobrowska, was a well-educated and sensitive woman who fully entered into her husband's interests and surely aided in his political activities. Co-accused of conspiracy, she was imprisoned, then with young Conrad followed Apollo into exile (on May 8, 1862) in Perm Province, not far from the Ural Mountains. Once in exile, Mme. Korzeniowski, frail, consumptive, and poverty-stricken, became steadily weaker and died less than three years later at the age of thirty-two.

Apollo himself in these years was a curious mixture of the romantic, practical revolutionary, landed nobleman, and poet. Many of the characteristics we find in the older Conrad, qualities both personal and political, can be discovered in his father. In many respects, Apollo was wholly admirable, a man ready to forgo personal glory for the greater good of an oppressed Poland. On the other hand, his activities against the Russian behemoth must have seemed foolhardy when Conrad looked back in retrospect at his checkered childhood. The dislocation, isolation, and discontinuity in his early life he, most certainly, attributed to his father's excessive zeal. Conrad's own political ambivalence—his predilection for anarchy and alienation co-existing with his desire for traditional values and social commitment—appears based on the divisions which began with Apollo's exile in 1862.

Without sufficient money to support himself or the young Joseph, Apollo was almost wholly dependent upon his less than sympathetic brother-in-law, Thaddeus Bobrowski. He retained, however, through all his misfortunes a love of literature. At this time he translated *The Two Gentlemen of Verona* and Victor Hugo's *Travailleurs de la Mer* into Polish. Removed from politics and immersed in literary work, yet broken in health and disappointed by his failures, Apollo died in Cracow in 1869, only eight years after he had arrived in Warsaw as an active partisan against the Czar. The funeral brought forth a huge display of patriotism on the part of those who remembered Apollo's political activities. The young Conrad, living in his father's strange world of broken careers, had occupied his lively imagination with books, which were almost his sole companions. Certainly a large part of Conrad's later emphasis on individual responsibility and his own strict self-control can be traced to his lonely, somewhat morbid childhood.

At twelve, Conrad was enrolled at St. Anne's Secondary School in Cracow, where he would have studied classics and German, but probably he never attended, another indication of the disruption in his early life. By this time, he was familiar with French, in which he became fluent in his later years. From 1870 to 1874, his studies were supervised by Adam Marek Pulman, a student at the University of Cracow. The discontinuity and irregularity of his schooling and family were beginning to tell on his health. He suffered from migraine headaches, and his excessive nervousness, according to Zdzisław Najder, may have indicated an epileptic condition. In his more mature years, Dr. Bernard Meyer tells us, Conrad suffered from an incurable disease of the joints. It is possible to speculate that his detestation of Dostoyevsky was partially based on the kinship he sensed with the Russian, extending even to their common physical ailment of epilepsy, although in Conrad the disease came to be manifest chiefly as nervous disorders or fits, without the classic symptoms.

It was during these years that Conrad confided to his uncle-guardian, Thaddeus Bobrowski, that he wanted to go to sea. All attempts to dissuade him were futile. No doubt his early love for the sea was a literary love, for in his father's personal library he had read a wide selection of sea and travel books. He became acquainted with the sea stories of James Fenimore Cooper, perhaps those of Marryat, as well as James Bruce's *Travels*, David Livingstone's journeys to South Africa, Sir Leopold McClintock's voyage to the Arctic, Hugo's *Travailleurs de la Mer* (which he knew in his father's proofs), and Mungo Park's *Travels in Africa*. Exile also enabled him to escape conscription into the Russian army. Certainly the most important reason for his decision was a need to escape confinement, a need, demonstrated in so many of his protagonists, to seek personal meanings, and a sea career offered one way. Conrad was early possessed by the desire to experience other countries. There is the now familiar and perhaps apocryphal story of his putting his finger on a blank space in a map of Africa and saying, "When I grow up I shall go *there.*" The *there* was the Belgian Congo, and his trip became the basis of "Heart of Darkness" and a major turning point in his life.

On October 14, 1874, two months before his seventeenth birthday, Conrad left for Marseilles and a sea career, armed with a few introductions and a small monthly allowance from his reluctant uncle. Shipping out from Marseilles, Conrad voyaged on French ships to the West Indies and to Central and South America; the frail factual basis of *Nostromo* was formed here, and it was on the *Saint-Antoine* heading for South America that he had his first experience with gun-running. Between voyages he found no difficulties in entering Marseilles café life. To his uncle's consternation, he spent his allowance liberally and soon went into debt. Most of his time was passed along the docks with fellow sailors, although in his more serious moments he attended performances of the operas of Rossini, Verdi, and Meyerbeer. Conrad also traveled in higher circles; in the salon of M. Delestang, the banker with whom he had been given credit, Conrad met several Royalists, and these meetings led to his smuggling activities on behalf of the Carlist cause, activities which he related in *The Arrow of Gold* (1919).[3] It was also here, his friend and biographer, G. Jean-Aubry, tells us, that he met a mysterious girl, the Rita de Lastaola of *The Arrow of Gold,* with whom he had a brief love affair. Reputedly the former mistress of Don Carlos himself, Rita was much sought after, particularly by a southern American gentleman, the Blunt of the same novel. Conrad, conceiving of himself as a romantic hero, as G. Jean-Aubry relates the story, fought a pistol duel with Blunt and was seriously wounded. A more recent biographer, Jocelyn Baines, argues persuasively, however, that Conrad's serious wound was not the result of a duel but of an attempted suicide because of gambling debts.[4] According to Baines, the duel was an invention of Conrad's and Thaddeus Bobrowski's to cover the suicide attempt, which was of course a mortal sin for a

[3] See also the section called "The *Tremolino*" in *The Mirror of the Sea.*
[4] The first indication comes in the "Document" compiled by Conrad's maternal uncle, Tadeusz (Thaddeus) Bobrowski. The entry for February 1878 reads, in part: ". . . I got news from Mr. Fecht that you [Conrad] had shot yourself." Later, in a letter to Conrad (for 26 June/8 July 1878), Uncle Tadeusz reproaches his nephew: "You were idling for nearly a whole year—you fell into debt, you deliberately shot yourself. . . ." Even more conclusively, Tadeusz Bobrowski wrote to his friend Stefan Buszczyński (12/24 March 1879): ". . . wishing to improve his finances, [Conrad] tries his luck in Monte Carlo and loses the 800 fr. he had borrowed. Having managed his affairs so excellently he returns to Marseilles and one fine evening invites his friend the creditor to tea, and before his arrival attempts to take his life with a revolver. (Let this detail remain between us, as I have been telling everyone that he was wounded in a duel. From you I neither wish to nor should keep it a secret.) The bullet goes durch [through] and durch near his heart without damaging any vital organ." (The documents above are translated by Zdzisław Najder in his *Conrad's Polish Background;* London: Oxford University Press, 1964.)

Catholic as well as a great embarrassment for his family. In any case, after his recovery, he saw no more of Rita and ended his Marseilles sojourn. Having spent four years in the French merchant service, four years in which he drifted from one berth to another with no idea of advancement, Conrad shipped out on the English steamer, the *Mavis,* on April 24, 1878, bound for Constantinople.

On the return of the *Mavis* to Lowestoft, Conrad first stepped on English soil, hardly understanding a word of the language. Little past his twentieth birthday, he decided, as he points out in *A Personal Record,* that if he was to be a seaman, he would be an English seaman and no other. It was, he said, "a matter of deliberate choice." After two years, in 1880, he passed his examination for third mate, and subsequently in 1883 and 1886, for mate and master. Two years later—and ten after entering the English merchant service—he had his first command, the *Otago,* from January, 1888, to March, 1889.

Just when Conrad started to write is not clear. In 1886, he began what is generally considered to be his first piece of fiction, a short story, "The Black Mate," unsuccessfully submitted for a prize competition in *Tit-Bits.* In the years 1887-1888, he perhaps kept a diary while at sea, just as he later kept a Congo diary. But when he began his first novel, *Almayer's Folly,* in 1889, he was still a seaman and by no means a dedicated writer. Conrad himself wrote in *A Personal Record:*

> The conception of a planned book was entirely outside my mental range when I sat down to write; the ambition of being an author had never turned up amongst these gracious imaginary existences one creates fondly for oneself at times in the stillness and immobility of a daydream.

It was soon after Conrad had begun *Almayer's Folly*

that he was designated captain of a Congo steamer (in late 1889), an expedition (June 13-Dec. 1890) into Africa that became the source for "Heart of Darkness," and perhaps had as much effect on maturing his outlook as the trip to the Sakhalin Islands had on Chekov's. The Congo experience, Jean-Aubry and all future biographers have believed, turned Conrad from the sea to a literary career. Broken in health by malarial fever and a disease of the joints, but impressed by the desolation and base meaninglessness of what he had seen, he continued to write while recuperating. Moral, physical, and psychological breakdown, the focal point of his Congo adventure, was to become the major theme of his fiction.

When his health permitted, he returned to sea on the *Torrens* until July 26, 1893. It was as chief of the *Torrens* that Conrad first met John Galsworthy, and with this meeting their close friendship began. It was on the same ship that Conrad, on his last voyage, showed the manuscript of *Almayer's Folly* to a young Cantabrigian, W. H. Jacques, who encouraged him to finish the novel. When Conrad left the *Torrens*, he was never to go to sea again, although it was not for lack of trying.[5] *Almayer's Folly*,

---

[5] A record of Conrad's sea career follows:

Mont-Blanc, from Marseilles to West Indies, June 23, 1875–Dec. 25, 1875, as apprentice; *Saint-Antoine*, from Marseilles to South America, July 8, 1876–Feb. 15, 1877, as steward and junior officer; *Tremolino*, gunrunner from Marseilles to Spanish coast, March–Dec. 1877, Dominic Cervoni as captain; *Mavis*, from Marseilles to Sea of Azov, back to Lowestoft, England, April 24, 1878–June 18, 1878, as ordinary seaman; *Skimmer of the Sea*, from Lowestoft and Newcastle, round-trip, July 11, 1878–Sept. 23, 1878, as ordinary seaman; *Duke of Sutherland*, from London to Australia, Oct. 15, 1878–Oct. 19, 1879, as ordinary seaman; *Europa*, from London to Mediterranean ports, Dec. 12, 1879–Jan. 30, 1880, as ordinary seaman; *Loch Etive*, from London to Sydney, Australia, Nov. 24, 1880–April 24, 1881, as third mate; *Annie Frost*, Conrad injured, served for eight days as third mate, June 5–13, 1881; *Palestine*, from London to Far East, Sept. 21, 1881–March 15, 1883, as second mate; *Riversdale*, from meanwhile, was finished and submitted to the publisher T. Fisher Unwin on July 4, 1894, where Edward Garnett, then a young publisher's reader, was greatly impressed with the manuscript. The novel was accepted, and Conrad, encouraged by Garnett, soon turned to writing another. While the evidence shows that Conrad was trying to obtain a command as late as September, 1898, he nevertheless continued to turn out nearly a volume a year for the next thirteen years. His entry into professional writing appears to have been a decision similar to the one he made when he chose a sea career: the need to seek his own valuation apart from the ties a man normally experiences.

Conrad's writing life extended for twenty-nine years, from 1895 until his death in 1924[6]; during this time he wrote thirty-one volumes of novels, short stories, essays, and plays, in addition to over 3,000 letters. Even with growing popularity, he remained, nevertheless, isolated

---

London to Madras, India, Sept. 13, 1883–April 17, 1884, as second mate; *Narcissus*, from Bombay, India, to Dunkirk, June 3, 1884–Oct. 16, 1884, as second mate; *Tilkhurst*, from Hull to Singapore and Calcutta, April 27, 1885–June 17, 1886, as second mate; *Highland Forest*, from Amsterdam to Java, Feb. 1887–July 1, 1887, as first mate; *Vidar*, from Singapore to Borneo, Aug. 22, 1887–Jan. 5, 1888, as chief mate; *Otago*, from Bangkok to Sydney, Feb. 9, 1888–May 7, 1888, also for several months in Australian ports, as master; *Roi des Belges*, on Congo River, Aug. 4, 1890–Sept. 14, 1890, as first mate and master; *Torrens*, from London to Australia, several passages, Nov. 20, 1891–Oct. 17, 1893, as first mate; *Adowa*: Conrad signed on as second mate in Nov. 1893, but never sailed.
[6] In the year of Conrad's death, another Pole, Wladyslaw Reymont, won the Nobel Prize for literature. Conrad was, however, offered a knighthood by Prime Minister Ramsay MacDonald, an honor which he declined for personal reasons. Najder argues that Conrad refused the knighthood because he was already a nobleman. I sense in his refusal a feeling of condescension toward MacDonald and a disdain for formal honors. He may even have recalled Matthew Arnold's lines in "Growing Old": "It is—last stage of all— / When we are frozen up within, and quite / The phantom of ourselves, / To hear the world applaud the hollow ghost / Which blamed the living man."

from many of the principal writers and movements. He was an intellectual writer rather than an intellectual. For a major novelist, his circle of friends, although intelligent and devoted, was curiously limited to those of the old guard. His tastes tended to be conservative and safe. There were of course some exceptions—H. G. Wells and Henry James among them—but they were not in the circle in the same sense as Edward Garnett, R. B. Cunninghame Graham, John Galsworthy, W. H. Hudson, Hugh Clifford, or Edmund Gosse. Conrad seemed almost entirely unaware of Freud's work and the new advances in science, and entirely ignorant of older, established writers like Meredith and Hardy or modernists like Joyce, Lawrence, Virginia Woolf, and other experimenters in the novel whose careers paralleled his own. Among contemporary European authors of the first rank, he knew only the work of Gide and Proust.

Certain questions about Conrad's personal life, although interesting to the biographer, must perhaps always remain partially unanswered or open only to conjecture: for example, exactly why he began to write in English and not in French or Polish, why he first turned to the sea and then gave it up for writing, why he was antagonistic to his father's politics, and why, once famous, he remained almost completely detached from the chief currents of English intellectual life. At the beginning of Conrad's literary career, there was, perhaps, little more than force of will and an ability to draw upon all sources and all experiences. His great power, like George Eliot's, lay in his ability to fashion strength of will into moral idea; and his life's work was devoted to "seeing" the moral idea from as many aspects as possible, until the idea became, as it were, the thing itself. Possibly, Conrad, already an exile in a strange country, perceived early that only in this area could he realize his talent, and any departure from it, he found, made him uneasy and unsure of himself.

Writing to Cunninghame Graham about Kipling, Conrad revealed just how frail his own hold on art was:

> Mr Kipling has the wisdom of the passing generations—and holds it in perfect sincerity. Some of his work is of impeccable form and because of that *little* thing he shall sojourn in Hell only a very short while. He squints with the rest of his excellent sort. It is a beautiful squint; it is an useful squint. And—after all—perhaps he sees around the corner? And suppose Truth is just around the corner like the elusive and useless loafer it is? I can't tell. No one can tell. It is impossible to know. It is impossible to know anything tho' it is possible to believe a thing or two. (Aug. 5, 1897, Dartmouth U. Libr.)

I I I

The common claim that the modern novel has approached (but not reached) the state of lyric poetry gains credence when we observe that as an ever-developing genre the novel in many of its aspects has attained the conscious refinements of poetic form. Because of their detail and their subtle changes in tone, the novels of Lawrence, Virginia Woolf, Joyce, and Faulkner call for the same close attention that readers have often brought only to poetry; and it is this reliance on the small and the seemingly casual as organic elements of the novel that we find also in the work of Flaubert, James, and Conrad.[7]

[7] Cf. Ralph Freedman (*The Lyrical Novel*, 1963): "Whatever its difficulties, the lyrical novel developed a new orientation toward experience: internal without being necessarily subjective; reflective without being essayistic; pictorial or musical without abandoning the narrative framework

Modern poetical criticism is a response to the demands a complex poem makes upon the reader; and more recently a new type of criticism that is aware of the importance of detail and form has begun to grow around the novel. This type of criticism must of course guard against the claim that the most complicated novel or the most "written" novel is necessarily the most significant. And while it should be recognized that no single critical approach is the whole answer, the new criticism of the novel does demonstrate that certain novels need attentive and close readings before they yield their meanings.

Because several of Conrad's major works fall into this category, during my discussions of his fiction I shall frequently refer to his use, among other things, of major and minor symbols, terms which must be defined carefully lest the symbol be mistaken for the whole work and Conrad be thought of solely as the author of symbolic novels. The importance of symbols in Conrad is no different from that in any writer who uses them artistically; symbols obviously are of little value unless they are necessary structurally, precisely as any other device is irrelevant unless organic. Symbols are simply the means through which an author chooses to express his personal vision. To understand these symbols is to understand the author and to be able to evaluate, at least in part, the degree of his seriousness and attention to detail.

In a pioneering article on Conrad, Morton D. Zabel commented on the power of these symbols:

> Every time we hear anew of Jim's jump from the boat into the "everlasting black hole" of his remorse, every time the bark of Flora's dog sounds again, every reappearance of

---

of the novel" (p. 279). Freedman writes particularly of Hesse, Gide, and Virginia Woolf.

Mrs. Schomberg's shawl, means that the significance of these irrefutable facts is deepened in a fresh consciousness, a more intense vision, of the event.

With the exception of Jim's jump, the symbols Zabel mentions—Flora's dog (*Chance*) and Mrs. Schomberg's shawl (*Victory*)—are what I shall call minor symbols. To these one may add Miss Haldin's veil (*Under Western Eyes*), Rita's golden arrow (*The Arrow of Gold*), Lena's use of her voice (*Victory*), the statue of Spontini's "Flight of Youth" (*Under Western Eyes*), Lingard's ring (*The Rescue*), Aïssa's veil (*An Outcast of the Islands*), the statue of Rousseau (*Under Western Eyes*), and many others. A minor symbol, as I define it, has only situational importance; that is, it may recur for one or two (possibly more) scenes while relating the characters and their actions and making clearer certain aspects of the total situation. Although the minor symbol may soon disappear, it leaves behind reverberations which are indispensable in Conrad's conception of a given novel or story. If, for example, we take one, Miss Haldin's veil in *Under Western Eyes*, we can see that the veil works as a complement to her feelings toward Razumov: the initial raising of the veil by Miss Haldin is her way of opening her heart; when she drops the veil at her feet she means Razumov to open his heart to her; after she recognizes his guilt, her veil— like her feelings—lies dormant and still; Razumov's sudden seizing of the veil conveys his strong feelings for her, for after this he makes of it something of a fetish; and the veil finally becomes the covering for Razumov's journal in which he reveals his daily life since his act of betrayal. Through Conrad's use of the veil in relation to Razumov and Miss Haldin, a tangible object suggests a psychological comment; the veil is a minor symbol which gives greater intensity and drama to a significant scene, and its application, we soon realize, is little different from its use by Victorian or earlier novelists.

A major symbol, on the other hand, is not only important for the immediate situation but also provides a spine to the entire book or story. Such major symbols are, for example, Jim's jump from the *Patna* (*Lord Jim*), the silver of the mine (*Nostromo*), the ever-present city background of London (*The Secret Agent*), the pictures and books of the elder Heyst (*Victory*), and the Congo as it weaves in and out of "Heart of Darkness." These symbols reverberate to a far greater extent than do the minor symbols, and provide an all-important order for both the form and content of their respective books. As part of Conrad's personal doctrine, a sense of order was the sole way he could control aberrant individuality in his characters, an order which precluded that excessive egoism he saw as self-destructive.

In Conrad's literary doctrine, the use of a central major symbol could give that sense of calculated restriction which both he and Ford early recognized as necessary if anarchy in prose fiction were to be eliminated. In *Thus to Revisit*, Ford remarked that Conrad's search for a new form in the novel was an answer to the episodic formlessness of the nineteenth-century serialized novel. The novel in Conrad's hands, said Ford, was to get its unity from "one embroilment, one set of embarrassments, one human coil, one psychological progression." Conrad, Ford repeated, was successful in wedding technical factors to content in his fiction; in his literary and personal beliefs, in every form whatsoever, he eschewed anarchy.

Besides the major and minor symbols which run through Conrad's books, there is also what I shall call the central symbolic scene; for example, the cab ride through the London streets to the charity home (*The Secret Agent*),

Decoud and Nostromo on the lighter (*Nostromo*), Razumov's confession to Miss Haldin (*Under Western Eyes*), the scene in the Brussels Company Office ("Heart of Darkness"), Almayer in his begrimed office (*Almayer's Folly*), the scene between Lena and Heyst under his father's picture (*Victory*). These scenes, which have literal as well as metaphorical functions, bring together the major threads of the work and act as epitomes of the entire novel or story. The cab ride in *The Secret Agent*, for instance, symbolizes the grimness and meanness of a London scene which involves the inhumanity of innocent people to each other. This short scene comments dramatically on the human elements in the novel in a way that discourse alone could not. Through this scenic presentation which gave him a central focus for character and event, Conrad could, like Henry James before him, suggest his principal themes. Taken together with the major and minor symbols, the symbolic scene imparted order and outline, and most important of all allowed Conrad certain significant reference points as he tried to construct new forms in the novel.

Now, many years after his death, Conrad's emphasis upon structural subtleties and upon symbols and symbolic scenes has been widely recognized as of particular relevance to the twentieth-century novel; and his work has indirectly influenced many of this century's major novelists, although direct influences are almost impossible to establish. His realization that the novel needed new life and his willingness to experiment, together with his treatment of the genre as a profound and mature undertaking, gave new dimensions to what he thought was a fading late-Victorian form.

As we read Conrad's early letters, we see his repeated attempts to treat the novel seriously and to find for it a new form, precisely as James and Flaubert had before him. In a characteristic letter, this one to Galsworthy late in 1901, Conrad firmly chided his friend for a certain lack of fidelity of purpose in *The Man of Devon and Other Stories,* saying: ". . . you must preserve an attitude of perfect indifference . . . you seem, for their [the characters'] sake, to hug your conceptions of right and wrong too closely." (Nov. 11, 1901, original at Birmingham [England] U. Libr.) One must, in brief, be true to his vision and yet be objective and impersonal in his treatment. In the oft-quoted Preface to *The Nigger of the "Narcissus,"* Conrad insisted that no single formula and no single point of view are sufficient to give the detachment every work of art requires. Accordingly, all of Conrad's artistic devices, if they were to be listed categorically, would perhaps come together under the major classification of aesthetic distance or impersonality. One can see the central narrator, the doubling of characters, and the symbols themselves as ways of securing detachment for the author. This was part of Conrad's revolt against the relative formlessness of the Victorian novel.

An emphasis on impersonality may have social as well as literary ramifications, but in its literary aspects impersonality finds twentieth-century echoes in the work of Proust, Joyce, Hemingway, Camus, and Faulkner, among several others. Nevertheless, technical devices, no matter how ingeniously used, Conrad well realized, obviously are valuable only if they help convey exactly what the author means. Writing of Maupassant's fiction, which he greatly admired, Conrad praised the Frenchman's way of working: "He thinks sufficiently to concrete his fearless conclusions in illuminative instances. He renders them with that exact knowledge of the means and that absolute devotion to the aim of creating a true effect—which is art."

Conrad's own body of work carries several meanings,

some of which are singularly commonplace and some intrinsically as well as historically significant. The world of *Victory, The Secret Agent, Nostromo,* "Heart of Darkness," and *Under Western Eyes* is non-variable, true in Conrad's time and true now because the author was able to suggest a definition of universal values. The following chapters will show that many of Conrad's meanings and his ways of attaining them were in the forefront of the modernistic movement in fiction. Without possessing the flexible powers of language of Joyce, Virginia Woolf, or Faulkner and without originating a single new technique, Conrad was able through the arrangement of his material and the force of his vision to influence both directly and indirectly the forms of the novel after 1900.

When the passage of time erases literary boundary lines, Conrad, along with Joyce and Lawrence, will surely join with his European and American contemporaries, Mann, Proust, Gide, James, Kafka, and Faulkner, as worthy successors to the major nineteenth-century writers, all of whom helped the novel to bloom into a profound and serious art form.

chapter 1

The Working Aesthetic

Experience is never limited and it is never complete; it is
an immense sensibility, a kind of huge spider-web of the
finest silken threads suspended in the chamber of consciousness, and catching every air-borne particle in its tissue.

Henry James,
"The Art of Fiction"

He [the artist] speaks to our capacity for delight and wonder, to the sense of mystery surrounding our lives; to our
sense of pity, and beauty, and pain: to the latent feeling of
fellowship with all creation—to the subtle but invincible
conviction of solidarity that knits together the loneliness of
innumerable hearts, to the solidarity in dreams, in joy, in
sorrow, in aspirations, in illusions, in hope, in fear, which
binds men to each other, which binds together all humanity
—the dead to the living and the living to the unborn.

Joseph Conrad,
Preface to *The Nigger of the "Narcissus"*

Any examination of Conrad's attitude toward literature in general and toward his own work in particular must take into account the curious lack of consistency between his early statements—those found in his
literary essays, letters, and the Preface to *The Nigger of
the "Narcissus"*—and his later, and one would suppose
more mature, Author's Notes to each volume of his Collected Edition. Many critics have been tempted to seek
Conrad's aesthetic in these Notes, but the Notes prove,
upon examination in their context, to be among Conrad's

lesser accomplishments. Unlike his cicerone and master, Henry James, in his Prefaces to the New York Edition, Conrad conceived his Notes with his eye more on his reading public than on his art.

Henry James believed that his Prefaces had an interest and a body apart from any relation to his work and that they would prove to be a virtual *Poetica* of the novel. Both James' Prefaces as well as Conrad's Notes were written for Collected Editions that came late in their respective lives. James, however, came to this edition at the height of his power, soon after the publication of *The Wings of the Dove, The Ambassadors,* and *The Golden Bowl.* As these books were models of how the novel was to be written, it is likely that in the Prefaces James wanted to create, as a supplement, a Bible of criticism.

Conrad's Notes, on the contrary, came in a period of creative decline and show upon even cursory examination that as a self-critic he was not of James' stature. His was not a great critical mind and his is certainly not a criticism that can stand aside in separate distinction, as does Arnold's, Coleridge's, or some of Eliot's. His most trenchant remarks do not afford a profound insight into literature, but at their best, like a great many observations of James' and Eliot's, lead back only to himself, to his own way of conceiving and dramatizing experience. The comparison with James must therefore be made, for to the mature and professional Conrad, James was ever a model and an inspiration on how a thing should best be done; Conrad, in a letter to Galsworthy, speaks of James the short story writer:

> Technical perfection, unless there is some real glow to illumine and warm it from within, must necessarily be cold. I argue that in H. J. there is such a glow and not a dim one either. . . . The outlines are so clear, the figures so finished,

chiselled, carved and brought out that we exclaim—we, used to the shades of the contemporary fiction, to the more or less malformed shades—we exclaim—stone! Not at all. I say flesh and blood,—very perfectly presented—perhaps with too much perfection of *method*. (Feb. 11, 1899, Polish Libr.)

But once it is clear that Conrad recognized James as the more relentless tactician, it is equally evident that Conrad approached his Collected Edition in a spirit quite unlike James'.

James carefully pruned novels and stories from his canon, works which he judged unworthy of inclusion in the New York Edition. Conrad included everything he had written. Whereas James, although well over sixty, approached his edition in a spirit of strength and vigor, Conrad came to his with almost an air of lassitude; by now he too was close to sixty years old, having spent most of his literary career in an uphill struggle to meet expenses. One can almost be certain that Conrad, familiar as he was with James' work, was aware of the Prefaces, had read some of them, and was cognizant of their high intentions (letter to James, Dec. 12, 1908). But it is equally certain Conrad realized he lacked the type of mind required for sustained literary criticism. Having always disclaimed a formal critical faculty, he surrendered any idea of duplicating the Jamesian Prefaces. His approach was, instead, to the backgrounds of the novels, to the real-life models for his leading characters, to the geography and climate of the books rather than to their substance as art.

Conrad's Author's Notes were, then, almost weary for a major novelist intent on the seriousness of his craft. It is not, therefore, to these Notes to his Collected Edition that we must turn, but more suitably to his essays and letters and to his 1897 Preface to *The Nigger of the "Narcissus,"* to the early comments thrown out when he was still a vigorous novelist. For as Conrad's novels declined in power, his critical comments—as evidenced by the Notes—also manifested a loss of serious intent. The debility that marked his last ten years of creative work carried over into the Author's Notes written during the same period. It is necessary to return to the apprentice writer to seek his working aesthetic.

II

In a revealing letter to Edward Noble, a former seaman and now a writer also at the beginning of his career, Conrad spoke of his conception of fiction writing:

> You must squeeze out of yourself every sensation, every thought, every image—mercilessly, without reserve and without remorse: you must search the darkest corners of your heart, the most remote recesses of your brain—and you must search them for the image, for the glamour, for the right expression. And you must do it sincerely, at any cost.

Conrad's belief in his craft, his commitment to what he called the agonies of composition, his realization that a novel must be "fully written"—all these mark his early letters and suggest the anxieties that led to his best work. Mixed in with these anxieties are recurring statements by the hard-headed seaman trying to justify his seriousness by the necessity of making money and making it quickly; but, as Conrad himself realized, these statements were only rationalizations of his earnestness.

Affixed to his third novel, *The Nigger of the "Narcissus,"* was an Author's Note,[1] the later Preface, which more than

[1] The book was serialized in the *New Review*, XVII (August-December 1897), ed. W. E. Henley. The Author's Note appeared after the final installment in December 1897.

any other account established the terms of Conrad's attachment to literature. By 1897, Conrad's two novels, *Almayer's Folly* and *An Outcast of the Islands,* had received encouraging reviews and his work, while not universally praised, had been recognized by the English and American press. But even after 1897, with three novels and four serialized stories behind him, he was not prepared to give up a sea career. Conrad only turned to professional writing when he found that his sea career was ending in deferred hopes. Still, he was personally pleased with *The Nigger,* and his staunch defense of art and the artist in the Preface bespoke the writer and not the seaman. It is difficult to believe that after the forthrightness of *The Nigger* credo he could forgo the novel, even had his search for a command proved successful. It is rather to be believed that the fervor of the Preface displayed as much a resignation from the sea as a commitment to a life of letters.

So close in spirit, despite certain differences in intention, are Conrad's Preface to *The Nigger* and James' essay "The Art of Fiction," published nine years earlier, that one is tempted to compare them in parallel columns. James, in arguing for heightened realism, had pleaded for intelligence in the novel and a seriousness of purpose that had often been brought only to poetry and poetic drama. The novel's *raison d'être* to James is no less than to represent life, and the novelist's very calling stimulates, he says, fidelity to a sacred office. Trollope is castigated for his sense of "only making believe"; his betrayal of a great trust is "a terrible crime." James spoke of fiction as producing an illusion of life, a semblance which is the very air of reality. The novel, like music, is united in texture and interwoven; in each part should be found something of other parts. The absolute wedding of the parts themselves is stressed by James, as it was by Flaubert before him and

Conrad after him. For the artist, for the novelist, experience is never finite, his imagination is always catching new hints. His subject matter is all ways of seeing and feeling. James' famous dictum: "Try to be one of the people on whom nothing is lost," is a plea for the novelist to expand his horizons, to be devoted to his craft at all times, in all places. The province of art is "all life, all feeling, all observation, all vision." Art, says James, is created by men enjoying the freedom of unlimited experience and the freedom of its re-creation in whatever form that particular experience suggests. The mind of imagination, says James, the mind of genius operating freely, "takes to itself the faintest hints of life," converting "the very pulses of the air into revelations." Experience is "an immense sensibility." James implies that under these conditions of fidelity to art, beauty and truth are sufficient; and that if the intelligence is fine, the art will be fine, while the moral and aesthetic unite into a whole.

When we come to the Preface to *The Nigger*, we cannot ascertain whether Conrad obtained this idea of the alliance of the moral and the aesthetic from James, Flaubert, and Keats, or else derived it from his earlier French reading or from the literature of the late 1890's. Conrad speaks of the artist "snatching in a moment of courage . . . a passing phase of life" and bringing to bear upon it an imagination bathed in tenderness and faith; the artist must show life's "vibration, its colour, its form; and through its movement, its form, and its colour, reveal the substance of its truth—disclose its inspiring secret: the stress and passion within the core of each convincing moment." Whoever holds to these convictions, says Conrad, cannot be faithful to any one of the temporary formulas of his craft. All the gods of Realism, Romanticism, Naturalism, and even sentimentalism must abandon the artist on the threshold of his struggle with his own conscience. At that moment the temporary formulas are left behind and only the individual intelligence remains: "In that uneasy solitude," says Conrad, "the supreme cry of Art for Art itself, loses the exciting ring of its apparent immorality. It sounds far off. It has ceased to be a cry, and is heard only as a whisper, often incomprehensible, but at times and faintly encouraging."

Conrad echoes James on the necessity of artistic awareness, remarking that to show intelligence at every moment and to search out the fundamental, the essential, and the enduring are the work of the artist. The artist appeals to what is in us a gift and not an acquisition. All art appeals emotionally, primarily to the senses—to our senses of pity and beauty and pain and mystery. And how, Conrad asks, can art—particularly fiction—catch this air of sensory reality; how, in short, "does it penetrate to the colors of life's complexities?" Art must, he says, in a passage reminiscent of Pater,

> strenuously aspire to the plasticity of sculpture, to the colour of painting, and to the magic suggestiveness of music— which is the art of arts. And it is only through complete, unswerving devotion to the perfect blending of form and substance; it is only through an unremitting never-discouraged care for the shape and ring of sentences that an approach can be made to plasticity, to colour, and that the light of magic suggestiveness may be brought to play for an evanescent instant over the commonplace surface of words: of the old, old words, worn thin, defaced by ages of careless usage.

Conrad then made his now famous declaration of intention, which repeats James' dictum that the artist should "produce the illusion of life"; Conrad said: "My task which I am trying to achieve is, by the power of the written word, to make you hear, to make you feel—it is, before all, to make you *see*." It is to catch in stasis each passing moment and to reproduce that moment so that it arrests the interest of men; that function, he says, is the aim "reserved only for a very few to achieve." At that moment, the artistic aims of the creator assume a moral importance, achieving a sense of grandeur and of something fully *done* which captures the moral significance of the moment.

Conrad, in his essay on James (1905), makes the Aristotelian distinction between Poetry (Fiction) and History; documentary History is based, Conrad says, on second-hand impressions, whereas Fiction, or human history, is based on the reality of forms and the observation of social phenomena; Fiction, therefore, is nearer the truth, and the novelist is a historian of human experience. James, as a writer of fiction, as the "historian of fine consciences,' becomes something of a moral hero to Conrad for his heroic struggles with his materials, for his ability to record them "with a fearless and insistent fidelity to the *péripéties* of the contest, and the feeling of the combatants." Fiction, says Conrad, can penetrate into the supra-real; History must record the mundane. Fiction gives a semblance of truth in all its variety; History, the facts alone.

I I I

In his emphasis on the mysterious interconnection of things, on their "solidarity in mysterious origin," on that "uncertain fate" which binds men together, Conrad is voicing a doctrine familiar to many nineteenth-century French poets. From Baudelaire to Rimbaud and Mallarmé, we find a working doctrine similar to Coleridge's division of the Imagination: the primary Imagination as the conscious sense experience of the manifest world, and the secondary Imagination as a quasi-divine faculty which perceives intuitively the secret and hidden connections between things. Both Coleridge and Baudelaire saw eternal analogies, and recognized the secondary Imagination as a unifying faculty which "dissolves, diffuses, dissipates, in order to recreate," what Conrad later defined as a power that is "enduring and essential."

In this connection, Ford Madox Ford commented that Conrad was always in search of new ways of infusing energy into the novel. Conrad was, he says, "seeking most of all a new form for the novel, and I a limpidity of expression. . . ." Both authors worked tirelessly on ideas, style, language, narration, reportage of conversation, the color and texture of prose, toward what Rimbaud had prophetically called an all-unifying fiction. Conrad himself prophesied in an early letter that imaginative prose work would be in a new form, but "a form for which we are not ripe as yet." In an even earlier comment suggestive of Rimbaud's theory of the *voyant*-poet, Conrad, writing to E. L. Sanderson (October 12, 1899), lamented fiction writing as a career and emphasized the unearthly nature of the enterprise: "One's will becomes the slave of hallucinations, responds only to shadowy impulses, waits on imagination alone. A strange state, a trying experience, a kind of fiery trial of untruthfulness."

William Butler Yeats, writing in 1900, repeated—either directly or indirectly—what Conrad had stated three years earlier in the Preface to *The Nigger*. In common, they emphasized the language and form of the work as a means of making the reader see; they stressed the interlinking of things in their solidarity and pointed to the contact between the visible and what can be suggested in the not-visible; and both recognized the necessity of new forms to describe things beyond sensory experience. Conrad's emphasis on the individual artist's conscious mind as guide to his artistic conceptions, finds its echo in Yeats' plea for the exploration of new territory. Conrad implies that each writer of fiction must discover anew the tools which are significant for him alone. This method of working—essentially an anti-traditionalist position—puts the artist in isolation, a familiar throwback to the aesthetic 1890's, the time of Conrad's apprenticeship.

In his nervous concern with choosing the exact word— the word free from secondary meanings and undesirable connotations, the word free and pure—Conrad was reflecting his background of French reading. In the same essay on Maupassant cited above, Conrad praised the French writer's sense of exactness, remarking that actualities rendered are the stuff of the novelist who deals with the concrete in order to glean realities from a "universe of vain appearances." Conrad praised Maupassant's diligence in polishing his work to obtain "the vision of its true shape and detail," for seeking its inscape, which can be only one true form from an infinity of possibilities; Maupassant's aim, like Conrad's, was that the subject be adequately seen.

Conrad carried this emphasis on detail to his reading tastes. His mixed reaction to Dickens was caused by the latter's "sloppy technique" and moralizing tone. At the same time he recognized Dickens' great power. And Melville's *Moby Dick,* Conrad thought, was full of "portentous mysticism," perhaps because of its lack of surface concreteness. But in Stephen Crane, Conrad found an approximation of the ideal: Crane was a man inspired, "a seer who saw the significant on the surface of things. Crane worked from the concrete to the unstated and could suggest a scene by an odd simile. Notwithstanding Crane's ability to reach into life's truths, within appearances and forms, it is, says Conrad, as if "he had gripped you with greased fingers. His grip is strong but while you feel the pressure on your flesh you slip out from his hand."

Crane's ability, however, to see beyond the surface was also the virtue of the French, particularly Maupassant and Flaubert. We see that Maupassant meant many things to Conrad: his steadfastness during the long years of apprenticeship to the writing craft; the slow development of skills and the never-forgotten goal of excellence; the lack of compromise with style and subject matter; the patience in finding the *mot juste* without flaunting a verbal facility —"a tranquil excellence," Conrad called it; the courage to face mankind with compassion and still maintain detachment while not qualifying his view of reality; the trusting of "his senses for information and his instinct for deductions"; and most of all, that "exact knowledge of the means and that absolute devotion to the aim of creating a true effect—which is art."

Everything Conrad says about Maupassant also applies to Flaubert,[2] whom the young seaman had read and reread "with respectful admiration" by 1892. Although he wrote no essay on Flaubert, Conrad's letters are peppered with allusions to the French writer's major novels. As early as

[2] Conrad's devotion to Flaubert was perhaps equaled by his feeling for Turgenev whom he read in French and English translations. Of the latter he wrote: "Every gift has been heaped on his cradle: absolute sanity and the deepest sensibility, the clearest vision and the quickest responsiveness, penetrating insight and unfailing generosity of judgment, an exquisite perception of the visible world and an unerring instinct for the significant, for the essential in the life of men and women, the clearest mind, the warmest heart, the largest sympathy—and all in perfect measure." (*Notes on Life and Letters*, 1921, p. 48) Turgenev, said Conrad, wrote about human beings, not "damned souls knocking themselves to pieces in the stuffy darkness of mystical contradictions." This is obviously an allusion to Dostoyevsky and parallels his attitude toward Melville. But Turgenev was an ideal to Conrad, a constellation to be looked to for inspiration, while Flaubert was to be analyzed for practicalities.

1914, Richard Curle compared Conrad with Flaubert, and in a later critical study Edward Crankshaw pointed out psychological similarities between Conrad's first novel, *Almayer's Folly*, and *Madame Bovary*. It was, however, not Flaubert the realist nor Flaubert the symbolist who attracted the young Conrad, but the Flaubert who in "his unworldly, almost ascetic, devotion to his art" was "a sort of literary, saint-like hermit." In Flaubert's combination of surface detail and constant suggestion through concrete images, Conrad found that Hellenic balance which he recognized as the imaginative faculty, that balance perfectly maintained by Turgenev and Maupassant as well as Flaubert. Conrad's neurotic compulsion towards writing itself was partly based on his fear of losing this delicate balance of imagination, what he at various times called manner or style. He referred to style when he remarked in *A Personal Record* that in "this matter of life and art it is not the Why that matters so much to our happiness as the How. As the Frenchman said, '*Il y a toujours la manière.*'" Conrad constantly felt an almost Coleridgean dejection at the frailty of his own imagination. In his early letters to Garnett, he wrote of his difficulty in dragging ideas out of himself, for his impressions, he said, are now faded and like "romantic ruins pervaded by rats." He complained that he is continuously haunted by the necessity of style, that his fortitude is being shaken by doubts that are monstrous and have begun to devour him. Each day he finds less substance in his work, each day it becomes more difficult to write and conceive.

Any prolonged study of Conrad's style must eventually return to Flaubert, for in both writers the awareness of style and its possible stagnation became part of their creative processes and helped to mold their aesthetic. Conrad, in a frantic letter to Edward Garnett, lamented that whil' other writers can lean on dialect or tradition or even the fad of the hour, he has only his personal uncertainties, his "impressions and sensations," to draw upon. In Flaubert, the development of a style likewise signified the relinquishment of props, personal and societal; he speaks of himself as alone in a crowd, "wrapped in [his] bear skin"; yet while exploiting personal doubts, the artist, Flaubert continues, must "stand to his work as God to his creation, invisible and all powerful; he must be everywhere felt but nowhere seen."

Both Conrad and Flaubert stressed the impersonality of the creator as a way of preserving the uncertainty, the "half-knowledge"—what Keats called Negative Capability —necessary to all points of view. Flaubert wrote to George Sand that "high Art is scientific and impersonal" and that by an effort of the imagination one must transfer oneself into one's characters. Similarly, Conrad advised Galsworthy to be more skeptical and more impersonal and to preserve an attitude of perfect indifference toward his characters. Conrad had also warned Arnold Bennett that the latter stopped just short of being absolutely real because he was too faithful to his dogmas of realism: "Now realism in art," Conrad said, "will never approach reality." Conrad's writing was based on the variability of human nature and human action. A work of art, he said in a letter to Barrett Clark, "is very seldom limited to one exclusive meaning and not necessarily tending to a definite conclusion."

This staunch belief in incertitudes placed Conrad under personal as well as professional apprehension. His early letters to Edward Garnett, to Richard Curle, and to Mme Poradowska are sufficient evidence of the power of uncertainties and doubts to pervade both the man and the writer. On September 16, 1899, he wrote to Garnett:

All is illusion—the words written, the mind at which they are aimed, the truth they are intended to express, the hands that will hold the paper, the eyes that will glance at the lines. Every image floats vaguely in a sea of doubt—and the doubt itself is lost in an unexplored universe of incertitudes.

For Conrad, as for Flaubert, the pledge to artistic creation was too serious to allow for relaxation or humor; both their public and artistic lives were directed toward creating a personal aesthetic.

I V

In those early letters and essays cited above, Conrad emphasized the qualities of suggestion in his work and de-emphasized its literal significance. In his essay on James, he spoke of all creative art as "magic, [as] evocation of the unseen in forms, persuasive, enlightening, familiar and surprising. . . ." Conrad maintained that the writer can only suggest, that he must leave "final meanings" to imagination, that no word is adequate to convey every nuance he intends, that "the *whole* truth lies in the presentation," and that this attention to veracity of expression "is the only morality of *art* apart from *subject.*"

Without developing a systematic aesthetic and certainly without identifying himself with any particular critical thought, Conrad placed himself in a general position we may consider "modern." He saw fictional art as the manifestation of a fluid and ever shifting world responsive to immediate intuition but inaccessible to the intellect. His refraction of time and his frequent use of durational or psychological time were merely two ways of defying surface reality. In experimenting with new forms in the novel, Conrad, along with Flaubert and James, extended

the boundaries of the genre and helped to inform the
twentieth-century novel.

Conrad was, in his way, grappling with what Bergson
called the vital or intuitional part of man's mind and what
Cassirer in his *Essay on Man* called "a new *dimension* of
reality" or "the symbolic system." As Cassirer pointed out,
this new dimension exists somewhere in the human character between the receptor system and the effector system.
It is anti-behaviorist, anti-rational; it operates on intuition, on imagination; it is above biological needs and practical interests, and without it man's life would be like that
of the prisoners in Plato's metaphorical cave.

A symbolic method, says Cassirer, suggests that aesthetic experience "is pregnant with infinite possibilities
which remain unrealized in ordinary sense experience."
He posits art as symbolic language without a rational basis
of signification in rational action. Art teaches us how to
visualize—not merely to conceptualize or utilize—a more
vivid and colorful image of reality. "Art," he says, "gives
us an ideal description of human life by a sort of alchem-
ical process; it turns our empirical life into the dynamics
of pure forms." By dramatizing his experience, man can
synthesize and universalize his humanity and build it into
what Cassirer calls a "symbolic universe."

These quotations from Cassirer are so little different
from Conrad's remarks in the Preface to *The Nigger* as to
make the passage of fifty years between the two works a
matter of small consequence. Conrad's insistence—here
and in his letters—on visualization, on suggestion, on
forms, colors, shadows, on the senses as opposed to intellect, on the aesthetic faculty, all point to man as a symbol-
making and not a rational animal.

Accordingly, we see that, as he worked into his fruitful
middle period from *Nostromo* to *Victory*, Conrad inte-

grated and objectified his use of images; so that image gradually became symbol in its suggestivity and fancy was transmuted into imagination. Conrad learned to conceptualize his material even while recognizing that subjectivity, *qua* subjectivity, did not necessarily preclude effective fiction. But he did realize, as Mrs. Langer (in *Feeling and Form*) states it, that: "It is usually with the advance of conceptual competence that an artist becomes able to find material outside his own situation, because he becomes more and more apt to see all things, possibilities as well as actualities, half-wrought already into expressive forms in terms of his own art." In his letters, Conrad recognized that the kind of subjectivity that fails to project emotive knowledge into objective forms, that fails to transmute mere discourse into the illusion of moral illumination, that fails to recognize the variability of experience—all these kinds of subjectivity are the province of journalism and not of art.

This ability to conceptualize sets off, as Mrs. Langer writes, the essential illusion from "the surrounding world of actuality," and articulates "its form to the point where it coincides unmistakably with forms of feeling and living." The artist, in brief, creates semblances and articulates vital form. From Flaubert and Turgenev to James and Conrad, we find this stress on the transformation of personal material into impersonal masks, to use Yeats' phrase, achieving what has since been called "aesthetic distance." In 1912, Edward Bullough had spoken of the separation of "personal affections, whether idea or complex experience, from the concrete personality of the experience, its filtering by the extrusion of its personal aspects, the throwing out of gear of its personal potency and significance." Bullough called this process of conceptualization "psychical distance," and, translated into literary composition, it approximates Yeats' use of the mask and Conrad's emphasis on impersonalizing personal experience.

In trying to travel the rocky literary path between an 1890's "code" of artistic anarchy and a Victorian code of professed didacticism, Conrad took refuge, as did Flaubert and James, in that devotion to craft wherein art and morality meet in commitment, responsibility, and lawfulness. By creating the semblance of events lived and felt so that their organization constitutes a completely experienced reality, what Mrs. Langer calls "a piece of virtual life," the artist fulfills his duty to himself and to society. It is only through projection, through dramatization, through conceptualization that all-important feelings can be communicated. Only artistic projection could bring forth works like *Nostromo* and *Victory*, which are based on the frailest of personal experiences.

When Conrad in the Preface to *The Nigger* and in his letters inveighs against the naturalists, the realists, and the romanticists, he is opposing the categorization of art, art that he later said can be only "a wonderful power of vision" which reaches into "life's appearances and forms, the very spirit of life's truth." He says that the scientist and thinker appeal to our common sense and intelligence, always to our credulity, but that it is otherwise with the artist. The artist, says Conrad, appeals to that "part of our being which is not dependent on wisdom . . . and, therefore, [is] more permanently enduring."

The other side of the coin is the position of H. G. Wells, who in his famous statement of self-indictment disdained playing the artist and put himself solidly on the side of the journalists. Wells equated education with rationality and chided Conrad for never admitting "that a boat could ever be just a boat." The impressionist was uneducated and, even worse, somewhat ridiculous for forsaking surface reality. Conrad, Wells says, was "always trying to penetrate below my foundations, discover my imaginative obsessions and see what I was really up to." Writing to James, Wells said: "When you say 'it is art that *makes* life, makes interest, makes importance,' I can only read sense into it by assuming that you are using 'art' for every conscious human activity. I use the word for a research and attainment that is technical and special. . . ."

Wells of course was making fidelity to fact and fidelity to truth one and the same. As a journalist he was able to make them identical. But James and Conrad made the distinction between journalism and literature when they deplored "the fatal futility of fact" alone and opposed to it the forces of imagination. Fact is fidelity to reality, but truth, said James, suggests a world that gives the semblance of reality and includes *more*. To work toward this "more" is a mark of literary devotion; to succeed in reaching it is the mark of the artist.

V

When, however, we turn to the Author's Notes Conrad wrote for the first Collected Edition, we find a wavering in his aesthetic position which parallels his loss of creative power. *Victory*, written from 1911 to 1914, was his last major full-length work. Of the remaining ten volumes he published before his death in 1924, only *Chance* and *The Shadow Line* can command our serious interest, and even then as something of a farewell to former power. It is important to remark that these Author's Notes are *a posteriori;* Conrad was looking back and defining himself to his newly acquired reading public, and not trying to establish a *modus vivendi* for the young Joseph Conrad.

As Conrad's power to conceptualize and his ability to imagine his material began to wane, he relied increasingly upon the props of strictly realistic fiction. These Author's Notes abound in attempts to root the story in direct reality: to provide real people as his models, to substantiate the geographical location of his fiction, to underplay the suggestiveness of his work while emphasizing factual and tangible details. In the Note to *Lord Jim,* Conrad speaks of its theme as simply "the acute consciousness of lost honour." In a further remark on the novel, Conrad's emphatic denial of the book's morbidity is a virtual denial of its very power; for in its finer moments the book offers a view of life which is nothing if not morbid.

In the disappointing Note to *Nostromo,* Conrad skirts the suggestive qualities of the novel and jumps from anecdote to anecdote about the origins of the book. In the Note to *Victory,* the emphasis is on a few generalities about man and his power of detachment and adaptation, with a documentation of the flesh and blood models for Heyst, Lena, Jones, and others; once again, Conrad is hesitant to talk about the novel. In the Note to *The Secret Agent* Conrad speaks principally of the origin of the novel; he traces it to three things: to the Greenwich Observatory incident, to a remark by a friend about those involved in the bomb attempt on the Observatory, and to a book of recollections of an Assistant Commissioner of Police. Conrad suggests that the real story is not about anarchists and anarchy, but he tends to shrink from significant comment on the novel itself. In one part of the Author's Note, it is true, he calls London a "monstrous town," a "cruel devourer of the world's light," with "darkness enough to bury five millions of lives"; alone in these remarks does he suggest, and that only briefly, the major theme of the novel. In the Note to *Chance,* Conrad touches on the prevalence of chance in life, on his roundabout method of telling the story, on his pleasure at the sale of the book, and finishes by noting that man is more responsible for his intentions than for the results of his actions. Remarks which, in effect, say little. In his Note to "The Secret Sharer," Conrad says that the basic fact of the story was the common possession of the whole Eastern fleet, and that he had heard of it in his first years of deep-water service. He concludes by pointing out that "The Secret Sharer" and *The Shadow Line* are his only two calm-water pieces.

The Note to *Under Western Eyes* is concerned chiefly with justifying the old language teacher as narrator, with the necessity of detachment from personal involvements, and with Conrad's equal distaste for autocratic imbecility and Utopian "revolutionism" (sic). Only in the Note to *Youth* does Conrad allude to a broader intention than that afforded by the surface realities of the work. Concerning "Heart of Darkness," he says that it was "like another art altogether. That sombre theme had to be given a sinister resonance, a tonality of its own, a continued vibration that, I hoped, would hang in the air and dwell on the ear after the last note had been struck." Even here, however, we find an evasion of the serious intent we expect in a major novelist.

If we judge by these Notes alone, Conrad is surely the most disappointing of major authors as self-critics. While prompting little relevant comment, the Author's Notes do, however, provide some clues to Conrad's psychology at this time. As we sift the Notes to the key novels and stories, we find an almost total lack of that "aesthetic feel" running through the Preface to *The Nigger* and the early essays and letters. Conrad evidently approached the Notes as informal essays, as letters of introduction to his newly established public. A spirit of weariness is ever present, the same sense of exhaustion that seeped into his fiction of this period. There is good reason, therefore, to believe that he had lost the nervous energy which had maintained him during the difficult early years. That desire to return to peace and quiet and rest, typified by the rover Peyrol returning home to die, may have signified a general intellectual lassitude in Conrad's later years. The memories were running out, and the remaining props of personal experience were far in the past; the initial energy had been expended, and the pressures of nervous attacks were as frequent as always. Furthermore, popular praise was greater than ever before with the resultant rise in sales.

Apart from these personal misgivings, Conrad had always disdained the critical spirit *per se*. The writer is a critic of life, not of other writers, he would say. In searching out Conrad's aesthetic, we must remark his own hasty retreat from any prolonged or involved critical analysis. He was frankly suspicious of literary criticism and relegated it to another level of mind, different from and implicitly lower than the creative mind. Conrad openly admitted that he was not a literary critic, and perhaps this frank realization of insufficiency extended to his lackluster comments on his own work. Only occasionally do the Author's Notes break through and reveal the ideas that impregnated his most important work, and only occasionally do they disclose a mind concerned with the novel as serious art. More often, the Notes reveal almost a complete breakdown of those aesthetic ideals painstakingly suggested twenty years earlier.

Perhaps, as indicated above, Conrad's Author's Notes suffer unduly from inevitable comparison with James' Prefaces. James' work, as we have seen, was accomplished at the height of his powers; Conrad's came when he was already in decline as a novelist. If, therefore, we want to seek the working aesthetic, that individual approach to the novel which resulted in the best of Conrad's work, we must go back fifteen or twenty years. Just as the amateur seaman had become the professional seaman, so the amateur writer had become the professional novelist, but with literary professionalism came a decline in power, and a loss of the adventure of experiment. In 1912, Conrad triumphantly spoke of those early years as full "of devoted practice, with the accumulated anguish of its doubts, imperfections and falterings in my heart. . . ." But in looking back to his abandonment of *The Rescue* in 1897, Conrad speaks of having then lost for the moment "the sense of the proper formula of expression, the only formula that would suit." It was during a similar loss of conceptual power that he created his later fiction and wrote the docile Author's Notes rooted as they are in fact and not in imagination.

V I

Conrad believed in the high seriousness of art and his aesthetic ideas were catholic enough to include many authors not necessarily sympathetic to his own mind. The high points of fiction were, in his eyes, the sea novels of Marryat and Cooper, the work of Flaubert, Turgenev, James, Chekov, Maupassant, and Proust, and a mixed appreciation for his contemporaries, W. H. Hudson, Cunninghame Graham, and Edward Garnett, an admiration no doubt heightened by his close personal relationship with these men.

The incongruity of these tastes—placing James and Turgenev with Cooper and Marryat, for example—demonstrates that his respect for these writers struck as deeply into their motives as into their results. He had to find not only a sense of responsibility, but also a formed and ordered surface. Part of Conrad's distaste for Dostoyevsky, apart from his antipathy to the latter's Pan-Slavism and Czarist politics, came from his recognition of the Russian's formlessness and his "confusion and insanity," the same qualities which had also tempered his enthusiasm for Dickens. Doubtless mixed in with this attitude, as Richard Curle pointed out, was an unconscious recognition on Conrad's part that he lacked the "tremendous personal feelings on elemental questions that lift the creations of the Russian to a pitch of epic grandeur." Dostoyevsky, nevertheless, was ever Conrad's tormentor to whom he returned again and again in his own characterization of the dark underside of twentieth-century man.

For Conrad, if art and beauty were to unite as moral factions, then there would have to be virility as well as verbal skill, sincerity as well as devotion, responsibility as well as sensitivity, and integrity as well as involvement. He was harsh to those he thought pseudo-artists, those who went through the motions without the substance, the fire, the restraint, and the detachment that could transform everyday facts into an artistic vision and the particular into the universal. If the imagination were to bear fruit, it must be an imagination rooted in responsibility, a conception of the world in moral terms presented indirectly through a non-didactic surface that derives every nuance and possibility from the arrangement of the material.

chapter 2

From Theory to Practice

The man replied, 'Things as they are
Are changed upon the blue guitar.'
                                 Wallace Stevens

Ezra Pound said that what Flaubert had done to change
French prose, Conrad and Ford did to transform English
prose, and he, Pound, was trying to do in order to reshape English poetry. Conrad's use of *phanopoeia*—the
piling up of imagistic details which replaced, in part at
least, a direct narrative—was, said Pound, the way of
the Imagists. The breakup of the conventional novel's
narrative into small scenes makes the scene function like
an image in poetry, in a way like the images in Pound's
own early poetry.

As Pound astutely remarked, Conrad and Ford had
arrived at some general principles, a kind of unwritten
manifesto of the New Novel, which in practice profoundly influenced the course of the genre in English.
Method in the novel, according to the two experimenters, was as important as in poetry; technique was
congruent with style. Technique, says Mark Schorer in
"Technique as Discovery," an essay that clearly echoes
Conrad and Ford, is what Eliot means by convention:
that is, "any selection, structure, or distortion, any form of
rhythm imposed upon the world of action: by means of
which . . . our apprehension of the world of action is en-
riched or renewed. In this sense, everything is technique
which is not the lump of experience itself." Schorer con-

43

tinues: "Under the immense artistic preoccupations of James and Conrad and Joyce, the form of the novel changed, and with the technical change, analogous changes took place in substance, in point of view, in the whole conception of fiction."

The object of Ford and Conrad was through appropriate technique to create a semblance of actual experience. Conrad himself, as we noted, had said earlier, perhaps with Walter Pater's words in mind, that the novel must "strenuously aspire to the plasticity of sculpture, to the colour of painting, and to the magic suggestiveness of music—which is the art of arts." He added that it is "only through complete, unswerving devotion to the perfect blending of form and substance . . . that an approach can be made to plasticity." Robert Penn Warren, among others, remarked this blending in *Nostromo* when he noted that the rhythms of that novel seem to suggest the very process of creation. Conrad achieved this, Warren continues, through his use of vista, landscape, time sequences, historical process, anecdote, and language itself.

Ford and Conrad, in their numerous sessions together, worked out their idea of the "planned novel," in which each step in the novel points toward a predetermined effect and leaves nothing to chance.[1] Every word and every

[1] Ford's numerous autobiographies and memoirs make more than passing reference to his relationship with Conrad. The collaboration began in October, 1898, according to a letter from Conrad to Galsworthy (Jean-Aubry, I, 253). A number of legends have accrued about the relationship, one of which—vociferously maintained by the pro-Fordists—claims that Ford all but taught Conrad English, a claim denied by Ford himself on many occasions. This pro-Ford position was attacked by Mrs. Conrad, who said that Conrad gave far more than he received. Certainly her many wifely virtues did not contain a far-reaching toleration of Ford as her husband's friend. The original controversy between the two factions commenced with a letter Conrad had written to Edward Garnett in

action, they said, must carry the story forward—what they called a novelistic *progression d'effet*—wherein the intensity increases as the story develops. This attempt to convey increasing urgency and intensity in the story would involve, said the authors, an assiduous study of all factors relevant to the pace of the novel. One idea, however, always predominated: to unsettle the conventional narrative sequences which had hitherto prevailed in the novel, and by so doing to create new interest in what the two authors feared was now a faded genre. This method meant slow and calculating work, paying unflagging attention to the effect of each scene and character, and maintaining always strict control. Conrad, with his enthusiasm for the French novel and possessing the French penchant for experimentation and analysis, was especially fitted for this role.

The first step was their mutual agreement that a poem was not what was written in verse but anything, "either prose or verse, that had constructive beauty." The emphasis both placed on the interdependent parts of the novel demonstrated that they considered its form like that of an edifice in which beauty and solidity are interrelated elements. In the construction of a novel, the basic rhythm has to be suggested, they said, in the opening paragraph. The opening part, in fact, should prefigure the entire work. *Romance* (1903), their second and lengthiest collaboration, begins *in medias res*, the (chronological)

---

which he referred slightingly to Ford, and even though Conrad asked that it be destroyed Garnett published it with Mrs. Conrad's permission.

Douglas Goldring, a close friend of Ford's, in his *Trained for Genius: The Life and Writings of Ford Madox Ford* (New York, 1949), makes the most sensible estimation of the controversy, saying that only Conrad could have commented upon the success or failure of the collaboration. The supposition is rightly taken that each man gained from the other, although their works written together are surely pedestrian.

opening scene not appearing in full context until page 76. But *Romance*, despite its elaborate trappings is only a simple adventure story, and all the high-minded theories applied to its development do not disguise this fact. The true test of their theories does not come in the collaborations, but in Conrad's individual works; and it is to understand these that we shall examine some of the conclusions reached by the two experimenters.

I I

As Ford remarked, the opening scene, although disconnected from its true context, should plunge in to suggest dramatically the substance of the work to come. This use of a disjointed initial scene influenced Conrad's later refraction of chronological time sequences, especially those in *Nostromo* and *Chance*, whereby he enters with suggestions and fills out the scene only after roving back and forth into anterior and future time. Replacing a direct narrative with fragmentary scenes is like the poet's use of images, particularly the way the nineteenth-century French poets proceeded. Poems like Rimbaud's "Le Bateau ivre," Mallarmé's "Hérodiade," "Cantique de Saint Jean," and "L'Après-midi," as well as Baudelaire's "Le Voyage," "Les Petites Vieilles," "Le Cygne," and others, are, in many ways, sequences of brilliant and startling images whose juxtaposition often replaces a conventional narrative. This method of poetic breakup applies not only to the narrative structure of the novel but also to the presentation of character. If the trouble with the English novel, according to Ford and Conrad, was that it always went forward, then the obvious thing was to go forward and backward; so that once a character has been introduced strongly enough to be remembered, his past is to be caught up *while* his present and future are being projected. Axel Heyst's past (in *Victory*) is filled in only after his present activities have been set into motion, and Nostromo's activities are picked up almost solely by fragmentary comments for nearly two hundred pages. Similarly, Flora de Barral in *Chance* is the center of a number of concentric circles, and before we can reach her we must pass through numerous protective layers of commentators.

What was achieved with narrative structure and character development, the collaborators realized, could also be effectively accomplished with speech. Conrad and Ford, perhaps influenced by Flaubert's experiments with interrupted speech, decided that to avoid boredom long speeches must be broken down, interspersed with narrative, and bolstered by little "jumps" in the pace of the novel. These "jumps" would provide, they said, a "constant succession of tiny, unobservable surprises" which would alleviate the monotony of incessant speech. But Conrad, as an admirer of James, was unable to eliminate altogether the lengthy dialogue. The best he could do on occasion was, like Flaubert, to temper a lengthy conversation with the bustle of the passing scene as, for instance, in *Chance* when Marlow and Flora talk amidst jostling people and passing carriages in front of Captain Anthony's hotel, or in *Lord Jim* when Marlow first meets Jim in the center of confusion at the court inquiry. Despite these specific instances, however, Conrad frequently broke away from this self-imposed limitation and piled conversation upon conversation, often losing all sense of pace—more than 150 pages of *Under Western Eyes,* for example, consists of lengthy dialogues, most of them consecutive, between Razumov and the various revolutionaries or between Razumov and the Haldins.

The object of all these efforts at control, as far as Conrad was concerned, was to lend an air of inevitability to his scenes and characters; so that what does happen must seem to be the only thing that could possibly have happened. Conrad, with his close attention to character development, always had in mind the intricate interactions of the minor personalities as complements to his major figures. Like Browning in *The Ring and the Book*, Conrad believed that a minor character might in the course of things affect the psychology of major characters and thus create a chain of external or internal events of some importance. In *Victory*, the villainous Ricardo, an essentially minor figure who is allied psychologically to Lena, sets off a series of events which result in the destruction of both Lena and Heyst. In *Lord Jim*, the brief scenes with Brierly, with the French naval officer, and with Stein are all of great significance for their relationship to certain elements in Jim's psychology. This theory of interaction maintains that everything that has gone before has some importance in the making and subsequent development of situation. Conrad, therefore, had to be especially careful to "prepare" the facts surrounding every new character and every change of pace; for in this sensitive arrangement of personalities, narrative, and speech, everything is of importance and nothing can be neglected. To get beyond the particular, Conrad realized, is to gain entrance into the total complex of forces acting in and beyond the novel. For beyond what the novelist explicitly states is a blurred mystery that can be reached only through new means. We call this blurred mystery "rich," "various," "like life itself," and it is toward this manifoldness of meaning that Conrad was striving.

Conrad conceived of the novel as history, psychology, sociology, fiction, and poetry cast into one structure and informed by the power of the imagination. As part of this conception came Conrad's belief that the writing of novels was the only pursuit worth while. In addition, this emphasis on inclusiveness meant that the novel had to become the receptacle of a large vision of human experience. Ford wrote that he and Conrad had agreed "that the novel is absolutely the only vehicle for the thought of our day. With the novel you can do anything; you can inquire into every department of life, you can explore every department of the world of thought." In making his characters themselves narrate the story, who thus, so to speak, create the novel, Conrad was moving toward a representation of history in the making. *Chance* and *Nostromo*, with their various points of view which carry the narrative backward and forward, are a sort of literary history in which the "facts" of the story are fictitious, but still their arrangement aims at historical and social truth.

As his letters amply testify, Conrad was skeptical of the accuracy of any single action. But by presenting several actions and points of view in conjunction with each other, he could weld them to the matter of the novel by building fugue-like scenes; so that the overlapping of characters—as, for example, in *Under Western Eyes* and *The Secret Agent*—ramifies their personal problems into universally felt situations. It is his insistence on inclusion which places Conrad in the line of major novelists of all time with their marked tendency toward comprehensiveness. The twentieth-century quest, in particular, for technical improvisation is perhaps part of the necessity to include as much as possible; certainly *Finnegans Wake* is the most inclusive of novels. New knowledge in every age is absorbed by the novel, and this knowledge, as Yeats once remarked, could be caught only by new rhythms and new forms.

III

In trying to arrange new forms for the novel, Conrad experimented with a central narrator who would provide both form and shape to his material. The use of a central narrator did not begin, however, with either Conrad or James; it goes back as far as storytelling. It appears in the early English novel, and was Sterne's way of achieving cohesiveness in *Tristram Shandy*. Not until James, though, was the method perfected with logic and care, and despite Conrad's repeated experimentation with Marlow or a similar figure, he never excelled James' use of Strether in *The Ambassadors*.

With Marlow, Conrad had a refractor of the material and not a character who experiences simultaneously with the reader. Marlow's role, therefore, is somewhat closer to that of James' Maisie than to that of Strether. In *What Maisie Knew*, the precocious Maisie is the center of a malevolent group of adults, and what Maisie knows—her experience of the facts and not what she does nor what is done to her—forms an important part of the dramatic tension of the novel. Similarly, in "Youth" and in "Heart of Darkness," it is what Marlow knows—the knowledge that he has gained through two separate experiences, one in youth and one in middle age—that becomes the nub of the stories. But it is the older Marlow who retrospectively refracts these experiences. The reader meets a Marlow who is interpreting the younger man, who is conveying an older man's reaction to an earlier series of events. The reader never does see the narrator Marlow *as* he is being changed, *as* the vision of Kurtz's "horror" alters Marlow's point of view and creates in him the knowledge of evil. In *Lord Jim* and *Chance*, we again meet a Marlow who interprets events that have already occurred, who looks back from the vantage point of his age to give meaning to the past.

Much has been made by numerous critics of the psychological necessity of Marlow to Conrad: that through Marlow, Conrad was able to detach himself from his subject matter; that Marlow gave Conrad a sense of artistic security and provided a literary convenience; that Marlow was a personification of the author's inner voice; that Marlow made possible an indirect injection of personal comment and allowed Conrad a freedom of presence; that Marlow is Conrad the seaman relying on intuition and not on sense or reason; that Marlow is a "prolonged hovering flight of the subjective over the outstretched ground of the case exposed." To these might be added: that the "Englishness" of Marlow gave Conrad a feeling for his adopted country; that Marlow's experiences demonstrated that life is a series of chances and rumors; that Marlow as the controlled narrator fitted Conrad's belief in the consciousness of the writing process, a process in which Marlow controlled the sequence of events as strictly as Conrad controlled Marlow and through him the book.

It is this latter point that I wish to emphasize, for I believe that Marlow chiefly fills an artistic function, though not by any means the chief one in Conrad's work—no more than Benjy's narrative in Faulkner's *The Sound and the Fury* is the author's sole device in that book. The psychological and personal reasons for Conrad's use of Marlow must inevitably be put aside, for they are based on speculation and not on evidence. If, however, Marlow can be placed securely among Conrad's principal *artistic* devices, then perhaps we have a significant index to his entire way of thinking. Through Marlow we enter into the creative process itself, into the collaboration between "many tellers and many listeners."

With his use of Marlow, Conrad has this, among other things, in common with novelists like James, Gide, and Faulkner: that he frequently shows the materials of the plot, so to speak the structural skeleton, beneath the completed novel. For example, in *Lord Jim,* the presence of Marlow, aside from his role as narrator, provides an ironic counterpointing to Jim's romantic view of life. Whenever Jim talks of romantic adventures, Marlow's bulky presence denotes the solidity of reality. Without the necessity of stating the obvious, Conrad through Marlow was able to emphasize one of Jim's chief failures, his romanticism. Not only Marlow but also Stein, Brierly, the French officer, and Brown are all ways of "seeing" different aspects of Jim, and in their bodily presence they provide a structural framework for the novel. Also, in *Chance,* Conrad was careful to fix eyewitnesses for all his scenes in order to display each element that went into the construction of the novel. In *Nostromo,* where Captain Mitchell assumes a Marlow-like role, Conrad assiduously "placed" his narrators and his facts: Decoud's letter, Mitchell's own narrative, Dr. Monygham's disclosures—all these elements working with symbol, setting, and language. But Captain Mitchell's main narrative serves another, more important, purpose. As an ironic comment on the sequence of events ending the Revolution, Mitchell's "triumph" shows what the immediate future of Sulaco holds—a materiality almost as oppressive and grievous as the previously avarice-ridden political state. As a man who has, as he repeatedly says, made Nostromo into the figure he is, Mitchell, in his righteousness and boorishness, is a brilliantly ironic counterpart to his adventurous and romantic protégé.

Following in part Conrad's use of the narrator, Gide, in *Les Faux-Monnayeurs,* gave to Edouard's intermittent comment a sense of discontinuity that is essential to the theme of the novel. But unlike Conrad, Gide did not allow his central narrator the omniscience of the novelist; he chose instead to destroy the realism of the fictional events by interposing himself in the lives and acts of his characters. Conrad, on the other hand, upheld a logic which precluded interference and necessitated a sustained point of view. He, therefore, was especially careful in "Heart of Darkness," in "Youth," in *Lord Jim*, and in *Chance*, to mention only those things it was logically possible for Marlow to know.

Pursuing the aesthetic logic behind Conrad's use of Marlow, I think one fact remains clear: Conrad's plan, as he developed it in the Preface to *The Nigger of the "Narcissus"* and in his early letters, was to convey a sense of actuality that partook of—without becoming the same as —the realism of the naturalists. Conrad wanted evocation, color, plasticity, and "the light of magic suggestiveness . . . to make you *see.*" He recognized that the "realest realism" is obtained through the most imaginative ordering of the material; he realized that "technical discovery," as Mark Schorer called it, is commensurate with the highest sort of realism. This notion has of course become common coinage through the work of Joyce, Wallace Stevens, Faulkner, Gide, and Virginia Woolf, among many others. But amidst the realm of the imagination, Conrad needed a human voice, and the presence of Marlow serves this function. Marlow is *there,* as if Conrad were actually afraid that too much "magic suggestiveness" without a recurring human voice might make the reader lose sight of the enduring human relationships. This point is particularly evident in *Lord Jim* when Marlow frequently interrupts his narrative to take a drink, light up a smoke, or interpolate a remark. Marlow's personality, surely not the most exciting among those of Conrad's characters, constantly pokes through in its reassuring and "safe" manner. Frequently, Marlow's remarks are windy and lackluster, particularly when he renders judgments in *Chance*, but his presence nevertheless provided a necessary human actuality for Conrad.

As a person who follows life wherever it leads rather than one who tries to change it, Marlow fits into Conrad's "scheme" of the illogical development of life and its experiences. This plan of Conrad's at first seems paradoxical for an author who maintained a tight and logical control of his novels. While trying to evolve an aesthetic for the novel, Conrad and Ford had outlined a series of exacting steps necessary for what would be the "new novel." Ford's reason for maintaining this strict hold on the novel's progression was, again paradoxically, the desire to convey that unsettled condition he found in life's experiences, to give a "sense of the complexity, the tantalisation, the shimmering, the haze, that life is." Marlow, in his attempts to come to grips with life, in his strivings to arrange his experience in some recognizable order for narrative purposes, becomes, then, part of this varied and complicated life that Conrad was trying to re-create. If the general effect of a novel must be the general effect that life has on mankind, then who other than Marlow is better suited to convey the bewilderment of a "feeling" person in his reaction to life? It will be noticed that all of Conrad's narrators—Marlow, Mitchell (*Nostromo*), Kennedy ("Amy Foster"), the language teacher (*Under Western Eyes*), Powell (*Chance*), the young Captain of "The Secret Sharer"—are each and all men of striking similarity: proper, simple in outlook, scrupulously honest, the very type of men who would go through life without understanding more than a fraction of it; in short, men with small imagination but with a keen sense of self-preservation. The Marlows survive, while the Kurtzes, Heysts, and Decouds die; and rightfully so, says the judicious Stein, who realizes that man must consider self-preservation more important than imagination.

IV

It is perhaps paradoxical that the novel, which exists as a protean and amorphous form for material that cannot be fitted into any other category, should have received such attentive formal treatment. Unlike the sonnet and the sestina or any other confined poetic form, the novel cannot be enclosed within specific limitations. E. M. Forster, in exasperation, permitted everything over 50,000 words in prose to be labeled a novel, and while this definition is perhaps more attractive than accurate, the dilemma remains real. Recognizing that a concern with prose fiction meant a concern with form, Conrad proceeded to attack the problem of structure with a bias that extended poetic techniques to certain aspects of the novel. When Conrad, like Flaubert and James before him, stated the action of the plot in terms of situation and scene and not from the point of view of the author, he was of course bringing to bear a poetic device upon the novel. Similarly, when Conrad, again like James, strove for the creation of pictures—especially those tableau settings that we find in Conrad's early Malayan works—he was using, so to speak, plastic images to "narrate" story and suggest themes. This mixture of the different arts was surely part of Conrad's effort to give form to so formless a medium as the novel.

In this connection, one of Conrad's letters to his friend, Mme Poradowska, is instructive, a letter in which while confiding to her his difficulties in writing English, he especially underscores his trouble in trying to put what he calls the "ideas of the novel" into definite form. He wrote: "I prefer to dream a novel rather than to write it. For the dream of the work is always much more beautiful than the reality of the printed thing." Conrad came to realize that a clear-cut and well-defined form for the novel was impossible of attainment and that his frequent use, for example, of the Chinese-box-like narration was an indication of his arbitrary procedures. No *single* procedure could be satisfactory. In the "dream of the novel," Conrad implied, the form is protean, and in contrast with reality, the dream has an attractive shiftiness. Form, he recognized, can be only the semblance of experience, but in artistic hands the semblance is often of greater intensity than the real. Conrad had always maintained that his "unconventional groupings and perspective" were purely temperamental, that they existed to give a shifting and fluid sense of effects, and that his entire art rested upon this fact. For these reasons, he particularly emphasized the plasticity of his character and scenic arrangements, which he felt were essential to realizing his literary technique.

Conrad's use of the ever-receding Chinese-box-like narration was not by any means original, Balzac and others having long preceded him in its use. In *Chance*, as I have suggested, the Chinese box, with its story inside further stories, is at its furthest development in a Conrad novel; Flora's tale is frequently thrice removed from the reader, and the quotes within quotes appear doggedly on every page. But *Chance* is a radical example, and in no other book did Conrad indulge his inclination for author withdrawal to this extent. In his other Marlow narratives, impersonality is obtained at a single or double remove. What, however, on a superficial look might seem extra-

neous or an exercise in virtuosity, becomes on closer view
a matter of importance. The involved method of seeing
the material, then, is another way of expressing what
Robert Penn Warren called "the urgency of experience,"
the trademark of the philosophical novelist or poet who
is always striving to "rise to the level of generaliza-
tion. . . ."

One sure way of proceeding from particular to general,
Conrad revealed late in life in a letter to Hugh Walpole.
In considering Flaubert's influence upon him, he pro-
tested that his only legacy from his French predecessor
was the latter's rendering of concrete images and visual
impressions. In the same letter, Conrad remarked that he
did not think he had really learned anything from
Flaubert. But of course Conrad's entire theory of surface
objectivity—the use of a particular image or scene to suggest circumstances beyond—is in a direct line from *Madame Bovary* and *La Tentation de Saint Antoine*.

In matters of tone, a quality or condition in which carefully selected language and images suggest sub-surface
rhythms, Conrad was an experienced practitioner from
Almayer's Folly, his first novel. In that book, his reliance
on figurative language and simile operated to give a tone
beyond that of surface realism. The spirit of generaliza-
tion was already at work. By tying images to a sense of
recall, like Proust in his great work, Conrad was able to
create a matrix of images and thus shape a work of considerable density. The image, with its reference to things
in memory, becomes evocative, abundant, and charged
with associational material. We find Conrad again and
again using images which as they reappear in new contexts with new clusters of meaning become relevant symbols. So we have the jungle and river of the early novels,
the silver of *Nostromo,* the city images of *The Secret*

Agent and *Under Western Eyes,* and the island setting of
Victory. Similarly, the major themes receive some of their
substance from a succession of concrete images which at
first may seem extraneous. "Heart of Darkness" and "Il
Conde," for instance, acquire their structural weight
through a series of significant background images, and
correspondingly all the major novels are heavily dependent on sequences of imagistic detail for their psychological import. The reiterative imagery increasingly qualifies
the bare verbal narrative until the story or novel in question becomes like a dramatic poem in its execution. These
recurring imagistic patterns work closely with larger
structural units—with time shifts and recurring characters and situations—to give an almost tactile quality to
Conrad's subject matter.

Nevertheless, despite his continual psychological probing toward the center of his subject, Conrad as a novelist
worked essentially from the outside. Through the accumulation of concrete imagistic details from as many sides as
possible, he created, as it were, a stream of consciousness
from the outside. His rich material, he somehow realized,
called for a device as psychologically creative as the
stream-of-consciousness technique; but without being able
to take that step, Conrad, with his proven ability to rove
back and forth into memory and into different time sequences through recurring images, developed (without
originating) a method that is almost equivalent to the
stream itself. If we agree that the stream works through
psychologically conceived images which relate to the outside world, then we can see that Conrad's method was
similar, although his procedure was to commence not with
internal facts but with surface images. In his hands, psychological associations are conveyed through outside detail, an impersonal process in which physical images bore

in toward the subject while carefully defining and particularizing their effects. (See Robbe-Grillet's essays.)

Commensurate with Conrad's attempt to suggest psychological depth through a surface of multiple images, was his desire for precision, a move away from abstractions and unwanted connotations, toward what we may call a realism of the word. Part of Conrad's endless dissatisfaction with the English language stemmed from its manifold connotations. He admired French for its clean edges and limpidity, for its freedom from secondary meanings and its exactness. As an example, he mentioned the word "oaken," which in its French equivalent signifies "of oak," while in English it has a variety of possible significations. Conrad desired surface clarity; he did not want his extensions of meaning to stem from verbal confusion but rather to be projections from his sense of scene and human psychology. Too often, he complained, the English word, full of potential ambiguity as it was, would cloud and not extend his meaning. Verbal clarity was essential for exactitude, and surely his inability to write rapidly derived from his need to convey the precise meaning and the precise connotation he wanted. That almost excessive feeling for the exact word and exact image was part and parcel of his attempt to view his material objectively, however difficult that might be when the subject matter was deeply felt.

Equally central to Conrad's technique was the emphasis he and Ford placed on the sense of the incongruous which, they said, should be based on the use of contrasts and comparisons. The incongruous situation could, through overlapping and repetition, dramatize combining or contrasting characters and themes, and at the same time keep the author at an objective distance from his material. *Lord Jim*—as I have pointed out—is full of characters whose personalities seem segments of Jim himself. Likewise, in *Nostromo* and *Victory*, we find characters and situations that hold the novel in balance through their interaction with previous characters or situations. Further, Heyst and Jones (*Victory*) complement each other like Jim and Brown (*Lord Jim*) and in some ways like Decoud and Nostromo (*Nostromo*). In *The Secret Agent*, the idiot boy Stevie, who draws circles of perfection when disturbed, is an ironic contrast with the "normal" anarchists who want to destroy while he wants to create.

This is how Conrad attained objectivity, imaginatively and not discursively, precisely without being journalistic, clearly without being obvious. When Conrad wrote to Hugh Clifford that no single word or method is adequate —that "the imagination of the reader should be left free to arouse his feeling"—he was of course suggesting that really big themes come through the novelist's awareness of all the potentialities of his subject matter. *Victory*, *Lord Jim*, *Under Western Eyes*, *The Secret Agent*, "Heart of Darkness," and *Nostromo* are the successful realization of this belief, and they endure as guides to all serious twentieth-century readers.

V

Thomas Hardy once claimed that his artistic aim was "to intensify the expression of things, so that the heart and inner meaning is vividly visible." In this remark, we have a recognition of the same problem which every novelist must face and which few can successfully resolve. Hardy's numerous old-fashioned and melodramatic devices have a curious power despite his pedestrian prose, but Hardy was not an experimenter in the technique of the novel as I believe that Conrad was.

Conrad could attain the "vividly visible" by investing each of his major characters with the illusions of the artist himself. A typical Conradian character is impelled by some illusion, be it repentance as with Jim, or reputation as with Nostromo, or a vision of beauty and love as with Decoud, or the wish for personal isolation as with Axel Heyst—all illusionists whose fundamental acceptance of life is not based on the truth of facts but on the truths that men make of facts. These illusions come from within and not from without; they are a personal standard whose efficacy for the person involved is based on self-justification, on a personal vision not of what the world is but of what the world is to be. These illusionists follow the dream, as Stein said they must, and to them the dream is reality; from this stems their grief. This belief in the dream becomes the very stuff of the various novels. In this way, each man is his own artist: each one is following an artistic vision of the facts, an imaginative re-creation of reality which, while it may be illusory and dream-like to the reader, is real to the believer and immerses him in the destructive element of life itself. The dream that the il-lusionists follow is commensurate with the dream every artist must pursue; so the personality of each character, in-cluding the illusions by means of which he survives, par-takes of the artistic personality which has created him, and each major character is in his way an artist trying to develop his material. The structure of a world full of illusions is transmuted, in the process, into the structure of a novel full of illusory facts. As Walter Wright has said, for Conrad "an illusion expressed the genius of artistic paradox."

chapter 3

Time in Conrad

O body swayed to music, O brightening glance,
How can we know the dancer from the dance?
> W. B. Yeats,
> "Among School Children"

Most readers and critics are aware that Conrad, Virginia Woolf, Joyce, and Faulkner—to name only the more important contemporary novelists—were and are preoccupied with breaking up conventional time, refracting it, and finally creating a "poetic time" in which the clock is servant of the mind. When, however, we try to fix the preoccupation with time as predominantly contemporary, we find that it did not begin with modern novelists, nor have modern scientific and philosophic concerns with time been the chief impetus. The novel has always been concerned with time. As Dr. A. A. Mendilow in *Time in the Novel* points out, the eighteenth-century novel contains all the main types of representative time techniques: he demonstrates that in the fifty years between *Robinson Crusoe* and *Tristram Shandy,* we have "the unities of time, place, and action, strict sequence, selective causality, and associationist irregularity, intercalated, preliminary, and distributed exposition, continuity and selection, immediacy and the time-shift"—the entire paraphernalia of a conscious time technique.

The concern of eighteenth-century novelists with time and allied artistic problems, Dr. Mendilow comments, is indicated in their critical prefaces and essays, in digressions in the body of the novels, in letters of intentions, and in dedications. In *Tristram Shandy,* the earliest example of experimentation with time in the novel, we find that a superficially haphazard form becomes upon closer examination very conscious, even precise. Enveloped by Sterne's highly complicated technique, Tristram is no more the central character than is Captain Mitchell in *Nostromo* or the old teacher of languages in *Under Western Eyes.* He is, rather, a coordinator and a narrator of the novel which does not essentially concern him. By means of a central observer, Sterne broke up the narrative into individual scenes through which he could project personal idiosyncrasies. This method gave him the chance to view his characters from a strategic point of vantage and to develop them through an accretion of detail rather than by means of a limiting chronological narrative.

Sterne's way of proceeding is akin to a modern technique and in particular to Conrad's, whose representative novels were constructed through the repetition of details, through constant allusions, and through the chance remarks of his characters, all of which appear at different points in time. Conrad's use of time, however, is more complex and subtle than even Sterne's. From time as a means, we pass to time as an end in itself, as an organic ingredient in the novel; and in *Chance* there is such variety of complex time sequences that frequently method overbalances subject matter.

Conrad's work with broken time sequences, however, began slowly and tentatively. His first two novels were more or less straightforward narratives, in which he used the conventional flashback to break up a progressing narrative. The time sequences in these books are similar to those of most nineteenth-century novels. Conrad's third novel, *The Nigger of the "Narcissus"* (1897), is strictly conventional in its use of time, almost a lesson in how to write a novel with a beginning, a middle, and an end. Further, the early stories which form the volume *Tales of Unrest* (1898) take few liberties with an orderly narrative structure. Not until *Lord Jim,* published in 1900, do we find that complexity of method and certainty of touch in time sequences that prefigure the great experiments of *Nostromo, Chance,* and *Victory.* Before analyzing Conrad's use of time in his major novels, however, I shall sketch in the background of a modern time theory.

II

The emphasis that Bergson placed on the *merging* of time is of course significant in any discussion of the modern novel. Melting time is not a surrealist discovery. The difficulty of measuring experience, the interpenetration of moments of consciousness, the impossibility of analysis without inevitable distortion and alteration—all these ideas, implicit in Bergson, help to define a modern theory of the novel and provide part of the base beneath modern technical experimentation. In the Bergsonian world, time is heterogeneous, always in motion, fluid, ever-shifting, and things in it are indistinguishable. Space, on the other hand, is homogeneous, still, measureable. Time, furthermore, cannot be characterized by separate moments— to do this, as some have attempted, is to measure what is indistinguishable and to replace time by space.

Through *durée* or psychological time, Bergson asserted a disbelief in the surface reality of life and stressed a time in which the clock is artificial and mental time is natural. T. E. Hulme, in his essay on Bergson, "The Philosophy of Intensive Manifolds," points out that in Bergson's "duration of time" you are in that stream of impulse which constitutes life. You are "inside the object" by means of intuition, an irrational process, rather than surveying the object from the outside, from a window, which is an intellectual and rational process. Bergson's idea of reality, says Hulme, conceived the world as a flux of interpenetrated elements unseizable by the intellect. This anti-mechanical mode of thinking places all time—all the past, as well as the present moment—in what Wyndham Lewis, a violent anti-Bergsonian, called "one concentrated *now*."

Historically, Bergson's *durée* and Croce's *historia* are not unlike, for both men are focusing their attention on similar dynamic aspects of reality. Croce's historian, together with Bergson's philosopher, believes that he is engaged in interpreting a present activity, and that all history is therefore contemporaneous. This identification of philosopher and historian is supported by the remarks of Dr. Wildon Carr, whose comments also clear the way for a literary application of *durée*, particularly for Conrad's use:

> To carry our past in our present action, we do not leave it outside and behind us. Not only is there no break between the present and the past, but both the form and the matter of present reality, what we now are and are now doing as individuals, or as nations, is in its essence *history*.

Wyndham Lewis in *Time and Western Man* attacked the time theory as "a glorification of the life-of-the-moment, with no reference beyond itself and no absolute or universal value"; he remarked that its ultimate significance is "Existence-for-Existence's Sake," a sensational and romantic doctrine that is "florid, unreal, inflated, self-deceiving. . . ." But Lewis was looking for absolutes, and the time theory was expressly based on the relativity of historical and philosophical truths. In literary terms, the time theory signifies the relative nature of human experience; most modern novelists, especially Proust, Conrad, Virginia Woolf, Beckett, and Faulkner, deny absolutes in human relationships, and the structural format of their work, in its emphasis on fluctuating time, mirrors their belief in the relational and non-absolute quality of experience and history.

Proust's *Le Temps retrouvé* is in part a treatise on time, an analysis which brings together and explains the main themes of the preceding six parts of his *A la Recherche du Temps perdu*. Marcel, in this seventh part, experiences those moments of insight and revelation (what he calls privileged moments) which project the flotsam and jetsam of the past into his mind and provide tension with his contemporary surroundings. This tension gradually melts into a continuity between past and present, an endless interpenetration of time which can only be "clocked" by art. Marcel says:

> And then a new light dawned within me, less brilliant, it is true, than the one which had disclosed to me that the work of art is our only means of recapturing the past. And I understood that all these materials for literary work were nothing else than my past life and that they had come to me in the midst of frivolous pleasures, in idleness, through tender affections and through sorrow, and that I had stored them up without foreseeing their final purpose or even their survival.

Only art can stop the flow of time and, as it were, contain it, the whole present and past, in one solid form.

When we read Conrad's words on Proust we recognize the curious affinity of these near contemporaries. Con-

rad strongly praised and admired Proust's characters for
"their plastic and coloured existence." He said that "all
the crowd of personages [in Proust] in their infinite variety through all the gradations of the social scale are made
to stand up, to live, and are rendered visible to us by the
force of the analysis alone." Proust made us see and feel;
but Proust had, in addition, drawn upon memory, and
Conrad's art, as he readily proclaimed, rested almost
solely upon recollection. Both the insulated Proust in his
cork-lined rooms and the isolated Conrad in his country
retreat had finished with the greater part of action, with
overt experience, and were drawing upon the already
lived and the already experienced. We remember Conrad
complaining that he had no props like other authors,
that he had only himself to face each day, and that his
fear was of the creative well running dry and leaving
him with a full pen and a quire of empty paper. Conrad
realized that these fading memories (those "romantic
ruins pervaded by rats")—the very stuff of his active life
—could be caught only in "the artifice of eternity."

Conrad would have concurred with Proust's emphasis
on "involuntary memory": that part of the mind which
stores sensations of the past, as it were, censored by voluntary memory, and which can be evoked, as Proust
claims, by "an odor, a taste, rediscovered under entirely
different circumstances." Voluntary memory paints "like
a bad painter using false colors," while involuntary memory (similar to the psychoanalytic subconscious) contains
a half-remembered, half-forgotten past which can be
called upon at any moment of sudden revelation, what
Proust later called privileged moments. In a revealing letter to Antoine Bibesco, Proust unfolded his theory of involuntary memory, which in its workings amalgamates
all time:

I believe that it is involuntary memories practically altogether that the artist should call for the primary subject matter of his work. . . . My novel is not a work of ratiocination; its least elements have been supplied by my sensibility; first I perceived them in my own depths without understanding them, and I had as much trouble converting them into something intelligible as if they had been as foreign to the sphere of the intelligence as a motif in music.

As a guide, then, to the reality of the past there is involuntary memory, which, as one of Proust's critics describes it, by launching "the mind on a voyage of introspection may carry it down below the superficial film" toward a vision of its own inner life in real time. Involuntary memory, so to speak, catches the imagination off guard without depleting the reserves of imagination in seeking a particular momentary recollection. Perhaps this sense of a subconscious force working in his imagination is what Conrad meant when he wrote to Garnett of his difficulties:

> The construction [of "An Outpost of Progress"] is bad. It is bad because it was a matter of conscious decision and I have no discrimination—in the artistic sense. Things get themselves written. . . . Things get themselves into shape—and they are tolerable. But when I want to write—when I do consciously try to write or try to construct, then my ignorance has full play and the quality of my miserable and benighted intelligence is disclosed to the scandalized gaze of my literary father. . . . I always told you I was a kind of inspired humbug. (Aug. 14, 1896, Colgate U.)

In practice, however, Conrad's complex techniques and his conscious use of time sequences belie an unconsciousness in which "things get themselves written." What Donald Davidson called "Conrad's Directed Indirections" is a calculated method of making traces of past time react upon and combine with present circumstances. Long before Eliot's observation that "the past should be altered by the present as much as the present is directed by the past," Bergson, Proust, and Conrad were using time in much the same way psychoanalysts were using memories and experiences from the past as indications of present actions. Chronology, then, in Conrad's work becomes a strategic supplement to mood and character. Time, however, rarely dominates so completely in Conrad as it does in Proust; it rarely becomes the very philosophy of the novel. But it is another component, another ingredient in the making of a construct, a solid block of experience compact in itself and air-tight; one way of conceiving an isolated "little world made cunningly."

III

It is possible to speculate that inadequate time techniques in Conrad's early novels placed too much responsibility on language itself, which, as a result, became prolix. Conrad's later use of time—which, incidentally, has much in common with the use of montage in the film—is a word-saver in a very particular sense. Two illustrations immediately occur of simple juxtaposition of past and present which makes the scenes speak for themselves. In *Nostromo,* we are flashed into the background of Dr. Monygham and see his former degradation at the hands of the tyrant Guzman Bento at just the moment when by his present action he is trying to regain his mastery of self. The juxtaposition of scenes eliminates the necessity of discourse and at the same time provides the wary reader with the irony of the Doctor's situation. In the flashback, Dr. Monygham is *created* for us as a man in conflict who has always to act *against* his own failure.

A second example of the use of time as a silent commentator occurs in *Victory*. This novel, probing the ironies inherent in the conflict between a theoretical view of life which advocates withdrawal and a practical view of life which accepts events as they are enforced upon one, employs time sequences which derive the maximum from the two contradictory positions. At the moment Heyst has committed himself to an action—the protection of the girl Lena and her removal to his island—Conrad flashes into Heyst's mind the scene describing the elder Heyst's death. "Look on—make no sound" was his advice; and now Axel, in the midst of his responsibility to Lena, is "hurt by the sight of his own life, which ought to have been a masterpiece of aloofness." Time considerations of this sort abound in *Victory*. Heyst, in the midst of reading in one of his father's books that of "the stratagems of life the most cruel is the consolation of love," is confronted by the bewildered Lena who, after a short exchange, comments: "You should try to love me!" Heyst's only answer, after a movement of astonishment, is: "But it seems to me————." Juxtaposition makes the scene, and time is the ally of ironic comment. Heyst's sense of personal liberty is ever at war with the exigencies of everyday existence, and in this conflict time becomes a shadow-like second character.

What I have been illustrating is time juxtaposition at its simplest and most apparent. Conrad and Ford Madox Ford, however, worked out a series of time sequences which they called the "time-shift technique" or "chronological looping." This technique entailed six major parts or steps: (1) a careful selection of details to give an idea of the passage of time; (2) the indirect and interrupted method of handling interviews and dialogues to give a sense of the complexity of past and present meet-

ing; (3) a keen sense of paralleling and opposing situations which provide time conflicts and tensions; (4) getting a character "in" and then working backward and
forward over his past; (5) the use of a "gathered-up"
summary which permits the novelist to sweep from past
to present and break into the chronological narrative;
(6) the use of time to provide the general effect that life
has on mankind—as an illustration of the latter, Ford
provided a clear description of their aims:

> A novel must therefore not be a narrative, a report. Life
> does not say to you: in 1914, my next door neighbor, Mr.
> Slack, erected a greenhouse and painted it with Cox's green
> aluminum paint. . . . If you think about the matter you will
> remember, in various unordered pictures, how one day Mr.
> Slack appeared in his garden and contemplated the wall of
> his house. You will then try to remember the year of that
> occurrence and will fix it as August 1914 because having
> had the foresight to bear the municipal stock of the city of
> Liege you were able to afford a first-class season ticket for
> the first time in your life. You will remember Mr. Slack—
> then much thinner because it was before he found out [etc.
> etc.]. At this point you will remember that you were then
> the manager of the fresh fish branch of Messrs. Catlin and
> Clovis in Fenchurch Street. What a change since then! Milli-
> cent had not yet put her hair up. . . . [etc. etc.]

Henry James had something similar in mind when he
complained that the time scheme of *Roderick Hudson*
was inadequate. He felt that the hero, Roderick, falls to
pieces too soon and relinquishes his hold upon our understanding and sympathy. The book, James said, was
ill-paced, "too scantily projected and suggested" for Roderick to turn around. That sense of passage of time necessary to give the feel of life, that complexity of change
and variation which only "duration of time" implicit in

the time-shift technique can give, was missing from the novel.

Beginning with *Lord Jim*, Conrad became master of a time technique, and steadily matured in his ability to use time as simple past, as narrative and as character, as ironic comment, and as history. Using these categories, many of which overlap, I shall illustrate Conrad's significant awareness of time in his major novels. The categories are flexible and in no sense are they intended to "define" a particular novel; they exist only for the sake of the novel. (The reader not freshly familiar with Conrad's individual works should read the following remarks in conjunction with the novels themselves, or else turn back to this section after having first read the book-by-book analyses in later chapters.)

I V

In his early work, Conrad relied almost solely on flash-back for his manipulation of time sequences. Even in his later work, flashback remained paramount, although frequently united with other time techniques. As I mentioned above, his first two novels, *Almayer's Folly* and *An Outcast of the Islands*, are straightforward narratives except for one major flashback in each. *Almayer's Folly*, similar in structure to the Flaubertian novel in which unity of plot predominates, is a radical departure from the multiple plots of the Victorians, and, along with *The Rover*, is perhaps the simplest of Conrad's novels. The narrative is uncomplicated, for here descriptive language provides comment, whereas in the later work time techniques often replace discourse. The simple flashback of Almayer's mind to a period when his hopes were still high is tinged with an irony that is not as yet sharply focused;

later, in *The Secret Agent,* for example, the ironic use of time becomes a way of "seeing" the material. As in *Almayer,* flashback in *An Outcast* serves a narrative and not an imaginative purpose.

If we skip to Conrad's last completed novel, *The Rover,* we find a curious return to the uncomplicated construction of his earliest work. Except for certain minor shifts, the narrative of *The Rover* is simple and even. Conrad is no longer trying to organize his material technically; he is writing *directly* of what he knows, and the lack of imaginative thrust is evident. The traditional episodic method of storytelling now seems sufficient to him. When Conrad relied too heavily on simple flashback, as he did in *The Rover,* his material often is thin, unconvincing, and obvious.

The Rescue, begun in 1896, but not completed until 1919, contains all the stylistic mannerisms from Conrad's early experimental period to his relatively uncomplex last works. This novel makes frequent use of flashbacks and of shifts in time and space. Flashback, however, is used expositorily—to sketch in the backgrounds of the characters, to re-create a prior sequence of events; in general, to enlarge the field of action beyond the particular point of the present. With all its shifts of time, *The Rescue* nevertheless remains almost a conventionally narrated book, a characteristic common to most of Conrad's work after *Victory* and before *Lord Jim.* The time methods here are only a way of telling the story; they never become the Why and How of the novel. Time, in *The Rescue,* creates surface complexities without sub-surface depth and variety.

Specifically, the climactic action of *The Rescue*—the complete destruction of Lingard's plan and with it his honor—is unfolded in a series of flashbacks, working from a narrator at the center of the action through a series of relay narrators to the reader himself. The device, though, is no more than what is popularly called a "gimmick"; for Conrad, it was an escape from direct participation and direct narration into simple recapitulation. Long before the climax, moreover, the dramatic sense has been lost, and this telescoping device seems evasive whereas elsewhere it is often integral. *The Rescue*, like many other Conrad works of his early and later periods, manifests what Mark Schorer in another context called "a failure of technical discovery"—that inability to find suitable form for one's material, with the result that form never becomes part of and "in of" the material.

The use of a complicated time sequence is, of course, no clear index to the success or failure of any given work. "Heart of Darkness," for example, contains an almost direct narrative, and yet it is one of Conrad's most successful stories. While forsaking an involved narrative in "Heart of Darkness," Conrad invested the story with numerous images which gradually assume the narrative line. There is poetry of word implicit in this treatment, but that fine sense of poetry of scene, reached through intensity of image in "Heart of Darkness," could usually be achieved by Conrad only by a more imaginative technical organization. "Youth," another work of the same period, fits into direct flashback treatment: the frame, the reminiscence, and then the coda.

It is, usually, the combination of effects that produces a gratifying semblance of reality. In novels like *Chance*, *Nostromo*, and *Victory*, the flashback into simple past is only one thread in a richly conceived fabric. The first 352 pages of *Nostromo* are in part used to catch up and fill in the past; at the same time that the story line is moving ahead, past events are moving in, as it were, crablike, and the result is a thickly textured narrative. *Victory,* like *Nostromo,* attains its richness through an aggregate of devices, not the least of which is an astute use of flashback. As the novel's present moves forward, we are constantly thrown into Heyst's background until the tension between past and present in interaction forms the knotty vertebrae of the book. In *Lord Jim,* the first of Conrad's major technical experiments, the use of flashback is no doubt enriching. With this novel, however, Conrad clearly extended the boundaries of his use of time as simple past, and *Lord Jim* rightfully belongs in a more technically advanced category.

V

In nearly all his novels and in many short stories, Conrad makes frequent use of a narrative device which, for lack of a more suitable term, I call the developing sequence: namely, the repeated allusion to a character or event that is then developed through repetition in succeeding pages until the entire sequence finally becomes clear to the reader. Through this technique, time determines the author's presentation of the characters and at the same time assumes the narrative weight of the novel. As a device, it is purely conventional, employed regularly by every novelist with a sense of pace and development.

In *Lord Jim,* though, Conrad employed the developing sequence to create a fugue-like quality, the polyphony of several voices counterpointing each other. Once the novel has moved less than half-way into the first part, Conrad, at one point, is expanding five sets of circumstances, none of which has as yet been fully developed:

(1) *The frame and its setting: Marlow as he narrates the story and comments upon it to his listeners.*

(2) *The setting of the initial conversation between Marlow and Jim.*

(3) *Jim's version of the* Patna *incident.*

(4) *The gap between the "facts" of the court story and the "real" circumstances on board the* Patna.

(5) *The novelist himself in the background controlling Marlow.*

If we compare the chronological sequence of events in one column with the novelist's conception of the sequence in the other, we can see what Conrad did with the developing sequence in Part I:

The Chronological Order	The Novelist's Order
1. *Patna* voyage.	7. Jim as water clerk.
2. Hitting the derelict.	1. *Patna* voyage sketched.
3. Desertion of the *Patna*.	2. Hitting the derelict.
4. Court of inquiry.	4. Court of inquiry.
5. Jim's sense of defeat.	6. Marlow's interference in
6. Marlow's interference in	Jim's life.
Jim's life.	5. Jim's sense of defeat.
7. Jim as water clerk.	3. Desertion of the *Patna*.

Conrad, however, went further than to keep each element in suspension while he worked part by part. Using a sequence of direct juxtaposition, like that of Flaubert's Agricultural Fair scene in *Madame Bovary,* he placed the initial meeting between Jim and Marlow against the background of a ridiculous assault and battery case in the courtroom. The whole confusion of Jim's case fans out, becoming one of universal misunderstanding, symbolized by his misinterpretation of Marlow's intentions taken together with his mistaking the chance remarks of a bystander—and ever in the background the natives involved in the assault upon a money-lender.

We nevertheless feel here, as I suggested above, in the remarks on *The Rescue,* that lack of sufficient technical invention which would have conveyed the flow of experience more smoothly. The lack is even more conspicuous in a later scene in Patusan, in which we are presented with a time sequence that shifts from past perfect to present perfect while the narrator is ranging back and forth from past to present. In his effort to catch all pastness and presentness in one even flow, Conrad was approximating what later became in other hands the stream-of-consciousness technique. It is evident that Conrad's attempt to integrate past and present in the narrative called for a still further emancipation from the forms of the nineteenth-century novel, a breakaway he was not as yet prepared to make in *Lord Jim.*

Conrad referred to *Nostromo* as a "great fraud" and an "audacious effort," by which he meant it was an ambitious and daring experiment. Time, although used here to convey history in the making, also has its traditional narrative functions. As pure narrative, the chronological sequence controls the flow of experience. To cite an example: the flight of the Costaguana ruler, Ribiera, is used as a reference point, first mentioned on page 11; referred to on page 130, in the context of a large cluster of related details; hinted at on page 145, with some additional background details; further explained on page 352 ff. in Captain Mitchell's narrative. Ribiera's flight, however, is just one of the time pegs on which Conrad suspended the narrative; the ever-present silver mine itself weaves in and out of the narrative and helps to fix the tempos of the novel. Through these reference points, all scrambled in a conscious time sequence, Conrad was able to control the flow of action. These "jumps" in time remove the onus of direct narration from the author and place it on the reader, who must reconstruct the action. Whenever Conrad simplifies, however—as he did in the latter part of *Nostromo* after the revolution—he minimizes the experiential quality of the book.

Even a superficial view of *Chance* reveals Conrad's most involved manipulation of time as narrative and time as character, in which both elements unfold according to what I have called the developing sequence. But perhaps the thinness of the novel—as if in defiance of its elaborate technique—rests with our awareness that method tends to inundate subject matter. Always in mind is the vague fear that intricate trappings have overburdened a relatively simple story with all the mechanics of a pretentiously conceived epic. *Chance,* nevertheless, was highly praised by Henry James in "The New Novel" as a "marvel of method applied to a particular end in view"; but James' praise was tempered by misgivings. He perceived that content seemed to be fighting system, and that while system triumphed, the challenge appeared to have come from without and not as a mystic impulse from within. Despite all this close attention to method, Conrad in this novel never essentially advanced his technique much further than that of *Lord Jim.*

Only in his more ambitiously conceived novels, like *Nostromo, Victory, Under Western Eyes,* and *The Secret Agent,* does time technique work along with a profound comprehension of subject to provide that rich meaning which justifies an elaborate method. In *Chance,* on the contrary, there is a great show of method whose function is relatively simple. The numerous shifts between past and present are no great matter in themselves, with the sole exception that Conrad's present time is not the reader's present, and his past time is divided into many groupings. *Chance,* accordingly, is full of experiments in the juxtaposition and fragmentation of scenes which indirectly create the narrative line and develop character. Often, the narrative line is suspended by lengthy interchanges between characters two and three times removed from the reader, who must himself take the necessary steps down the chronological ladder. On page 280, for example, the reader must synthesize the following sequences: (1) the conversation between Franklin, the chief mate of the *Ferndale,* and Powell, as repeated by (2) Marlow and Powell, as repeated by (3) Marlow and "I," the novelist.

If we compare Conrad's arrangement (column II on the following pages) of the "facts" of *Chance* (in Part One) to a direct chronological narrative (column I), we can obtain some idea of the intricate interweaving of time sequences, an intricacy, as I said above, which enfolds the relatively uncomplex subject matter in the webbing of a great and pretentious design.

I. *Chronology of events in Chance*	II. *Novelistic order in Chance*
(1) The de Barral family, Flora and her governess; background of de Barral's fraud and his sudden demise.	Chapter III. pp. 68-87 IV. pp. 96-133
(2) Flora is with the Fynes.	Chapter II. pp. 35-40 pp. 40-66
(3) Flora deserts her cousin and returns to the Fynes, goes off again with her cousin and re-returns, goes off to Germany, and once again comes back to the Fynes.	Chapter VI. pp. 163-186
(4) First intimation that Flora and Captain Anthony, the	Chapter III. pp. 67-68 VII. pp. 206-238

brother of Mrs. Fyne, have
eloped.

(5) Marlow meets Flora for the first time in his initial visit to the Fynes.	Chapter II. pp. 40-66 pp. 206-238
(6) Subsequent visits of Marlow to the Fynes after Flora has eloped with Captain Anthony. All these visits take place over a short period of time before Marlow and Fyne go up to London.	Chapter III. pp. 87-95 IV. pp. 96-133 Chapter V. pp. 134-154 V. pp. 154-162 VI. pp. 163-195
(7) Marlow, once in London, speaks at length to Flora on the pavement in front of the hotel where Fyne is facing Marlow and ostensibly trying to split the couple. Flora tells Marlow about her stay with the Fynes (5) and about her attempted suicide (5).	Chapter VII. pp. 196-199 VII. pp. 199-238
(8) Fyne comes from the hotel and speaks with Marlow; Fyne tells of de Barral's release from prison and of Flora's love for her father and not for Anthony. Just then, Marlow sees Flora enter Anthony's hotel.	Chapter VII. pp. 238-253
(9) Powell, one of the sources of information for the novel, along with Marlow and Franklin, the chief mate of the *Ferndale*, obtains a berth	Chapter I. pp. 25-34

on that ship, of which Anthony is captain.

(10) The novelistic present: Mar-   Chapter I. pp. 3-34
low, Powell, and "I," the nov-   II. pp. 35-40
elist. The emphasis is on Pow-
ell's having obtained passage
on the *Ferndale* in the distant
past.

(11) Powell leaves, and Marlow   Chapter II. pp. 40-66
remains to speak with the   VII. pp. 253 ff.
novelist about the past in re-
lation to the Fynes and to the
girl Flora—memories called
to mind by Powell's reference
to the *Ferndale*.

This column-by-column comparison is of course a simplification; for within each category there are numerous
interruptions by several of the narrators, many side comments by Marlow, and many small shifts between
past and present. By alluding to the central situation and
central characters from various sides, Conrad was able to
present the materials as "experienced," the characters as
"met," and the interactions of people as they occurred.

Nevertheless, even if we rightly feel that *Chance* is no
more than a narrative *tour de force,* withal lacking in
substance, we must recognize the ingenious development
of character that results from refracted time sequences.
Our view of Anthony, until the latter part of the book,
is almost totally from outside; again and again, he is
"seen" through comments of others. When we finally
come upon him in the flush of his experience and he exhibits the sensitive awareness of a man walking a tight-
rope, then we know him to be "there," trapped by his own

generosity and loneliness which he had disguised to himself as love. As Marlow comments: "Anthony had discovered that he was not the proud master but the chafing captive of his own generosity." Anthony, ostensibly a bluff sea captain, is always more than the sum total of his virtues and vices and never less than a figure of some import, although neither intellectually satisfying nor emotionally profound.

Our initial ideas of Flora are formed in like manner, more through her acquaintances than through herself. Not until the long and central scene with Marlow in front of the hotel do the fragments which are called Flora become a flesh and blood personification. Then, page by page, our awareness of her sensibility grows, until her fortune is decided in that critical scene when she conclusively selects Anthony rather than her egocentrically insane father. From a position of isolation and mistrust she gains love and security. Flora, although fragile and even wispy at times, is perhaps Conrad's most fully developed female character. Yet her creation is almost totally from the exterior; encircled by passing events and chance remarks, her characterization unfolds by bits and pieces.

Conrad was not by any means employing this method of character development for the first time. His Nostromo —in this respect like Molière's Tartuffe—is a "constructed character": that is, one who is seen from outside, created almost apart from his physical being, and then presented in person at the climax of his acts. In Nostromo, we hear of the titular character in a fragmentary manner, but we know a great deal about him by the time he assumes central importance. Through an encircling time sequence that shuttles between the novel's present and various shades of the past, Conrad is able to surround his characters with comments and actions which construct their personalities for us. Of course, he is never completely able to avoid the chief danger of this method, which is the failure to achieve that intellectual and emotional depth that can be gained only by a closer acquaintance with the character.

We find in *Under Western Eyes* (1911) an attempt analogous to the Tartuffe-like character development of Nostromo, but with this difference: Razumov is presented early, rather than late, in the plot and his precarious position is dramatically defined at the outset. Once the hopelessness of his situation is made clear to him, Razumov disappears from active participation in the novel for nearly two hundred pages. So ends Part One. Conrad then shifts sharply from the Russian setting to Geneva, where Razumov inevitably is to arrive as a counter-agent. Before we meet him again, Conrad has circled closer and closer *around* his situation, introduced us to the Haldins in Geneva, and created the personalities of that revolutionary world who are to raise Razumov to great success and then let him drop to his doom. Razumov becomes a character created by circumstances. Similarly, in Conrad's other novel of anarchy, *The Secret Agent*, Verloc—like Razumov in this respect—after a short introduction disappears for nearly a hundred pages. His person, in fact, is seen very little; yet he is ever-present through indirect references and through sequences of events that are constructed about him.

By means of these significant shifts in time, Conrad was often able to charge his narrative with the actuality of experience and create characters who live because of method and not despite it. All these examples, however, demonstrate simple and traditional time sequences; but when we turn to the next category we see that time can create an entirely new dimension.

V I

The Secret Agent, if compared technically to *Chance*, is a relatively simple book, but without question it yields more upon second or third reading. One of the reasons, perhaps, for its greater profundity is Conrad's repeated use of time-based structural ironies to supplement verbal irony.

After Verloc's conversation with the Embassy agent Vladimir, in which they discuss the possibility of bombing Greenwich Observatory, we are left with the sense of an impending, though still distant, crime. Soon after, Verloc drops out for one-third of the book, and we first hear about the bomb-attempt casually from the anarchists Ossipon and the Professor. Ossipon is speaking:

"Then it may be you haven't heard yet the news I've heard just now—in the street. Have you?"

The little man shook his head negatively the least bit. But as he gave no indication of curiosity Ossipon ventured to add that he had heard it just outside the place.

From this suggestion of crime we pick up the police investigation of the case, their suspicions, and their concrete evidence saved from the explosion—the address of Verloc's shop sewn to a fragment of Stevie's coat. Before we know the facts of the explosion, before we even know Verloc's part in it, the police have already traced it to him and are ready to interrogate him. Through a subtle time-shift technique, the whole stupidity of Verloc's fumbling action is ironically pointed up; and without any verbal comment Conrad has, by means of the very structure of the novel, intimated the irony inherent in the bomb-attempt.

Not until page 190, fully 127 pages after the conversation between Ossipon and the Professor, does Conrad pick up Verloc on the day of the bomb-attempt. The sequence of the book, then, is the opposite of the detective story; the element of chase is not paramount, and the ingenuity of the criminal is not a factor. Speaking indirectly through shifts in time, Conrad implied that his subject was not merely a story of anarchism and definitely not the "Simple Tale" of the subtitle. The temporal order of the book makes us realize that the real center is not a bomb-plot or machinations of anarchists, but, rather, everyday human tragedy, as symbolized by that significant cab ride of Winnie's mother to the charity home.

In *Under Western Eyes*, through building around Razumov a framework of conflicts waiting to receive him, Conrad has, with clear ironic overtones, created an atmosphere of tension which the reader—the only one in possession of all necessary facts—re-creates imaginatively. The time device constitutes, as it were, a ready-made mold which encloses Razumov's past, present, and future, and disallows even his temporal escape from the events fashioned for him by his sudden decision to betray Haldin. The time device becomes a working part of Conrad's sense of human irony, his belief in the inevitability of an endless sequence of events following hard upon one another once an initial judgment has been made. When the time theory operates, as it does here, in the service of a novelist's beliefs, then we find a perfect integration of a novel's form and substance.

The circling method of narration in *Victory* provides

an implied ironical comment through the juxtaposition of dissimilar situations. In an early exchange between Davidson, that solid knight, and the much persecuted Mrs. Schomberg, we learn that Heyst and Lena have run off to their island retreat. We continue to pick up fragments of the flight and learn its effects on the villainous Schomberg, who had chosen Lena for himself. We then see the plotting of Schomberg and the amoral Jones to destroy Heyst, the reputed possessor of a vast treasure. Yet Heyst had been presented to the reader as a solitary hermit whose only dedication is to the philosophy of indifference. Nevertheless, his commitment to Lena is a commitment to life, and his act, like Razumov's—that other hermit who wanted solitary success—sets off a series of events which enfold and eventually doom him. As a consequence, we experience in the narrative line at least four simultaneous levels of action which are created by time sequences, each one an ironic comment on the other: (1) Heyst the Hermit, influenced by the philosophy of his father; (2) Heyst committed to the rescue of Lena; (3) Heyst being slandered by Schomberg as a thief and murderer; (4) Heyst, the victim of plotting by Schomberg and Jones. In addition to these major characters and events, there are also numerous minor characters and minor threads of action operating at the same time. The structural irony works to point up the withdrawn and solitary Heyst ever encircled by events and decisions which he is temperamentally unable to handle. This is the verbal point of the book, and it is also part of the structural organization.

But this category of time as irony does not by any means exhaust Conrad's time philosophy. Certain elements of *Victory* and *Nostromo*, and to some extent *Under Western Eyes*, carry time technique further. In this

chapter 4

Early Conrad: From Almayer to Typhoon

Part I

Must I not serve a long apprenticehood
To foreign passages, and in the end,
Having my freedom, boast of nothing else
But that I was a journeyman to grief?

KING RICHARD II

As a first novel, *Almayer's Folly*[1] paradoxically displays the exhaustion and "sucked-out" quality of a very old and disillusioned novelist. Published in 1895, it manifests the language, the tones, the characteristic rhythms, and most of the mannerisms of *fin de siècle* literature. *Almayer's Folly* is a prose counterpart of 1890's poetry, of early Yeats and Dowson, of Arthur Symons and the siftings of the pre-Raphaelites, in particular the softness of D. G. Rossetti and otiosity of William Morris. Conrad's novel,

---

[1] According to a letter to Mme Poradowska, *Almayer's Folly* was begun in September, 1889, in London and finished in first draft April 24, 1894. Published by T. Fisher Unwin (London, 1895), *Almayer's Folly* was not necessarily Conrad's first written work; a short story, "The Black Mate," was written in 1886 for a prize competition in *Tit-Bits,* but the version we have in *Tales of Hearsay* (1925) probably shares at most only the title and theme of the 1886 version. Although Conrad's wife said he claimed the story as his first work, it is of such inconsequential stature that beyond matters of chronological interest it merits no discussion in its own right.

as befitting its background, is one of decadence and breakdown, a pageant of retreat, of dreams, of filmy torpor and fatigue. His method of developing this theme of exhaustion is through emphasis on a certain type of language and through his choice of characteristic images.

Conrad's settings in *Almayer* and his second novel, *An Outcast of the Islands,* are exotic, full of jungle scenes, semi-civilized natives, and violent emotions. These images—the basic stuff of his early work—are found later in new settings but with the same purport, transformed into the storm images of *The Nigger of the "Narcissus,"* the natural descriptions of *Nostromo,* the city backgrounds of *The Secret Agent* and *Under Western Eyes,* the island backdrop of *Victory.* No matter what the setting—in city or jungle or sea—Conrad used imagistic devices as objective correlatives to create the narrative.

The chief images in *Almayer* are those of languor—a languor of character, of language, and of setting. *Almayer's Folly,* despite its thinness, is a mine for those interested in viewing Conrad in his apprentice stage, for his literary devices were certain even in his first novel. This is a sure book, a "written" book, although what is obviously lacking is a large enough canvas. But the basic themes and devices are here.

It is of some significance to note how Conrad organized his material to suggest the novel's pervading theme of the old and the exhausted, that lack of spirit and energy which characterized much of the 1890's prose and poetry. Many of the early reviewers paid tribute to Conrad for his adventurous use of language and recognized the importance of his sense of the word, although they were undecided whether or not it was advantageous to the theme. As the reviewers suggested, it is surely through a careful selection of language that Conrad explored his basic themes of man and nature, of greed, survival, and courage. Malaya and Africa in the early novels are as much a mirror of the late nineteenth-century world as the more mature works set in Europe and the Americas are of the twentieth.

In his manner of presentation, the apprentice Conrad was not unlike the young Yeats or the young Melville. As their vision deepened their verbal style changed, Yeats becoming leaner and harder, Conrad and Melville less embellished and more conservative. Conrad's early enameled prose has many striking similarities to Yeats' "woven" world. The long drawn-out vowel sounds of the following passage suggest the languorous setting:

> . . . the big open space where the thick-leaved trees put black patches of shadow which seemed to float on a flood of smooth, intense, light that rolled up to the houses and down to the stockade and over the river, where it broke and sparkled in thousands of glittering wavelets, like a band woven of azure and gold edged with the brilliant green of the forests guarding both banks of the Pantai.

In the same section Conrad speaks of the "smell of decaying blossoms" and the "acrid smoke from the cooking fires," of the "clear blue of the hot sky," "the light puffs [of breeze] playing capriciously" and the "faint rustle of trees"—the relaxed dormancy of a hot afternoon beneath a sweltering sun, the sensuous retreat into sluggishness and apathy.

So overwhelming is the presence of the jungle and so overpowering the slow rhythm of this vast primeval slime that the people in contrast seem mere pawns in the grasp of uncontrollable forces. Conrad's description of background drives home their severe isolation; the vast swamp of trees and roots and mud seems to suck up every semblance of life and to reduce man to insignificance. Supplementing the jungle, Conrad uses the symbol of storm, an oft-repeated phenomenon in his later work, as an epitome of nature's power and man's insignificance. The wild fury of the storm—first its "oppressive calm," "furious blast," "fantastic shapes," "driving roar," then the "tormented river" and the turmoil of "leaping waters"— all these images are natural background for man's relatively minor agonies, for man's impotence against cosmic forces.

After the storm, as if in sluggish opposition, there is once again the near-silent jungle which murmurs and hums—those onomatopoetic words suggesting the same sense of primeval drowsiness which we find in Yeats' characteristically soft poetry of the mid-1880's and early 1890's. Yeats spoke of a "drooping brow," of "great boughs," "quiet boughs," "heavy boughs," and of "great boughs [that] drop tranquillity"; his poems were filled with murmuring seas and "the water's drowsy blaze," taken together with "the feathered ways" and "vapoury footsoles" of a hushed evening.

In a passage reminiscent of Yeats' Indian poems, Conrad, in his description of the slave girl Taminah—that pitiful double of Almayer—approaches the perfection of pure silence and pure languor:

> Then she paddled home slowly in the afternoon, often letting her canoe float with the lazy stream in the quiet backwater of the river. The paddle hung idle in the water as she sat in the stern, one hand supporting her chin, her eyes wide open, listening intently to the whispering of her heart that seemed to swell at last into a song of extreme sweetness. . . . And when the sun was near its setting she walked to the bathing-place and heard it as she stood on the tender grass

of the low bank, her robe at her feet, and looked at the
reflection of her figure on the glass-like surface of the creek.
Listening to it she walked slowly back, her wet hair hanging
over her shoulders; lying down to rest under the bright stars,
she closed her eyes to the murmur of the water below, of
the warm wind above; to the voice of nature speaking
through the faint noises of the great forest, and to the song
of her own heart.

Taminah's pre-Raphaelite figure caught in a narcissistic
pose is characteristic of the lazy, measured beat of this
fin de siècle work. Moreover, her sense of peace and
tranquillity amid potential violence is a significant prefiguration of Almayer's own position.

Those early critics who pointed to Conrad as a strikingly new figure working in English failed to see continuity between the poetic language of the 1890's and
Conrad's early work, and failed to recognize how completely he was part of the 1890's spirit. The work of Arthur Symons, a central nineties figure who, Jessie Conrad
said, was the only poet Conrad read with pleasure, is
full of "sea moans" and "dark shivering trees," "sickle-
moons" and "delicate ivory"—that whole paraphernalia
of late nineteenth-century poets who combined the vivid
mannerisms of English romanticism with a misunderstood
and misused French symbolism. Like Ernest Dowson,
that frail figure of washed-out manhood who wrote of
pale and faded roses, long-dead leaves, the pallor of
ivories, the "drear oblivion of lost things," "languid
lashes," and a vast assortment of exhausted objects, Conrad, similarly, wrote of the murmuring river behind the
white veil, the soft whisper of eddies washing against the
river bank, and the breathless calm of the breeze. As
much as Yeats and Dowson, Conrad learned his literary

English at the end of the century, and was only able to make it leaner and more pungent as he developed a more mature style.

Of greater importance, however, in Conrad's later development as a novelist is his parallel use of another type of image: the image of despair. Among Conrad's contemporaries, this imagery had of course gained prominence—in the necropolis of James Thomson's nocturnal imagination, in Dowson's personal laments, in Beardsley's nihilistic sketches, in the pessimism of John Davidson's distorted visions; it would reappear in Housman's *A Shropshire Lad* (1896) and come to fruition in Conrad's own "Heart of Darkness" (1899), in which a personal malaise became objective and gained epic proportions. In *Almayer*, this image supplements the languor of the jungle, but it is essentially a city image, a civilized image transferred to an exotic setting. In that scene, for example, portraying *Almayer's* desolation, his exhaustion, his life-come-to-nought, we have a virtual wasteland of sterility and dust:

> He went towards the office door and with some difficulty managed to open it. He entered in a cloud of dust that rose under his feet. Books open with torn pages bestrewed the floor; other books lay about grimy and black, looking as if they had never been opened. . . . In the middle of the room the big office desk, with one of its legs broken, careened over like the hull of a stranded ship; most of the drawers had fallen out, disclosing heaps of paper yellow with age and dirt. . . . The desk, the paper, torn books, and the broken shelves, all under a thick coat of dust. The very dust and bones of a dead and gone business. . . . He started with a great fear in his heart, and feverishly began to rake in the papers scattered on the floor, broke the chair into bits, splintered the drawers by banging them against the desk, and

made a big heap of all that rubbish in one corner of the room.

In a similar vein, we have an earlier scene of the deserted Almayer, forsaken by all, living in a ghost house, a significant harbinger of one type of neurosis-ridden late nineteenth-century individual.

At his feet lay the overturned table, amongst a wreck of crockery and broken bottles. The appearance as of traces left by a desperate struggle was accentuated by the chairs, which seemed to have been scattered violently all over the place, and now lay about the verandah with a lamentable aspect of inebriety in their helpless attitudes. Only Nina's big rocking-chair, standing black and motionless on its high runner, towered above the chaos of demoralized furniture, unflinchingly dignified and patient, waiting for its burden.

. . . A couple of bats, encouraged by the darkness and the peaceful state of affairs, resumed their silent and oblique gambols above Almayer's head. . . .

The language of desolation joins the language of exhaustion and retreat to fix the atmosphere of *Almayer's Folly* and to give substance to its ghostly characters. The description of a once active working office and once-inhabited house is as much an epitome of Conrad's world as the passages of torpor and languor.

In his conception of character as well, we find that same sense of desolation, frustration, and exhaustion. The comedy of Almayer—a man of great hopes and only moderate abilities, an expedient man who found out that circumstances were set to destroy him—is played out against a vast panorama of natural forces which he is unable to control or even understand. It is an old Almayer we see falling further and further into personal and social isolation; an Almayer separated from his wife and child by race, suspected by the Dutch authorities of illegal activities, opposed by the Arabs and Malay natives, enemy of the vestigial jungle and ever-present river which brought in the Arabs and took away Nina and Dain, deserted by an old and ineffectual Lingard who is beset by his own sense of failure; an Almayer who lives with his old shrewish wife and tries to deal with those predatory statesmen of Sambir, old Babalatchi, old Lakamba, and old Abdulla. Only Nina and Dain are young, and significantly they escape to another place, away from the decaying jungle world, away from the aged and desolate to a rebirth among new surroundings. Remaining is an Almayer sunk so low in the human scale that his only friend is Taminah, the slave girl beaten and ostracized by the others. In their common suffering and insufficiency, they find momentary identification but never real sympathy or feeling. Defeated, unimportant, shrunken in size, Almayer is, like the century itself, ready to die. Victimized by his own greed, Almayer rarely gains even pity, for he is clearly a figure of debility and fitfulness, never one of defiance or strength.

The structure of the novel is simple, one of the simplest in Conrad's canon. Most of the book is a straightforward narrative, two flashbacks filling in Almayer's earlier relationship with Lingard, with his Malayan wife, and with his "white" background. The comparatively simple narrative is a natural method of telling a story of essentially uncomplicated people caught in a dramatic but not tragic situation. Almayer is surely an object more of pity —if even that—than one of tragedy. His is an ironic end, rather than one fraught with the convulsive feelings of a Heyst or Kurtz. Almayer is, as we have seen, too much a figure of debility to attain tragic standing by his victimization. He lacks original stature, even though the real Almayer (William Charles Olmeijer) made a vivid impression on Conrad as an example of "that discord between the imagination in man and his ability to perform." Evidently this Don Quixote-like theme haunted Conrad from the beginning of his career, for it became one of the dominant patterns in his more important novels. But at this time, Almayer is certainly not of sufficient consequence to sustain a novel of large dimensions.

The seemingly facile narrative would appear to belie the great difficulties Conrad had with this first novel. John Dozier Gordan's indispensable study of early Conrad manuscripts and typescripts lays bare many of Conrad's dissembling remarks about his ease in writing *Almayer*. Dr. Gordan also shows that between the typescript and manuscript the entire relationship between Almayer and Dain Maroola, the young native, comes to life; that in the first version Conrad had no clear idea of their relationship; and that he worked slowly and uncertainly toward the right conception of Almayer's ruin. My own study in Chapter Five of the manuscript, typescript, and various published versions of *Nostromo* will show how Conrad revised his work as he went along, changing the verbal structure of entire passages and scenes, saving and transposing words, sentences, whole paragraphs, always the master craftsman who was rarely satisfied with his own work.

Notwithstanding Conrad's assiduity, the contemporary reviewers justifiably attacked his excessive use of rhetorical and descriptive passages seemingly for their own sake. In the following passage, for instance, Conrad makes palpably obvious use of flame and fire as imagistic comments on the feelings of Dain and Nina Almayer as the couple passionately comes together:

A small blue flame crept amongst the dry branches, and the crackling of reviving fire was the only sound as they faced each other in the speechless emotion of that meeting; then the dry fuel caught at once, and a bright hot flame shot upwards in a blaze as high as their heads, and in the light they saw each other's eyes.

This overwritten passage with its conspicuous appeal to stock feelings characterizes much of Conrad's early prose, particularly when he must meet a situation directly. Surely, Conrad's major successes came because he conceived scenes which eschewed stock responses and because his language avoided clichés. But as yet in *Almayer's Folly* as well as in his second novel, he was unable to judge his effects.

I I

As a sequel in reverse to *Almayer's Folly*, Conrad's second novel, *An Outcast of the Islands*,[2] goes back to an earlier period in the lives of the characters of the first book. The structure and language also return to those of *Almayer* rather than suggesting any new developments. That same sense of debility and exhaustion prevalent in the earlier book is present in *An Outcast*, but here attached to a dominant death theme; for the jungle has gained in malevolence, and the sea is an ambivalent force of life and death.

Conrad began *An Outcast* not as a novel, but as a short story, and perhaps its thinness and deficiency of substance can be traced to its original conception. The vast panorama of jungle creates a scenic background far in excess of what the characterization can sustain. Similarly, many

2 Finished September 16, 1895, and published in 1896 by T. Fisher Unwin, London.

of Conrad's other early works, except "Heart of Darkness," are constructed with the force of an epic around an essentially puny center. The conflicts of Willems, Lingard, Aïssa, and Almayer simply do not seem of sufficient import for their pretentious background.

The novel proceeds almost consecutively from its beginning with Willems at the peak of his power to his decline into futility, frustration, and, finally, death. Willems is a study of a man of vain pretensions brought to isolation, sensory exhaustion, and personal impotence, like the pitiful Almayer at the end of Conrad's first novel. Most of the novel is told through the omniscient author, with little character participation in the narration. Two narrative summaries pick up Willems' past, but once he arrives in Sambir his passion for Aïssa, the native seductress, dominates the action, and the narrative proceeds directly. Off the center of the stage are a younger Almayer, his hopes now ruined by Willems' treachery in disclosing the river route to the Arabs; a vigorous Lingard, vainly trying to salvage his trade; and those politicians of Sambir—Abdulla, Lakamba, and Babalatchi. A book of little subtlety, *An Outcast* is of the same stuff as *Almayer*.

Willems, who is by no means a tragic hero (almost an anti-tragic hero, in his way a clown), is related by Conrad to a Hell-Death motif, and his collapse is imagistically suggested in many scenes which imply both living-death and real death. When early in the book Aïssa veils herself against Willems' wishes, she seals off real contact between them and becomes an enclosed mummy "of cheap cotton goods" who sucks in Willems' will, leaving him "lost in abominable desire" and doomed as a human being, cut off from civilization and civilized feeling. A similar image is intensified later in the book as Willems and Aïssa are caught in a trap of frustration and emotional exhaustion, cognizant that there can be nothing between them now that even passion has been extinguished. Aïssa suddenly lets down her hair, literally, and it falls "scattered over her shoulders like a funeral veil. . . . she rested her head on her drawn up knees . . . and she sat in the abandoned posture of those who sit weeping by the dead, of those who watch and mourn over a corpse." As the relationship between Willems and Aïssa reaches its blackest moments, Conrad by a series of striking images and by a lavish use of description implies their "No-Exit" frustration, their sitting by the river Styx in their own personalized hell. Conrad pictures them as shades, as the living-dead who wait hopelessly at the nadir of despair:

> Those three human beings [Willems, Aïssa, and an old and decrepit serving woman, who is "a shrivelled, an unmoved, a passive companion of their disaster"] abandoned by all were like shipwrecked people left on an insecure and slippery ledge by the retiring tide of an angry sea—listening to its distant roar, living anguished between the menace of its return and the hopeless horror of their solitude—in the midst of a tempest of passion, of regret, of disgust, of despair.

That old serving woman—that ever-present Fate out of *Macbeth*—seems in her sorceress' caldron to be boiling out Willems' last moments:

> The water in the iron pan on the cooking fire boiled furiously, belching out volumes of white steam that mixed with the thin black thread of smoke. The old woman appeared to him through this as if in a fog, squatting on her heels, impassive and weird.

A like image, supplementing Willems' despair of Aïssa, is conveyed in the scene between Lingard and Almayer when their inability to kill a wily housefly symbolizes the frustration of their urgent attempts to escape the situation: "Lingard struck at it with his hat. The fly swerved and Almayer dodged his head out of the way. Then Lingard aimed another ineffectual blow." The fly continues to evade the two men who lunge at it and swing their arms to no avail. "But suddenly the buzz died out . . . leaving Lingard and Almayer standing face to face . . . looking very puzzled and idle, their arms hanging uselessly by their sides—like men disheartened by some portentous failure." As the fly evades their efforts to trap it, so does Aïssa and all she stands for elude Willems, until life becomes meaningless for him with or without her.

The Hell-Death motif which characterizes both *Almayer* and *An Outcast* is nowhere better seen than in man's ineffectual efforts to sustain nature. Conrad's jungle background, despite its torpor, is also a snare, a den of struggle for survival in which man is worn down and subjected to inhuman forces. Towering over Willems and emphasizing his isolation, the trees themselves look "sombre, and malevolently solid, like a giant crowd of pitiless enemies pressing round silently to witness his slow agony." Nature becomes the sole enduring thing, deathless in its omnipotence, and man in his struggles becomes frailer and more ephemeral. Willems literally surrenders his will to the unknown, to those unidentifiable forces, working within and without, which sap life and reduce resistance.

The sun in its oppression and cruelty becomes an ally of the will-sapping jungle. It is presented as a force which destroys all motion, buries all shadows, and checks all breath, whose powerful serenity penetrates to the earth and silences all within its range.

Strength and resolution, body and mind alike were helpless and tried to hide before the rush of the fire from heaven. Only the frail butterflies, the fearless children of the sun, the capricious tyrants of the flowers, fluttered audaciously in the open, and their minute shadows hovered in swarms over the drooping blossoms, ran lightly on the withering grass, or glided on the dry and cracked earth.

In his use of language, which differs little in essentials from that in *Almayer*, Conrad attempted once again to convey the mysterious and exhaustive powers of nature, although he was still too much a man of his day to go against the vocabulary and tones of the 1890's. While *An Outcast* may perhaps display less luxuriance and exuberance than *Almayer*, the language, as in the following passage, is still lush; particularly evident are the languid adjectives and slow-paced verbs which fill out the scene:

> . . . the landscape of brown golds and brilliant emeralds under the dome of hot sapphire; the whispering big trees; the loquacious nipa-palms that rattled their leaves volubly in the night breeze, as if in haste to tell him [Lingard] all the secrets of the great forest behind them. He loved the heavy scents of blossoms and black earth, that breath of life and death which lingered over his brig in the damp air of tepid and peaceful nights.

Contrasted with the languor of the jungle and the energy-sucking sun, is the river which leads to the sea, that river of freshness which in *Almayer* took away Nina and Dain. But, as Conrad describes it, the river can in turn "nurse love or hate on its submissive and heartless bosom"; it can be a "deliverance, a prison, a refuge, or a grave." To Almayer and Lingard, it is a river of misfortune and doom which brings death to their enterprises, but to Willems it is temporary life, for by divulging its rocky passage to the Arabs he gains access to Aïssa. The river, a significant participant, becomes ". . . a voice low, discreet, and sad, like the persistent and gentle voices that speak of the past in the silence of dreams."

Water—as in the river or the rain—is a prominent image in the novel: water as friend and water as enemy. In that charged scene between Lingard, furious in righteous indignation, and Willems, trying hopelessly to summon up some human dignity in his complete frustration, we have nature's comment in the form of a storm. It immediately seems to the fierce Lingard that "light was dying prematurely out of the world," and that each crash of thunder is the startled sigh of an anguished earth, the "low and angry growls" of the storm reflecting and intermingling with the angry growls of the two men. When Willems finally tries to run away, his bedraggled figure is carried back in that rush of water which "his heart was not stout enough to face."

But Willems persists in looking to the river for escape; "If there was any hope in the world," he thinks, "it would come from the river. . . ." Willems dreams of death "on the brilliant undulations of the straits," and his dream is correct—the river does bring violent death, but in a form he had never dreamed. His "shadowless horizons" are those of that meeting between Aïssa and his wife and himself. Almayer's revenge is fulfilled; that river which had defeated *his* hopes is also the source of frustration and finally of death to Willems.

Between the action of the river and the languor of the jungle, Willems, a "being absurd, repulsive, pathetic, and droll," is dead; Lingard—a god who had controlled destinies—is ruined; Aïssa is a mad, "doubled-up crone"; and Almayer is left, still waiting for his fortune to be made, a broken man in a world "that's a swindle," embittered by frustration, and ready to dwindle into the Almayer who lives with his Folly as goal.

These bulky background trappings are of course much in excess of Willems' tragedy, and Conrad's attempts to suggest a tragic situation break down in the insignificance of the central character. Even the pretentious epigraph from Calderón,

Pues el delito mayor
Del Hombre es haber nacito [sic] [3]

is pointed at a character of greater substance than Willems. He becomes lost in the very immensity of things, a circumstance which, while it is the central point of the book, at the same time paradoxically reduces him to comparative insignificance. In writing a short story, as this novel was originally intended, Conrad would perhaps have restricted himself to more direct treatment, but after 368 pages the atmosphere becomes too charged with mysterious forebodings for its slight central character. For a study in passion, there is too much of the expedient in Willems to convey the necessary tension. His passion is off the top of his senses, touching only the froth of his emotions, and not reaching into the center of the man where real passion in conflict with reason might have been effectively dramatized in the cosmic trappings Conrad employs. Willems, like Almayer before him, seems to be crushed by the weight of the dying century, whose great burden allows him little freedom of self-expression and no chance to attain tragic stature.

Almayer and *An Outcast* both show, then, only moderate movement toward a new style in the novel, preliminary steps as yet somewhat unsure of direction. Nev-

___

[3] Man's greatest crime is having been born.

ertheless, from the beginning, Conrad was writing like a poet, letting his images—hazy though many are—speak for him and become a part of the narrative line. Ever present, however, are the long descriptive passages and the lazy discursiveness of the language of the 1890's; ever present is the tendency to overwrite and to substitute purple passages for those sharp images which suggest, convey, and become part of the novel's organic movement. Conrad's style was still that of a traditional novelist, but the signs of a potential breakthrough are visible. In his recognition, for example, of the darks and lights of human nature and in his presentation of certain types of "under" and "have-not" characters, Conrad presaged his own later work and the direction the novel was to take after him.

III

Before taking up *The Nigger of the "Narcissus,"* I want to say a word about Conrad's uncompleted novel, *The Sisters*, abandoned evidently because of Edward Garnett's adverse criticism. Stephen, the artist-hero of the novel, is a typical *fin de siècle* disillusioned idealist, an early counterpart of Axel Heyst and Martin Decoud. Stephen draws back instinctively from personal contacts and seeks salvation in the pursuit of immortal masterpieces. This Alastor-like spirit, with the exhausted manner of Huysmans' Des Esseintes, suffers from a soul infected by ennui, torpor, and a mysterious longing for completion. In nature he seeks the sources of all inspiration, but with a sigh of "Not here! Not here!" he turns away to the "undesirable security of perfect solitude." This extant fragment of *The Sisters* is interesting, for it affords a view of Conrad dealing with an artist-type and fully carrying over the excessively ornate language and languorous characters of the late nineteenth century.

The Rescue, begun in March, 1896, was not completed until 1919 and will be discussed in its finished state in Chapter Eight, indicating Conrad's later state of mind, although in style and geography it belongs with *Almayer* and *An Outcast*.

In *Almayer's Folly* and *An Outcast of the Islands*, Conrad worked through imagery and description to create an obvious world of man and nature, of greed and passion —obvious because discursive and labored: in short, too talky and too stagey. But in *The Nigger of the "Narcissus"* —still about man and nature, greed and passion—we have Conrad's first significant attempt to understate, to create a world through less obvious verbalizations, and to comment through a construct and not through a patchwork of discourse. *The Nigger* is Conrad's first non-discursive work, full of suggestive overtones that are neither pushed nor forced.

The fact that Conrad decided to publish his now famous Preface after the serialization of *The Nigger* in Henley's *New Review* demonstrates his avowed confidence in his craft and his recognition that he was heading in a new direction. This Preface and the novel are a "Vita Nuova," although it has been clearly established that even at this late date (1897) Conrad had not forsaken his idea of returning to sea. The writing of this book, nevertheless, gave Conrad confidence to continue; he was reasonably pleased with the results, which he claimed went further than those of a sea story. In a letter to Henry Seidel Canby near the end of his life, Conrad was still insisting on what he considered to be his true subject matter: the suggestive quality of the work, its non-literal application, and its implied ideas.

In the *Nigger* I give the psychology of a group of men . . . the problem that faces them is not a problem of the sea, it is merely a problem that has arisen on board a ship where the conditions of complete isolation from all land entanglements make it stand out with a particular force and colouring. (April 7, 1924)

Even though *The Nigger of the "Narcissus"* was planned as a short story of about 30,000 words, it demonstrates a significant shift in Conrad's method of working, pointing ahead toward his more mature novels. A worthy part of his canon, it stands with *Victory* and *The Secret Agent* as one of his almost perfectly measured novels, one whose development was not thwarted by considerations of space, as were, for example, the swiftly-ended *Nostromo* and *Under Western Eyes*. This book, Conrad implied, is a microcosm of a universal situation; that is, the inarticulate confusion of men of vague convictions when confronted by fear and superstition; those who could only shake their fists at the ineffable while they "lolled about with the careless ease of men who can discern perfectly the irremediable aspect of their existence."

The structure of the book is simple enough; the story is told by an omniscient shipmate on the "Narcissus" who doubles as author-narrator and as participant in the action. But the logic of the storytelling shows that Conrad was lazy in his conception, or at least was not seriously concerned with the logic of the narration. Beginning in third person as a viewer, the narrator soon passes into the first-person "we" and "us." From there, he fluctuates between viewer and participant. The discrepancy or difficulty arises when as the "we" he participates in events at which he could not logically be present; or when as narrator he describes events and/or conversations from which he also is logically removed. But unlike many of

Conrad's later novels, the emphasis here is not on the How of the book, although questions of technique are of no little interest.

The first temptation in analyzing any work in which man and the sea fight an isolated battle is to interpret the story allegorically; but this view would only divert us from what is essentially a fragile human drama. Certain letters Conrad wrote at this time supplement the Preface to *The Nigger* by throwing further light on his aims and by suggesting how his ideas were intermingled with his continual search for suitable technique. We find Conrad now not as a novelist of sea and jungle, but as a receptor of certain moral ideas conveyed in the tense relationship between the Nigger, James Wait, and the crew of the "Narcissus."

Writing to Cunninghame Graham, Conrad spoke of the personal demon in each man which drives him to stupidity, drunkenness, murder, thieving, contempt, and, not least of all, to the reforming of others. The world, he said, is a place of "vain and floating appearances" in which cowardice is the rule and a belief in the perfectibility of man a foolish ideal. Conrad saw life in half-tones, incomplete in its joy, sorrow, heroism, rascality, and suffering, a life in which improvement is self-delusive and an ardor for reform and beauty only a "vain striking for appearance." Life, Conrad claimed, is mysterious and our own thoughts ephemeral and full of shadows; we can only recognize the push of events and the crowd of incidents in which nothing significant happens. What we must ever deal with is a series of uneventful incidents in which we never take to heart the fate of humanity, wherein salvation lies in being illogical, and the only reasonable attitude for the novelist is one of "cold unconcern."

Applied to *The Nigger,* these remarks afford insight

into the character of the novel. Conrad's concern at this time was with the ever-shifting relation between the individual and society, and the role that each must play in conflict with the other. One can remark that James Wait stands as a symbol of the ethical demand that human beings in distress exert upon others, for Wait's predicament upsets the solidarity of the crew and creates a disturbance that can be reconciled only in moral terms. This is like the situation in *Lord Jim,* reversed though it is in emphasis, in which the crew without any sense of honor or integrity—deeply rooted as it is in merely personal justification—causes and abets Jim's defection from the *Patna.* Wait, in his role of seagoing confidence man, finds his counterpart in the fraudulent Donkin and in the vague fears and susceptibilities of an ignorant and superstitious crew. How Conrad develops this relationship, how the nature of Wait's illusory attraction conflicts with a crew rooted in reality and survival, becomes the stuff of the book.

Within this dialectic of illusion and reality, Conrad has placed a representative group of characters who become symbols of their type. In Singleton, whose name suggests his character, we see a mythological figure, a man of duty of whose fiber gods are made (". . . colossal, very old, old as Father Time himself"), strong and mute, "effaced, bowed and enduring." The chief mate Baker is dutiful like Melville's Starbuck, and though lacking in imagination, stolid, fair, just, withal a good seaman, a "model chief mate." Captain Allistoun, while lacking the sensibility of Captain Vere in *Billy Budd,* has an implied complexity which results in a keen sense of moral values; as Captain, he of course makes his decisions in the "loneliness of command," a godly function of whose powers he is aware and of whose rights he partakes judiciously.

The crew as a whole, then, with its sense of duty, provides a stable background of moral conduct. It has that sense of team understood in its best sense by Singleton, who, in his aloofness and surety, seems to possess, Conrad says, "the secret of their [the men's] uneasy indignations and desires, a sharper vision, a clearer knowledge." The Singletons can physically collapse only when their duties are terminated successfully. These are the supreme realists and they live as they must; yet such is the persuasive influence of the illusionists that some of them are led away from the reality principle toward the illusive behavior of Donkin and James Wait, who can evoke beliefs and superstitions that lie deep beneath the surface of the crew's behavior.

Beneath every settled and ordered mind lies a stubborn anarchy which pokes through the surface under provocation. Donkin, together with Wait, is the first of a long line of Conradian anarchists; not men who throw bombs, but those who refuse their duties and know nothing of courage and endurance and loyalty; men who know only of their rights. Of Donkin, Conrad says that he knew well enough how "to conquer the naïve instincts of that crowd." This is illustrated when in a moment they "gave him their compassion, jocularly, contemptuously, or surlily. . . ." As a combination confidence man and troublemaker, Donkin preludes the introduction of Wait, providing a prefatory comment upon him and giving Conrad a scorching weapon of attack upon the anarchistic idea. Conrad's anarchists, so often misunderstood, are objects of ridicule not so much for active behavior against society as for their refusal to accept their duties in a common fate. If the common enemy is the wind, the sea, or some other form of travail, then the coöperation of each hand is necessary, and the funking of duty by a single person is an acceptance on his part of the anarchistic principle. It is just this chord of irresponsibility or rebellion in man that Donkin sounds. He offers the crew temptation—the forsaking of its duty—which in its way is the knowledge of evil. Outcast, tempter, criminal, and anarchist, Donkin of course cringes before the righteousness of law and order embodied in Captain Allistoun. To refuse duty, Conrad implies, is to be criminal, and in this sense the criminal equals the anarchist. The ship, then, becomes a prison, with Donkin and Wait the prisoners and Allistoun the warden, a prison in which the crew offers its chorus of approval first to one and then the other. In conjunction with Wait, Donkin is able to demoralize the men by breaking through their surface serenity to their inner fears. While Donkin strikes into their minds, Wait, as a complement, throws terror into their hearts.

Wait's introduction is auspicious enough, as his name, signifying a do-nothing, becomes literally a definition of what he is. Having missed muster, Wait calls out his name from a distance and the name, mistaken for the command, causes momentary disruption of the ship's affairs and sets the tone for his presence on the ship. As a destructive and sub-surface force, Wait appropriately enters aft and departs aft; in neither case do we see him in the fore part of the ship. In his skillful recognition of Wait as the crew's alter ego, Conrad is here subtler than in his more obvious use of this same psychological condition in "The Secret Sharer." For as surely as Singleton is the active and life-giving principle of the ship, Wait is the death-force who plays on and with the crew's inarticulate confusion. Supplementing this inarticulate fear is the great and inexpressible sea, for it too is a reservoir of mystery and superstition. Conrad speaks of the impersonal sea "that knew all, and would in time infallibly unveil to each the wisdom hidden in all the errors, the certitude that lurks in doubts, the realm of safety and peace beyond the frontiers of sorrow and fear." With the unfathomable sea outside and Wait working on the unfathomable within, the crew breaks into disorganized pieces on which the storm itself is more than sufficient comment.

The storm—excepting that of "Typhoon," perhaps the greatest description in sea literature in any language—baptizes the crew, in time unifies it, and further isolates Wait and Donkin, who lose identification through their refusal to coöperate. Although Wait retains his hold on the men by means of his very helplessness (virtually a Mother-Father and Child relationship), their sense of plight gives them a solidarity hitherto either missing or dormant. Only Singleton—that old man of the sea—is aware of the connection between Wait and the sea. Each is a concrete form of the death principle; Wait is described as a funereal figure who hastens "the retreat of departing light by his very presence . . . a something cold and gloomy that floated out and settled on all the faces like a mourning veil." Yet compared with the majestic sea in all its energy as well as in all its destruction, the lassitude of Wait and Donkin becomes doubly contemptible. The sea is tireless and immortal; Wait and Donkin are exhausted and very much of this world. The sea prevails, so does the crew, but Wait cannot.

In this relationship between the crew and Wait, a supreme irony develops which touches upon the theme of illusion and reality. The ironic play of parts contains a two-way possibility, the relationship of James Wait to himself on one hand and his relationship to the crew on the other. As a confidence man, Wait is anxious to mislead the crew and through a feigned illness to be relieved of his duties while still collecting his pay. His exploitation of his illness is as unscrupulous as Donkin's righteousness in the face of what he calls unjust treatment by his superiors. In facing himself, Wait—if we follow the original manuscript—suspected that his trafficking with death was not a matter of coincidence; but as one critic has pointed out, Conrad decided that Wait must "have no idea that he was playing in earnest the part of the dying man which he had assumed for convenience." The reworking of certain significant details demonstrates that the Nigger was in reality fooling himself while attempting to dupe the crew. Wait, as well as the crew, is the gull of his own fraud, but the reader never is; so Conrad can play a double game of irony.

In that central scene in which the crew attempts to save Wait entombed in his cabin, we have a symbolic presentation of Wait's relationship to himself, to the crew, and, finally, to the reader. This scene—like the cab ride in *The Secret Agent*—is an epitome of the entire book, summing up all the themes and gathering all the threads. Pounded by the sea at the height of the storm, the crew tries to get to Wait's coffined prison, only to find a wall of nails from the carpenter's stores covering the bulkhead beneath which the prisoner screams out his dread. Wait is, as ever, unable to act, able only to cry out in mortal fear, lacking will, entirely passive and acted upon. In his cabin-coffin, we see the real Wait, fearful of death and at the same time caught in a death situation, terrorized, but still able to terrorize his rescuers. Wait has given up; he is no longer the confidence man, his role is now real, lived. He becomes flabby, boneless, a helpless child unable to stand or even to clutch at his rescuers. They handle him like the prodigal son, hating him and mothering him: "The secret and ardent desires of our hearts was the desire to beat him viciously with our fists about the head:

and we handled him as tenderly as though he had been made of glass. . . ."

Ever present in the crew's subconscious is the sadistic relation that exists between the strong and the weak, the healthy and the sick. Wait plays on the crew's sympathy and eats so sharply into its latent fear of weakness that he tempts it into a show of strength as if to exhibit its capabilities in the face of his feebleness. Conrad writes that the crew hated Wait, scorned him, doubted him, desired to beat him, and yet always found itself succoring him. Wait appeals to everything that is bad and good in men, to their fears and weaknesses as well as to their strength.

In these central pages, Conrad, through a single dramatized scene, presents the major tensions and suggests the various aspects of the conflict. Like Jonah, Wait creates dissension among the men; in his own person, he symbolizes the anxieties that lie between life and death, between psychical fear and reality. If I were to cite one advance Conrad had made between *An Outcast* and *The Nigger*, I should point to his use of scene as symbol. It was surely on these grounds that Conrad asserted *The Nigger* was not a sea story but a psychological study of human nature under duress. As yet, however, Conrad was experimenting with a manner of representation, and it is not until *Lord Jim* that we meet innovations in the genre itself.

An early reviewer of *The Nigger* recognized that Conrad had the poet's trick of heightening and deepening, of modifying and exaggerating, of producing what the reviewer called "a harmony of untruth which is a powerful representation of truth." As a novelist often writing like a poet, Conrad has frequently been compared to Stephen Crane, in particular Conrad's *The Nigger* to Crane's *The*

Red Badge of Courage. The real similarity of the two authors—when it does exist—rests in their way of conceiving a scene. In a revealing letter to Edward Garnett in 1897, Conrad emphasized that Crane was an impressionist, and by that he meant Crane imagined his scenes apart from the literalness of facts; that Crane's final test of a scene was, "What has it meant in *my* imagination?" and "Have I reproduced imaginatively what I have seen imaginatively?" It is this quality in Crane—along with his "rapidity of action and that amazing faculty of vision" —that Conrad praised even while recognizing the lack of solidity in the American writer which made his work seem slippery. The conciseness of Crane, his ability to compress a mountain of human experience into a single image, is echoed in Conrad's use of the central scene with its network of implications which extend throughout the book.

I V

Three of the five pieces in *Tales of Unrest* published in 1898 [4] belong in language and tone with Conrad's Malayan period, and as stories they show little or no advance in technique or conception. These stories follow the course of his work prior to *The Nigger*, duplicating the ornate language of the Nineties and the straightforward form derived from the French novel.

"The Idiots" [5] and "The Return" [6] can be dismissed as works without sufficient complexity or merit to warrant further comment. A third story, "An Outpost of Prog-

[4] Published by T. Fisher Unwin (London, 1898).
[5] Published in Arthur Symons' *Savoy* (October, 1896) as Conrad's first magazine appearance.
[6] Never published serially, finished September 24, 1897.

ress," [7] was described by Conrad as "the lightest part of the loot carried off from Central Africa," and it suffers from inevitable comparison with "Heart of Darkness." The ironic tone of the story—an irony implicit in the title —is conveyed through wide-spread use of images, but the images are invariable and of a uniformity which forces the obvious. The scenic desolation is all there: the smudged and broken equipment, the empty, useless boxes, the torn wearing apparel, and the spiritually exhausted colonists. But the manner and meaning of the story are rarely more than its physical equipment.

"The Lagoon," [8] published six months after "An Outpost," is, according to Robert Wooster Stallman, Conrad's first symbolic work; but according to Conrad it is of the same stuff as his two Malayan novels. The narrative of passion, a man and woman escaping from responsibility in an attempt to find pure love, takes up where Willems and Aïssa left off. Conrad's early theme, that a man caught in passion loses his manhood—a condition characterized by loss of courage, loyalty, and responsibility— is familiar from *An Outcast* and is repeated in "Karain," the fifth story in the volume. The language of "The Lagoon" is full of the lazy verbiage of the early novels. While nature stands as backdrop for human endeavors and emotions, dark and light imagery plays over the surface of the story. Night and day stand in more than physical opposition: for the night harbors illusions and life; the day, reality and death. After the long night of vigil and with the coming of sunlight, Arsat's woman dies, and a white eagle carrying her soul soars toward the sun.

[7] Called "A Victim of Progress" in the MS. This story, published in *Cosmopolis*, VI, VII (June and July, 1897), was a product of Conrad's impasse with *The Rescue*.

[8] *Cornhill Magazine*, II, n.s. (January, 1897).

The story ends as Arsat stands poised lonely in the sun-light, peering beyond the light into the "darkness of a world of illusions." In this description, we have a recognition of what was to come in later Conrad: a world full of unrealities and illusions which are nevertheless necessary for life.

"Karain"[9] is Conrad's most ambitious story prior to "Heart of Darkness." The theme and language of the earlier "Lagoon" are repeated, but in the telling and conception Conrad carried "Karain" further, as he himself recognized. The rich tone of the story imparts substance to the ghost-ridden Karain, who had slain his comrade, Matara, in lieu of the woman they were chasing and is then unable to exorcise Matara's image. The sumptuous language tends, however, to overwhelm the frail story, and the background trappings are clearly pompous and overblown. At the outset, Karain is presented as an enigmatical and mysterious being who deals in immensities and is then described later as a neurotic Odysseus who wanders among illusions. The beginning of the story, with its long description of the bay as "a bottomless pit of intense light," is not unlike that of *Nostromo*. Then, shortly afterward, Conrad proceeds to a portentous storm scene (". . . and the great voice went on, threatening terribly, into the distance") that suits a story of greater import, a storm scene reminiscent of that in *Under Western Eyes*. Such descriptive virtuosity is wasted on a story that is self-limiting. "Karain," consequently, seems the result of some leftover material which was fitted to a theme not necessarily insignificant in itself, but lacking the qualities of a truly felicitous work.

Conrad's over-evaluation of this material can further be seen in his use of an epigraph for the volume: "Be it

[9] *Blackwood's Magazine,* CLXII (November 1897).

thy course to being [busy] giddy minds/ With foreign quarrels," which comes from the fine scene, in Act IV of *Henry IV, Part 2*, between the dying Henry IV and his son Harry, who is to succeed him. Henry advises Harry to divert the minds of the old king's followers by leading them on conquests, perhaps on a crusade, and in that way to make them forget by what means the king had attained power. In its pretentious application here, Conrad equates Henry's advice to provide diversion with the diversionary and giddy quality of passion which makes constant men unstable; but Conrad's early heroes, unable to play the heroic role, are only able to take the heroic pose.

Part II

Then plain and right must my possession be,
Which I with more than with a common pain
'Gainst all the world will rightfully maintain.

KING HENRY IV: *Part II*

Just prior to the publication of *Lord Jim*,[1] Conrad turned his back on a sea career and became a professional writer. *Lord Jim* was started while Conrad was trying to finish *The Rescue;* at the same time he was working on "Youth" and "Heart of Darkness" and beginning his collaboration with Ford Madox Ford on *The Inheritors* and *Romance*. It was a time filled with personal difficulties—what with illness and insufficient funds—as well as a trying period of professional misgivings. Conrad's references to *Lord Jim* testify to his troubles, probably because it contains more of his personal philosophy than

[1] *Blackwood's Magazine*, CLXVI (October 1899-November 1900). Published by W. Blackwood (London, 1900).

any other single work up to *Nostromo*. In a lengthy letter to Hugh Clifford in 1899 revealing his artistic preoccupations, Conrad spoke of the necessity of handling words with care lest the "image of truth abiding in facts should become distorted—or blurred." Conrad emphasized the inadequacy of words alone to convey the full thrust of imagination and warned Clifford to leave unsaid what the reader should do for himself.

As a technical achievement, *Lord Jim* displays almost all of Conrad's favorite devices: the time-shift technique, the use of a central symbol, the awareness of imagistic detail, the use of indirect narrative, the paralleling of characters and situations, the fugue-like quality of the narrative structure. Those critics who find *Jim* an artistic failure because of the split in the novel between the *Patna* episode and the Patusan section would do well to re-examine Conrad's method of combining the various parts.

The spine of the book is formed by the three decisions of increasing intensity that Jim must make; each decision shows Jim as a romantic hero who is a failure. Jim is a man of excellent motives possessing a mind drenched in ideals, a man enticed by a vision that constantly evades him. Unable to make the right decisions at the opportune time, he commits mistakes in judgment and makes hairline decisions dictated by predisposition and by the exigencies of the moment. In this way, Jim progresses through three successive stages, each of which is sharply defined by the necessity of decision.

The first is the training school incident which in itself conferred neither shame nor dishonor, but did instill a subconscious guilt that with enlarging circumstances in later years proved self-destructive. When Jim first missed his opportunity for heroics, he romanticized his vagaries, and then, as Conrad says, "felt angry with the brutal tumult of earth and sky for taking him unawares and checking unfairly a general readiness for narrow escapes . . . he exulted with fresh certitude in his avidity for adventure and in a sense of many-sided courage."

In Jim's hierarchy of decisions, the second is of course his abandonment of the *Patna* under the influence of the morally degrading ship's company. Jim's dreams of a heroic role slip from him as he moves from a purgatory of indecision into an active vision of hell when he jumps into the lifeboat, that "everlasting deep hole" which means eternal self-castigation.

The terms of Jim's third decision are far removed in time and space from those of the earlier two, but in its circumstances this decision is a natural development. In letting the predatory Brown escape from Patusan, Jim recognizes that a forceful decision cannot be made by an imperfect being and that his tainted past precludes making strictures against even a criminal. " 'Let us agree,' " says Brown, " 'that we are both dead men, and let us talk on that basis, as equals.' " Conrad comments that through their sparring there ran a "vein of subtle reference to their common blood, an assumption of common experience; a sickening suggestion of common guilt, of secret knowledge. . . ."

This hierarchy of decisions forms the frame of *Lord Jim* and creates an ever-expanding circle of adhesive material. In Chapter Three, I commented on the fugue-like quality of certain scenes, a quality that is conveyed by dissimilar sequences running parallel. This manner of presentation creates a flow of action in the novel that is comparable to the flow of later novelists who compressed time through refracting language and sentence structure. In this connection, a Spanish writer, Lilia d'Onofrio, made an astute comment upon the relationship between Conrad's sea experience and the rhythmic ebb and flow of his fiction:

> El mar había nutrido de recuerdos e impresiones el inconsciente de Conrad; por ese motivo hay en sus historias algo de la cambiente tonalidad y de las mutaciones incesantes de los estados del océano, semejante al alma humana; ella, como el océano, suele anunciar con bonanzas pasiones agitados.[2]

Stein's ring, an object of human solidarity, fulfills just this rhythmic function; a tangible object that has parallels throughout the novel, it imparts a uniform rise and fall to the sequences. Jim's breaking of trust on the *Patna* in the first part is commensurate, in its way, with his breaking of trust in connection with Stein's ring. When in the Patusan section Jim has failed again in permitting Brown to escape, he removes the silver ring and holds it in front of the native chief Doramin before dropping it disconsolately in his lap, waiting and watching as the ring rolls off onto the ground. That ring, which "had opened for him the door of fame, love, and success," is now tumbling in the dust, a symbol of Jim's romantic dreams which had thwarted him from the lost opportunity on the training ship to the failure of nerve in Patusan.

Paralleling the rhythmic quality of the scenes is the plasticity and fluidity of the characters, a fluidity partially obtained through the recurrence of psychological doubles, who in their way supplement the experiments

---

[2] "The sea had nourished Conrad's unconscious with memories and impressions; there is therefore in his stories something of the changing tonality and incessant mutations of the ocean's condition, comparable to the human soul; it, like the ocean, is accustomed to announce agitated passions with surface placidity."

with manifold time sequences and the repetition of structural similarities. Ralph Tymms, in his scholarly presentation of the historical background of the psychological double, points out the long literary use of doubles and notes how the practice was absorbed by Freud and Jung in their theories of the unconscious mind. The *doppelgänger*, widely employed by German romanticists who pictured a world tortured by split personalities and dependent alter egos, is of particular interest as we move chronologically toward Conrad's work, especially in Dostoyevsky's *The Brothers Karamazov*, which Conrad knew and roundly disparaged. In Dostoyevsky's presentation of the brothers, we discover a process of re-duplication; so that significant elements of Ivan's character, for example, are reproduced in various ways by Alyosha, Mitya and Smerdyakov. Each brother is, as it were, the allegorical *visibilis* of Ivan's psychological make-up, and the emergence of each one is in a way a throwback to and a comment upon the other brother.

On a lesser scale and with less artistic success, Conrad's circling about Jim creates a similar psychological involvement; the presence of each person is a psychological comment upon Jim's state of mind and situation. More than merely buttressing the story, these characters are molded to the rhythm of the novel; frequently, they assume the narrative function. In this way, we can explain Brierly, Brown, the French officer, the German skipper of the *Patna*, Stein, Jewel, and Marlow.

Brierly's suicide is a way of identification with Jim's failure. Brierly is a successful Jim who recognizes that failure is a condition of life and who destroys himself while still in good fortune, with his ship on course and his log up to point. Marlow realizes that Brierly had looked into himself when faced by Jim's defection and

found there "one of those trifles that awaken ideas . . .
with which a man . . . finds it impossible to live."

Similarly, Brown's treachery is equated in psychological terms with Jim's defection on the *Patna;* the French officer's sense of honor is Jim's dream now reduced to dust; Jewel's loyalty, as her name implies, is of a solidity and perfection which contrasts with Jim's tainted past; the German skipper of the *Patna* is the reality principle at its cruelest, and this is what Jim in the midst of his dream succumbs to, realizing in action his sub-surface fears and sense of failure.

If the German skipper represents the harsher side of reality, then Marlow himself stands for a gentler but ever staunch sense of reality; his attitude, in its almost dogmatic rejection of romance, is in sharp contrast with Jim's persistent spirit of adventure. Even when struck down by the *Patna* experience, Jim is still able to see it as an opportunity for heroism missed—"'Ah! what a chance missed! My God! What a chance missed!'" Marlow's comment is derisive: "'Ah, he was an imaginative beggar! . . . With every instant he was penetrating deeper into the impossible world of romantic achievements.'" Whenever Jim dreams of the might-have-been, whenever his imagination re-creates his dreams and not the actuality, the ever-realistic Marlow pulls him back almost cruelly, almost sadistically, to his former tragic decision and to the fatal consequences of withdrawal from reality. In the Conrad canon, this play of attitudes is not limited to the Jim-Marlow relationship alone, but recurs in the Decoud-Nostromo counterpointing and in the Lena-Heyst fencing in *Victory.*

By far the most pregnant figure in the book is Stein, whose awareness of both the imaginative and the real and their relative place in the modern world stamps him as one of that renaissance type which our own age has split into parts. The Germanic name, the granite placidity of the man in the face of decisions, the avidity for nature, the scholarly tendencies mixed with the involvement with man, and finally, the quotation from "Torquato Tasso"— all these suggest Goethe, who can survive because he partakes of *all* experiences while Jim must perish because his accomplishments are broken into fragments.

It is not surprising that the very center of the book is devoted to that scene of great consequence between Stein and Marlow. Against man's imperfections, a mankind perhaps spawned by an artist who "was a little mad," Stein offers the perfections of nature, particularly the beauty and delicacy displayed by the incomparable butterfly. Then in a statement central to Jim's character, central to the novel, and central to Conrad himself, Stein speculates on the relative merits of the butterfly and man. The butterfly clearly accepts reality, but man "wants to be a saint, and he wants to be a devil"; in short, man sees himself as he can never be. The question, adapting Hamlet's, is how to be; and the answer is to follow the dream which is self-destructive, to submit to what is an eternal condition of man, and in the submission, temporary though it is, lies the only relief, the only salvation.[3]

This doctrine is a recognition that man is limited by his own inferiority in an inexplicable world, a realization that violence and destruction are a concomitant of the will to live, and that the loss of self-protective illusions is the surest way to self-destruction. As Robert Penn Warren

---

[3] *Lord Jim.* "The way is to the destructive element submit yourself, and with the exertions of your hands and feet in the water make the deep, deep sea keep you up. . . . In the destructive element immerse. . . . That was the way. To follow the dream, and again to follow the dream— and so—*ewig-usque ad finem.*"

pointed out in his fine essay on *Nostromo:* "The last wisdom is for man to realize that though his values are illusions, the illusion is necessary, is infinitely precious, is the work of his human achievement, and is, in the end, his only truth."

Nowhere else has Conrad created a "god" figure like Stein, who can order human destinies through his superior wisdom and infinite capabilities. In his combination of the active and the scholarly, Stein, more than any other Conradian character, becomes not only a model of what the twentieth century wants, but also a wistful reminder of what the complete man could be. Strong man among Conrad's intellectuals, Stein has abilities the lack of which destroy Decoud (*Nostromo*), Heyst (*Victory*), and Renouard ("The Planter of Malata"), those men of excessive intellect with but jejune illusions.

Stein's sufficiency is such that he overshadows Jim, and rather than supplying merely a comment upon him, he engulfs and swallows up the young man in a way like that of the experienced professional in his relations with the green apprentice. What is clearly lacking is a sufficiently strong central character who can sustain this framework of technical proficiency. We realize that Jim is not enough, that he does not yield meaning, and clearly never will. This lack of depth is more Jim's than the novel's; and Conrad's attempts to dissemble the want of center are not completely successful. We are reminded that the original version of *Lord Jim* was to be a novella concerned solely with the *Patna* episode.

The lack of strong guide is what occasions the hollowness and stringiness of the Patusan section. In the first part, the *Patna* episode, we see so little of Jim that we believe more about him than we know of him. Conrad's method of indirect narration keeps us at a distance; and while Marlow himself is not excessively stimulating, the result is an idealized Jim seen almost solely from without. But in Patusan the situation has changed. The method is simpler, more direct, and our eye is upon Jim. Not all the rich language, nor the evocative scenes of adventure, love, and fidelity, not even the dramatic Jamesian dialogues can dissemble the simple surface reactions of the sailor-boy Jim. We know all when we know a little, and for Conrad to tell more is to go around Jim and not to penetrate further into him. Only with Heyst, and possibly Decoud and Razumov, is Conrad able to maintain his vision and probe deeply.

Conrad's characteristic use of nature is a fruitful part of *Lord Jim* and foreshadows the organic natural descriptions of *Nostromo*, which help determine the rhythms of that book. Much can be made of the Edenesque setting of the Patusan sequence, but often the jungle is closer in its function to an anti-Eden. Rather than finding man living in close harmony with nature, we see the constant struggle in nature which sharply underscores the conflict in man's affairs. Natural man—if such a thing existed for Conrad—is often equivalent to savage man or corrupted man who lacks the gentler tones of a moral character. Under natural conditions the will to survive unmasks every desire for decency and propriety. Even the sea, often a source of renewed energy and human solidarity, becomes the background of hate and treachery when man's natural fears are touched.

It is not the sea, however, but the jungle, that primitive repository of stagnation and torpor, which symbolizes man's hopeless struggle to keep afloat in life. The lush jungle of the early Conrad merges into the ironically idyllic backdrops of *Victory* and *Nostromo* and then becomes the city background of *The Secret Agent* and *Un-*

der Western Eyes. Jim in his semi-articulate and stumbling self-destructive way, in his sense of almost complete failure, is as much a guide to the modern temper as Heyst and Decoud with all their articulateness. The jungle which surrounds Jim is not an Eden of this world; it is, instead, filled with fatal temptations, with the "stumps of felled trees," with flowers destined for "the use of the dead alone," with "smells like that of incense in the house of the dead," with "white coral that shone like a chaplet of bleached skulls," and over all is a silence "as if the earth had been one grave."

The haunting presence of an indifferent or belligerent nature of course further isolates the human aspects of life and suggests tragic dimensions. Moreover, Conrad's organic use of nature goes even further; as a commentator upon humanity, nature becomes, so to speak, an active participant in Conrad's novels. The displacement of Jim from human society and his effacement in an anti-Paradise afford ironical comment: for here an anti-hero is trying to become a tragic hero against a backdrop that would frustrate the efforts of even a god. The unheroic surroundings contrast with Jim's futile quest for respectability and a sense of status. His continual failure to recognize that anonymity is impossible makes his quest lose its rationality; and his actions become those of a compulsive neurotic who seeks suffering while hoping that through physical and mental masochism he may efface what reason would tell him is a hopeless situation. In depicting the impossibility of the human quest for peace, Conrad was obviously probing a major theme in the literature and life of the present century. Nevertheless, the very terms of Jim's quest preclude a tragic sense, for he never knows exactly what he is doing. He acts from the top of his emotions, and the simple view he takes of his plight prevents any countering struggle. To the stimulus of criticism, Jim responds by running. Perhaps our only concrete memory of Jim can paradoxically be his very vagueness, the image that Marlow carries of his last sight of Jim:

> He [Jim] was white from head to foot, and remained persistently visible with the stronghold of the night at his back, the sea at his feet, the opportunity by his side, still veiled. What do you say? Was it still veiled? I don't know. For me that white figure in the stillness of the coast and sea seemed to stand at the heart of a vast enigma. The twilight was ebbing fast from the sky above his head, the strip of sand had sunk already under his feet, he himself appeared no bigger than a child—then only a speck, a tiny white speck, that seemed to catch all the light left in a darkened world. . . . And suddenly, I lost him. . . .

Jim, as we leave him, is a man of self-conceived romance and misplaced imagination who is perforce a failure. Suffering as he does from an excess of imagination, he resembles that greatly-admired hero of both Conrad and Flaubert, Don Quixote. Conrad called Jim a romantic, and perhaps he saw him as Henry James saw Emma Bovary—as of romantic temper and realistic adventures. Jim is clearly in the line of those romantic heroes whose awareness of reality never catches up with the roles they have idealized for themselves.

Stein, conversely, suggests reality, control, forethought. His advice that one must immerse oneself in the destructive element—a loose paraphrase of Novalis' "Most men will not swim before they are able to."—conveys his realization of man's limited powers. *Realization* is perhaps the key word in *Lord Jim*, as much as it is the key to tragedy. But only Stein, not Jim, *realizes*. The latter, because he beats against life without ever recognizing his role, will always consider himself a failure—and tragic heroes are made of other stuff. Stein's presence, then, is truly the destructive element, for his multifarious activities—his controlled romanticism, his grasp of reality, for example —allow alternatives to Jim's compulsiveness, and the alternatives, had Jim acted upon them and still failed, would have provided the stuff of real tragedy.

The novel, even if it lacks the tragic sense, still remains, of course, a rich and varied experience. Jim in his semi-articulate and stumbling way, in his sense of almost complete failure, in his inability to act powerfully and wisely, is a compelling guide to the modern temper; and his frustrated quest for personal salvation in an indifferent or hostile world is Conrad's distressing prophecy for the twentieth century. Of possibly even greater importance is Conrad's insight into hidden psychological forces which may operate regardless of one's conscious wishes. Jim often tries to ascribe reasons and motives to phenomena outside of himself, instead of seeking within for his motivation; but this evasion of the truth is, surely, the result of Jim's inability to fathom his own self-destructiveness, his desire, natural in itself, to find excuses beyond his own conscious choice of action.

The psychological possibilities of Conrad's handling of Jim are immense. *Lord Jim* is often called existential or at least discussed in existential terms. However, if we read Conrad correctly in this novel, unconscious impulses, such as Jim's self-destructive promptings, make hash of any existential interpretation dependent on man's conscious choices. Questions of identity, good faith, attitude, even of life style, have no significance if the impulses directing one's conduct derive from unconscious sources. Under such

conditions, one can only, like Jim, seek external explanation and yet continue to pursue a self-destructive course of
action.

In his psychoanalytic study of Conrad, Dr. Meyer
touches on these questions without trying to resolve them,
interested as he is more in Conrad than in Jim. He does
point out that Jim never really succeeds "in persuading
himself of his innocence," nor does he "accept his wishful
efforts to project the origins of his shame-ridden conduct
upon external agencies. For throughout the remainder of
his life he embodies the image of a man seeking to undo
his guilty deed." Psychologically unable to undo anything
—in fact, compelled to pursue whatever will destroy him—
Jim, like Kurtz in other ways, becomes our archetypical
modern outsider. To continue to speak of him in traditional terms of penance, expiation, "undoing," and forgiveness is to lose sight of this most important side of Conrad's
novel.

Although *Lord Jim* is often more imposing in its parts
than as a whole, it nevertheless retains a power and a force
rarely duplicated by Conrad's contemporaries or by Conrad himself in his later work; obviously, Conrad's way of
conceiving this novel makes *Lord Jim* his as yet most com-
prehensive statement on man. His ability to suggest and
evoke is evident, and from here to "Heart of Darkness" is
not a great step.

II

Contemporaneously with *Lord Jim*, Conrad wrote "Youth" [4]
and "Heart of Darkness," [5] two of three stories in *Youth;*

4 *Blackwood's Magazine*, CLXIV (September 1898).
5 *Blackwood's Magazine*, CLXV (February, March, April, 1899). Con-

the entire volume, including "The End of the Tether,"[6] was not, however, published until 1902.[7]

In reading "Youth," one is aware of how high its critics have placed it in the Conrad canon; yet it can rightfully be praised only in terms of a small job neatly performed within severe limitations. Marlow appears for the first time in a Conrad work, entering into the narrative after one page of frame introduction in which the barest excuse for a narrative is provided.

The language of "Youth" is rich, the thoughts are sentimental, and the whole, except for that justly famous description of the East, has the aura of a sentimental story for a family magazine. The descriptive passages are certainly among Conrad's more pedestrian achievements: he wrote about polished seas, a sea sparkling like a precious stone, the sea like a single gem, the sky as a miracle of purity, the earth as a jewel, and so on. The similes and metaphors are frequently somber and dark for a lightly-recalled memory, unless Marlow—that very serious man —is sporting with his own sense of adventure, an uncharacteristic attempt at humor. His obvious reflections and constant attitudinizing seem to be the major ingredients in a work of bursting sentimentality. Yet despite these frailties of conception, Conrad surely knew what he was doing when he climaxed the story with that revelatory passage of youth meeting the East in all its ambiguities. Full of detail and comment, this passage

---

rad's "Congo Diary: Notebook I," with entries from June 13, 1890, to August 1, 1890, can be found in *Last Essays* (London: Dent, 1926), pp. 238-253. Book II, 79 pages, consists principally of navigational aids and a few comments. The manuscripts of both Notebooks are preserved in the Library of Harvard University.

[6] *Blackwood's Magazine*, CLXXII (July-December 1902).

[7] Published by W. Blackwood (London, 1902), as *Youth: A Narrative, and Two Other Stories*.

with its lights and darks, its shadows and mysteries, its brilliance and color, shows Conrad at his descriptive best. The early Conrad, somewhat ornate but in full control of his still fresh memories, is able to re-create them in vibrant and rhythmic language. Conrad pictures a frozen scene of "brown, bronze, yellow faces, the black eyes, the glitter, the colour of an Eastern crowd," against the motionless background of the shore, with the bay and glittering sands beyond:

> . . . the wealth of green infinite and varied, the sea blue like the sea of a dream, the crowd of attentive faces, the blaze of vivid colour—the water reflecting it all, the curve of the shore, the jetty, the high-sterned outlandish craft floating still, and the West sleeping unconscious of the land and the people and of the violence of the sunshine.

From "Youth" to "Heart of Darkness" is indeed a step from youth to maturity as Conrad was aware. "Heart of Darkness," he said in the Author's Note, is "anything but the mood of wistful regret, of reminiscent tenderness," or the memory of romantic youth. To relate Conrad's development between the two stories to another author at another time, it is not unlike the passage from *Tom Sawyer* (1876) to *Huckleberry Finn* (1884) in Mark Twain's canon. The first is a study of a boy's growth which despite its preoccupation with the darker images of a youthful imagination is nevertheless a relatively light-hearted work. But its sequel, *Huckleberry Finn,* is a profound projection from a playful boy's world into an adult world of retributive and self-seeking evil. Dangers no longer lurk in the imagination but exist in the realities of the social world. From *Tom Sawyer* to *Huckleberry Finn,* there is implied a process of maturity which consists in facing-up to the real world. Twain, like Conrad with "Youth" and "Heart of

Darkness," moved from a youthful tone of "wistful regret" and "reminiscent tenderness" toward a larger and more mature view.

The comparison is not fortuitous. Behind *Huckleberry Finn* and "Heart of Darkness" there is a basis of similarity and a general kinship of idea, although the methods of each writer are frequently dissimilar. Central to both works is the passage along the rivers Mississippi and Congo respectively, and the relationship between the river and the shore. Using the freedom of the river as a vast symbol, Twain opposed it to the deceit and treachery of the shore. Built on a series of contrasts, the structure of *Huckleberry Finn* is kept in balance by the very undercurrent that maintains the balance of the raft—the rhythm of the river itself—a rhythm that conveys the tempos of the novel. Conrad's Congo does not have the purifying qualities of the Mississippi, but it does lead up to and away from the stagnant jungle, the river Styx leading into an Inferno, and by comparison with the shore it is less tainted, less evil.

When Huck grows toward maturity and responsibility, an entire society is undergoing the rites of baptism, either gaining a sense of right conduct or suffering the loss of humanity. As a view of society, *Huckleberry Finn* is a very sobering picture, no less than "Heart of Darkness," whose dismal images of breakdown and expedience have so strongly engaged the modern mind. As studies in human degradation touched by the possibilities of regeneration, both works symbolize an era.

"Heart of Darkness" is possibly the greatest short novel in English, one of the greatest in any language, and now a twentieth-century cultural fact. Like all great fiction, it involves the reader in dramatic, crucially difficult moral decisions which parallel those of the central characters, here

Marlow and Kurtz. It asks troublesome questions, disturbs preconceptions, forces curious confrontations, and possibly changes us. With Kurtz, we sense the allure of great power. With Marlow, we edge toward an abyss and return different.

Conrad himself recognized that this novella penetrated to those areas of darkness, dream, indeed nightmare, with which he tried to define the substance of his world. "Heart of Darkness" helped solidify a vision that rarely wavered in Conrad's later work, and one we now accept as uniquely modern. Here he limned the images one usually encounters in dreams or in war, and here he found that discontinuous, inexplicable, existentially absurd experience which was to haunt his letters and his work.

Based on personal impressions, his own Congo journey, "Heart of Darkness" welled out. As he wrote apologetically and hesitatingly to Elsa Martindale (Mrs. Ford Madox Ford):

> What I distinctly admit is the fault of having made Kurtz too symbolic or rather symbolic at all. But the story being mainly a vehicle for conveying a batch of personal impressions I gave the rein to my mental laziness and took the line of least resistance. This is then the whole Apologia pro Vita Kurtzii—or rather for the tardiness of his vitality. (Unpublished letter, December 3, 1902)

The novella, then, contains a vision so powerful that Conrad excuses himself for being unable (he thought) to control it. It was also, as Freud wrote of his own *Interpretation of Dreams,* an insight that falls to one but once in a lifetime. The reference to Freud and to *Dreams* is not fortuitous. It was of course chance that Freud and Conrad were contemporaries; but chance ends when we note the extraordinary parallelism of their achievements. Freud did his major work on dreams in the 1890's, the same time that Conrad was fermenting ideas about the Congo and personal and political expedience in a quicksand, nightmarish world. Freud's book, the culmination of his observations, appeared in 1900, only months after Conrad's "Heart of Darkness."

Chance is further reduced when we recognize that literature and a new style of psychological exploration have been first cousins for the last hundred years; that both Conrad and Freud were pioneers in stressing the irrational elements in man's behavior which resisted orthodox interpretation. Conrad's great contribution to political thought is his insight into the irrationality of politics, its nightmarish qualities which depend on the neurosis of a leader, in turn upon the collective neuroses of a people. Such an insight is timeless, but particularly appropriate for developments since 1900. For when has man tried so carefully to preserve life while also squandering it so carelessly? Conrad caught not only hypocrisy (an old-fashioned value), but the illogic of human behavior which tries to justify itself with precision, only to surrender to explosive inner needs. "Exterminate all the brutes," Kurtz scrawled at the bottom of his report. This is the politics of personal disintegration, uncontrollable personal needs, ultimately paranoia.

Confronting similar material, the scientist Freud was concerned with a logical analysis of seeming illogic—the apparent irrationality of dreams, on occasion of nightmares. Both he and Conrad penetrated into the darkness—when men sleep, or when their consciences sleep, when such men are free to pursue secret wishes, whether in dreams, like Freud's analysands, or in actuality, like Kurtz and his followers. The key word is darkness; the black of the jungle for Conrad is the dark of the sleeping consciousness for Freud.

In still another sense, Marlow, in his trip up the Congo, has suffered through a nightmare, an experience that sends him back a different man, now aware of depths in himself he cannot hide. The tale he narrates on the *Nellie* is one he is unable to suppress; a modern Ancient Mariner, he has discovered a new world and must relate his story to regain stability. The account is a form of analysis—for him and for Conrad. In a way, it provides a defense against Kurtz's vision.

Freud, too, returned from the world of dreams, an equally dark Congo—with an interpretation and a method, an attempt to convey order. His great discovery, like Conrad's, was surely that dreams, despite the various barriers the conscious mind erects, are wish-fulfillments of the hidden self. This sense of wish-fulfillment is evidently never far from Marlow—for the very qualities in Kurtz that horrify him are those he finds masked in himself. Kurtz's great will to power, Nietzschean and ruthless in its thrust, is also Marlow's. The latter, however, can hold back; his restraint, for Conrad, a mark of his Englishness. Marlow, however, only barely restrains himself, for, irresistibly, he is drawn toward Kurtz, readily accepting the latter's ruthlessness as preferable to the bland hypocrisy of the station manager. Even Marlow is seduced—he, too, hides secret wishes and desires, his dreams curiously close to Kurtz's; and so are those of us all, Conrad suggests. Kurtz's savage career is every man's wish-fulfillment, although by dying he conveniently disappears before we all become his disciples.

The secret longing, the hidden desire, the hypocritical defense, the hate covered superficially by love, the artfully contrived lie—all of these are intertwined in dreams. In this sense, Marlow's experience is a nightmare for creator, narrator, and reader. The jungle, that thick verdant cover, disguises all, but most of all hides a man's real existence from himself.

As a connoisseur of dreams, Conrad is a "dark" writer in the sense Rembrandt was a dark painter, Milton a dark poet. They begrudged the light, husbanded it, squeezed it out in minute quantities, as if it were filtered from between densely packed trees in a jungle setting. So the light in Kurtz's heart barely appears, overwhelmed as it is by the darkness of his needs, the exigencies of his situation. Light and dark, in this vision, are polarized; their antagonism runs parallel to the struggle for life in nature itself, a Darwinian battle for growth, power, supremacy.

The yellowish, wispy light, indeed the white of the ivory, later of Kurtz's very bald skull, exists against the fragmented darkness of the jungle—the contrast of colors giving Conrad a vast symbol for moral, political, and social values. And yet such is the knottiness and ambiguity of his symbol that the result is blurred, filled artfully with the illusions and deceptions that Conrad makes us accept as the pathos of existence. Marlow, that pillar of truth and morality, does Kurtz's work at the end, lies to protect the lie of Kurtz's existence, ultimately lies to preserve his (Marlow's) own illusions. In an impure, dirty world, he desperately seeks a compromise—and finds it in the pretty illusions of naïve women. The very ground on which he stands softens and shifts. Marlow has indeed peered into the heart of darkness, his own as well as Kurtz's, and found as a reflection the very nihilism he fears. Needing to believe, he lies to maintain that belief.

To create order from such shards of nihilism, negativism, distortion, deception, savagery, and, ultimately, fear, Conrad offered a dubious restraint. Somehow, one must find it within. It is an individual matter, and evidently either one has it or one doesn't. It is not solely a European quality by any means, since Kurtz, that pan-European, lacks it, and the Congolese tribal natives have it. Restraint —a kind of muscular courage *not to do*—marks the difference between civilization and capitulation to savagery. Yet where does it come from? How does one obtain it? Does the lack of it always brutalize? Neither Marlow nor Conrad knows the answers. Such mysterious reckonings make it impossible for us to see Conrad as a meliorist. Society as constituted means little—only the responsible individual counts. Possibly one acquires restraint as the sum total of what he is. Yet decency, indeed the future of civilized society, hangs in the balance.

In this respect "Heart of Darkness" is one of our archetypal existential literary documents in which all is contingency. It fits the categories; it has the right psychology. The reader can, if he wishes, see the novella as a delineation of absurdity—that term applied to man's skew relationship with objects, with his milieu, inevitably with the universe. The images of the narrative, like images of a poem, intensify man's sense of alienation—right into the appearance of the pale, white-skulled, ailing, then dying Kurtz, an elongated image of wasted power and fruitless endeavor, the humanitarian now inhuman.

Possibly it is this sense of absurdity and discontinuity which so impresses Marlow that he returns a changed man. All his inner computers have broken down. This gnarled seaman is surely one of the keys to the story, and much has been written about him, including much nonsense. He is, at least here, Conrad's Everyman, Bunyan's Christian updated. What he suffers and experiences is analogous to what we as judicious democrats would feel. Conrad made Marlow sentient, somewhat intelligent, but,

most of all, courageous—about himself, about life, about
man's social responsibilities—yet at the same time sufficiently cynical; in brief, very much like Conrad himself.
But the two are not congruent; among other things, Conrad possessed a literary intelligence that his narrator did
not. He surrounds Marlow as well as enters him. But even
if he is foremost a man of action, Marlow should not be
taken too lightly. His intelligence is displayed in his moral
sensibility. With a certain dogged charm, reminiscent of
many American presidents and statesmen, he wishes to see
the world based on English (or American) democracy. He
accepts private enterprise—with personal restraints. He
believes that imperialism must justify itself with good
deeds. He expects all men to be fair and decent. Such are
Marlow's preoccupations, and here Conrad demonstrated
to good purpose the contradictions and rifts between modern belief and modern practice. And here also is the source
of Conrad's irony—a quality that gives him considerable
advantage over Marlow.

Since he is a man of order and moral courage, Marlow
expects similar restraints to prevail elsewhere. As a captain
he of course knows that such qualities are essential to preserve life at sea. Carrying them over into civilian life, they
become for him psychological expectations. Marlow ac-
quiesces to the world's work as basically just and funda-
mentally good, even necessary, provided it is done by enlightened men. Like Conrad, he accepts the status quo,
but one maintained, he trusts, by just men. For both this
is the sole basis of the human contract—one does things in
an enlightened manner and develops his moral sensibilities.
This is a solid nineteenth-century philosophy, although for
us somewhat naïve. Marlow rarely questions whether particular work is necessary; for example, he never asks
whether white men should be in the Congo—for what-

ever reason. Rather, he assumes they should be—since they are—but they must come as friends, as helpers, and bring enlightenment. Even while they rape, they must be benevolent. He sees them as solid, progressive English-men, who helped to develop countries the better to plunder them, nineteenth-century "ugly Americans."

Marlow's great revelation comes when he sees that the world is not arranged this way—and here the Congo is a microcosm of the great world in which those who can, plunder those who cannot. Marlow's awareness of evil comes when he notes that many men, and those the most willful, do not share his belief in an orderly, enlightened society. Theirs is one of chaos, anarchy, "unspeakable rites." They approve human sacrifice, and they eat their victims. This is Conrad's existential wedge, so to speak. A law-abiding, morally sensitive man enters an avaricious, predatory, almost psychopathic world. For the moment he sees that civilization brings dubious rewards. He learns the harsh vocabulary of reality. He matures. The nineteenth century becomes the twentieth.

The long river that informs this world is described, like the Styx, in treacherous, serpentine terms—"deadly—like a snake," "resembling an immense snake uncoiled." The river is essentially a woman: dangerous, dark, mysterious, concealed, with the jungle also feminine, personified by Kurtz's savage mistress. Marlow is overwhelmed; his ideal of womanhood is clearly the girl back in Brussels, or his aunt—the brainwashed public—that naïve woman who believes "the labourer is worthy of his hire." Such womanly illusions Marlow wishes to preserve. But his experience in-cludes a treacherous, feminine river, an equally perfidious jungle that conceals its terrors, and, finally, a savage mis-tress—in all, an unspeakable sexual experience. Though the reticent, chivalrous Marlow never speaks directly of

sex, it lies heavily on the story, in every aspect of nature—
in *his* fears, in *its* demands. As much as Marlow fears the
attraction of power, he shies away from the temptation of
orgiastic, uncontrollable sex. He retreats into neutral shock.

Clearly, every facet of Marlow's experience in the
Congo, including his preliminary interview in the Brussels office, contains elements of the absurd—that is, elements that become a wedge between man's seeming rationality and a world suddenly irrational and out of focus.
The question is not Hamlet's, but how one should live. If
absurdity is acknowledged, what are a man's guidelines?
Does one concern oneself with morality or conscience?
And even so, what sustains a man when tempted by the
devil within, by corruption without? What is restraint if it
isolates?

In a letter to Cunninghame Graham, written while
"Heart of Darkness" was welling up, Conrad revealed his
most personal fears: that in a world of ever-shifting illusions, what ultimately, if anything, does matter? Who
finally, if anyone, does care?

> In a dispassionate view the ardour for reform, improve-
> ment for virtue, for knowledge, and even for beauty is only
> a vain sticking up for appearances as though one were anx-
> ious about the cut of one's clothes in a community of blind
> men. Life knows us not and we do not know life—we don't
> know even our own thoughts. Half the words we use have no
> meaning whatever and of the other half each man under-
> stands each word after the fashion of his own folly and con-
> ceit. Faith is a myth and beliefs shift like mists on the shore;
> thoughts vanish; words, once pronounced, die; and the mem-
> ory of yesterday is as shadowy as the hope of to-morrow—
> only the string of my platitudes seems to have no end. As our
> [Polish] peasants say: "Pray, brother, forgive me for the love
> of God." And we don't know what forgiveness is, nor what is

love, nor where God is. Assez. (January 14, 1898, Dartmouth
University Library)

"Heart of Darkness," then, is concerned with moral issues in their most troubling sense: not only as philosophical imperatives, but practically, as they work out in human
behavior. In a mechanical universe—"evolved out of a
chaos of scraps of iron"—what is flesh? The profusion of
metallic and mechanical images indicates that resistant
objects have superseded softness, flexibility, humanity itself; that, clearly, one must become an object, tough and
durable, in order to survive.

Once again to Cunninghame Graham (Feb. 8, 1899,
Yale U. Library), Conrad stressed apropos of "Heart of
Darkness" that he didn't start "with an abstract notion"
but with "definite images." Such images abound: from the
ludicrous French gunboat to its shells lobbed indiscrimi-
nately into the bush, then the metal of nuts and bolts and
decaying, overturned equipment, the rusted steamboat
settled in the mud, even the polished, unnatural ac-
countant at the station, with the land itself silhouetted by
withered natives, shades of themselves, victims of an im-
perialist Inferno, now dried, inhuman, lacking flesh or
spirit, too soft for modern life. And dominating all, the
smoothly metallic, white, luxurious ivory.

The sense of human waste that pervades the story is
best unfolded in the ivory itself. It is an object for the
rich—in decorations, for piano keys, for bibelots—hardly
necessary for physical or mental survival. In a way, it is
like art, a social luxury, and it is for art that the Congo is
plundered and untold numbers slaughtered brutally, or
casually. This view of ivory as art was surely part of Conrad's conception; a utilitarian object would have had its
own raison d'être. A relatively useless item or one selective

in its market only points up the horror; surely this, too, is part of Kurtz's vision. Possibly Kurtz's artistic propensities (he paints, he collects human heads, he seeks ivory) make him so contemptuous of individual lives; for art and life have always warred. In the name of art (pyramids, churches, tombs, monuments, palaces), how many have died, gone without, worked as slaves? Traditionally, beauty for the few is gained with blood of the many.

Where art rules, artifacts are a form of power. The art object takes on magical significance, becoming a kind of totem, the fairy-tale golden egg. Knowing this, Kurtz gains his power, indeed his identity and being, from the ivory he covets. In a world of art, the most greedy collector is often supreme; matter, not manner, counts. One source of Kurtz's fascination for Marlow is the former's will to power, Nietzschean, superhuman, and brutal. Kurtz has risen above the masses—of natives, station managers, even of directors back in Brussels. He must continue to assert himself, a megalomaniac in search of further power. Marlow has never met anyone like him, this Kurtz who represents all of Europe. The insulated Englishman now faces east, toward the continent. "I took great care to give a cosmopolitan origin to Kurtz," Conrad noted in a letter to K. Waliszewski (Dec. 16, 1903, *Lettres françaises*). "All Europe contributed to the making of Kurtz," we read.

He is indeed Europe, searching for power, maneuvering for advantage; and he finds it in the colonial adventure of ivory. No wonder, then, that his hunger for acquisition is so overwhelming. Having gratified forbidden desires, he is free of civilized taboos. In the Congo, where the white man—the civilized Belgian—ruled, he could do anything. His only prescription: produce results, send back ivory. Indeed, his very will to power, his confident brutality made him appear a kind of god—to the natives and other agents who feared him, to the Russian sailor who believed in him. The ultimate corruption is that Kurtz can go his way without restraint. All human barriers are down. Only power counts—no matter whether political or economic. In the jungle, as in enterprise, only the strong survive, and Kurtz obviously is one of the strong. He brings European power—all of Europe—into the jungle; his weapons encompass 2,000 years of Western civilization. And the consequence: corruption of self and death to "inferiors" on a monumental scale.

When a journalist informs Marlow that Kurtz would have been a "splendid leader of an extreme party," Marlow understandably asks, "What party?" "Any party," his visitor answers. "He was an—an extremist." With that, Conrad presents his grandest insight into the politics of our time—superficially totalitarian, but extending also to democratic powers. The absence of social morality, the desire to rise at everyone's expense, the manipulation of whole peoples for purely selfish ends, the obsession with image and consensus, and personal power, the absence of meaningful beliefs, the drive for advancement and aggrandizement without larger considerations, the career built on manipulation and strategies, not ideas—all of these have become the expected burden of the ruled in our century. The rapist here is Belgian, later German, Russian, American—with the scale varying. The great symbol of our times is the chameleon—one can be all things to all men. This, we are reminded, in a society proud of having turned the corner into democracy, decency, and dignity. The best lack all conviction, as Yeats was later to write, while the worst—they act.

In this conception of Kurtz, Conrad's powers as an artistic thinker were at their strongest. In reading Conrad it is often necessary to discriminate between pure thought and

thought embodied in a work of art. As a political and social theorist, he was antagonistic to modern developments,
deeply conservative in the sense that he suspected or
mocked new departures or experiments. As an artistic
thinker, however, he was at once caustic, subtle, broad.
His conception of Kurtz, slim on the surface, broadening
beneath, is a Cassandra's view of European progress, a
view both realistic and ironic.

Conrad was concerned with the rape of a people. The
Congo had been, since 1875, the private preserve of Leopold II of Belgium, a medieval kingdom for personal use,
organized under the deceptive title of the International
Association for the Civilization of Central Africa. Demo-
graphists estimate that hundreds of thousands, possibly
millions, of Congolese died in slavery or through brutality;
a beginner's course in Nazism. Kurtz, or his type of ex-
ploiter, was the rule, not the exception. Kurtz himself was
based roughly and loosely on one Georges-Antoine Klein
(Klein = small, Kurtz = short), whom Conrad had taken
aboard his steamer during *his* Congo days. Conrad's journey, as he relates in his Congo diary, was real, Kurtz and
his type prevailed, the land and the natives existed, the
facts are undisputed. Even if Conrad used symbols to excess, as he feared, each symbol is solidly grounded in fact.
Here is white against black, entrenched against primitive,
have against have-not, machine against spear, civilization
against tribe.

If Conrad's novella is to have artistic as well as political
significance, it must make broad reference to human motivation and behavior. One evident part of the application
comes with Kurtz's double shriek of "The horror! The horror!" The cry is far richer and more ambiguous than most
readers make it. We must remember that Marlow is re-
porting, and Marlow has a particular view and need of

Kurtz. As Marlow understands the scream, it represents a moral victory; that is, on the threshold of death, Kurtz has reviewed his life with all its horror and in some dying part of him has repented. Marlow hears the words as a victory of moral sensibility over a life of brutality and prostituted ideals. This "Christian" reading of the words is, of course, what Marlow himself wishes to hear; he is a moral man, and he believes, with this kind of bourgeois religiosity, that all men ultimately repent when confronted by the great unknown. Kurtz's cry, in this interpretation, fits in with what Marlow wants to know of human nature.

We are not all Marlows, however, and we should not be seduced into agreeing with him, even if he is partially right. More ambiguously and ironically, Kurtz's cry might be a shriek of despair that after having accomplished so little he must now perish. His horror is the anguish of one who dies with his work incomplete. In this view, Kurtz does not repent; rather, he bewails a fate which frustrates his plans. Indeed, at the very moment of death, he challenges life and death and tries to make his baffled will prevail. Like Milton's Satan, he prefers hell to compromise.

Conrad's grasp of moral issues remained unresolved; he always harked back to the individual devil in each man— perhaps as part of his Catholic background. He believed that men deceived themselves to the very end: "Our refuge is in stupidity, in drunkenness of all kinds, in lies, in beliefs, in murder, thieving, reforming—in negation, in contempt. . . . There is no morality, no knowledge and no hope; there is only the consciousness of ourselves which drives us about a world that whether seen in a convex or a concave mirror is always but a vain and floating appearance" (To Graham, Jan. 31, 1898, Dartmouth U. Library).

The irony of the story comes full turn. Returning from the world of the dead, Marlow—our twentieth-century

Everyman—cannot admit the full impact of the indecency he has witnessed, of the feelings he has experienced. Even this most honest of men must disguise what he has seen and felt. Like a politician he must bed down with lies. Only Conrad, who is outside both Marlow and Kurtz, can admit the truth, can limn the lie and see it as a lie. Only the artist, and his art, can triumph; all else is dragged down or forced to exist by virtue of untruths. Marlow, the narrator, controlled in turn by Conrad, the creator, can transform the horror of his experience into the human terms necessary for continued life. Conrad has succeeded in constructing a form which can, so to speak, hold the horror at arm's length and yet also touch us deeply.

In this and other respects, "Heart of Darkness" is a masterpiece of concealment. Just as Marlow has concealed from himself the true nature of his own needs, so too we can find concealment—in art, in nature, in people—in virtually every other aspect of the novella. The jungle itself, that vast protective camouflage barring the light of sun and sky, masks and hides, becoming part of the psychological as well as the physical landscape. Like the dream content, it forms itself around distortion, condensation, and displacement.

Post-Darwinian and overpowering, the jungle is not Wordsworth's gentle landscape, by no means the type of nature which gives strength and support in our darkest hours. Rather, it runs parallel to our anxieties, becomes the repository of our fears. The darkness of the jungle approximates darkness everywhere, adumbrating the blackness of Conrad's humor, the despair of his irony.

The persistence of the color sets the tone and elicits our response. We first meet the Romans, who penetrate *their* Congo—the English swamp, the savage Thames. Then we encounter the women in the Brussels office who knit black wool, suitable for Fates who send gladiators out to die in the jungle for the glory of empire. There are, we remember, only two Fates—Clotho and Lachesis—for the presence of the third, Atropos, would indicate Marlow's death. Their black is indeed morbid against Brussels as a "whited sepulchre." Later, when Kurtz paints in oils, he represents a woman, draped and blindfolded, carrying a torch, all against the somber background. She emerges from the dark, but only partially, for dark nourishes her. She is, in fact, a symbolic Kurtz—one contiguous with and defined by blackness. Then, just before Kurtz dies, he lies in dim light awaiting the end, despair writhing on his face, the blackness of the past merging with the mystery of the future. Once dead, Kurtz returns to the black of the Congo, his epitaph spoken by the manager's boy: "Mistah Kurtz—he dead."

The sarcastic understatement of the boy, his cruel indifference to Kurtz's prestige, all stress the contrast between Kurtz's desires and the blackness which receives him. The jungle itself will conceal him. Beyond every wish is the force of fate, the dark power which is both within and without, psychological needs and physical consequences. "Mistah Kurtz—he dead" becomes the epitaph of all those who die in jungles, their careers curtly reviewed in the contemptuous words of the boy, a bleak and black destiny.

Attached to each of these events—Kurtz's final words, his death, the report by the manager's boy, the darkness surrounding all, the frantic run out of the Congo, the meeting with Kurtz's Brussels fiancée—connected to all such events is the shimmer and nightmare of dream, Conrad's definition of modern life. No less than Kafka, he saw existence as forms of unreality stubbled with real events. And no little part of the dream-like substance of the tale is the Russian follower of Kurtz, like Marlow a mariner. Dressed

in motley, he seems a figure from another world, and yet
with his ludicrous appearance he is a perfect symbol for
Marlow's Congo experience. Befitting someone who worships Kurtz like a god, the Russian forgives his worst behavior and argues that a common man like himself needs
someone to follow. He is persuaded that Kurtz's will to
power draws in all those less capable, conveys hope and
substance to them.

There is, in his view, a void in every man that only
someone like Kurtz can fill. Without Kurtz, the sailor says,
he is nothing. "He made me see things—things." His ordi-
nariness is balanced by Kurtz's superiority—every disciple
needs a god. Like the natives, like the superb native mis-
tress who forgives Kurtz everything, the sailor follows
power. Conrad's prescience was never more trenchant.

To Marlow's accusation that Kurtz is insane, simply
mad, the Russian offers Kurtz's great intelligence, his ability to talk brilliantly, his charismatic qualities. To our ob-
jection that the sailor himself is mad, Conrad offers his influence upon Marlow—he strikes in Marlow precisely the
note of love-hate that Conrad's narrator has come to feel
for Kurtz. Although Marlow would like to anchor himself
solidly in the Russian's sea manual and reject the vapidity
of the Russian, he too is drawn into Kurtz's orbit. He
senses what the sailor voices.

In this strangely insane world, all alignments defy logic.
Loyalties, beliefs, love, women themselves take on new
shapes and attractions. Marlow, that neuter bachelor, is
fascinated by the jungle woman, by her wanton, demanding display of sex, by the "fecund and mysterious life" she
embodies, by the deliberate provocation of her measured
walk. He is further drawn to her sense of reality; without
illusion, without question, she accepts Kurtz for what he
is, as integrated with the very savagery which enfolds her.

For Marlow the pull of the primitive comes full circle. Again and again, he breaks off his narrative to assure his listeners that all this really happened. Even while he talks, this modern mariner, he must convey the depth of his experience, try to convince that it was as profound as he claims. Marlow knows what happened—yet to find the precise words is almost impossible. Returning from the dead, like Eliot's Prufrock, he now has to convince his audience that there is really a hell.

The problem of Marlow, as we saw earlier, is the problem of Conrad's art: to communicate the weight and depth of an experience which is uniquely felt. Some of the criticism of Conrad's treatment, particularly F. R. Leavis's, has been directed toward his "excessive" use of descriptives to suggest mysteriousness and unspeakable events. Possibly in some areas the language is too heavy, but to labor this point is to lose sight of the story as a whole. One might, in fact, argue the very opposite: that the words—adjectives and all—beat upon us, creating drum-like rhythms entirely appropriate to the thick texture of the jungle, a more sophisticated version of Vachel Lindsay's "Congo." When one confronts the artistry of the complete piece, Conrad's reliance on verbal embellishment appears a minor consideration.

The novella in fact has form: from the opening frame, with Marlow's somewhat ingenuous listeners, to the closing sequence, with Kurtz's innocent fiancée confirming her illusions. The use of a first-person narrative, through the agency of Marlow, was necessary so that Conrad could gain aesthetic distance and the reader could identify with an average man thrown into an abnormal situation. We must, Conrad realized, go through it with him and Marlow. Lacking the narrator, the story would appear too distant from the immediate experience—as though it had happened and was now over, like ancient history. From this safe distance, everyone was saved, and the evil force, Kurtz, rightfully had perished. But that is not at all Conrad's story; to make a morality play out of the tale is to destroy its felt sense. The story is concerned with hidden terrors in the normal heart, with the attractions of the unspeakable which we all experience, with the sense of power we wish to exert or identify with, ultimately with the underground existence each sentient being recognizes in himself. In this respect, Marlow as direct participant through his narration becomes indispensable.

So, too, in other respects did Conrad work out the shape of the story, in large and in details: through doubling of scenes and characters, through repetition, analogy, duplicating images, through differences of tone. From the beginning, when the ancient Romans on the Thames are contrasted with the modern Europeans on the Congo, Conrad used heightening and foreshortening, contrast and comparison to give the novella form. Most obviously, Marlow's peaceful setting on the *Nellie* is set off against his nightmarish Congo riverboat setting; in a different way, Kurtz's two fiancées are contrasted, each one standing for certain values, indeed for entire cultures, in conflict; further, the jungle is set off against the river, with jungle as death, river as possible relief; in another way, Kurtz is compared with other forms of evil, with the deceptive smoothness of the station manager, with the hypocrisy of the pilgrims; the pilgrims in turn are ironically compared with the savages they condemn, with the pilgrims less Christian than the pagan natives; within the natives, the tribal savages are contrasted with those exposed to civilization, detribalized as it were, the latter already full of wiles and deceit; light and dark, the painter's chiaroscuro, hover over the entire story, no less important here than in

Milton's Christian epic; day dream and night dream form contrasts, worked out in the play between expectation and consequence, between professed ideals and realistic behavior, between Kurtz's humanitarianism and his barbarism, between Marlow's middle-class sense of English justice and the Congo reality, between the fluctuating love-and-hate which fill both Kurtz and Marlow.

Out of the infinite possibilities facing Conrad, he chose these to give unity to his language and ideas. Such devices shape our thoughts and give form to our responses; they, too, become the substance of our awareness. Only in *Nostromo*, with his use of silver, or in *The Secret Agent*, with London city streets, did Conrad find comparable central images to the Congo.

To discover the rightful place of "Heart of Darkness" in European culture, we must leave English literature and compare it with Dostoyevsky's *Notes from Underground*, Kafka's *Metamorphosis*, Thomas Mann's *Death in Venice*, Camus' *The Stranger*—all relatively short fiction concerned with underground men in an underground existence who become, through force of character or vision of art, suffering creatures outside the mainstream of society. This is typically continental fiction, not English—Conrad's vision remained Slavic. At the heart of all is an anarchy that repels and attracts, where one toys with the unimaginable and contemplates mysterious rites, where one defies the edicts of civilization and suffers secretly.

What makes this story so impressive is Conrad's ability to focus on the Kurtz-Marlow polarity as a definition of our times. European history as well as the history of individual men can be read more clearly in the light of Conrad's art; for he tells us that the most dutiful of men, a Marlow, can be led to the brink of savagery and brutality if the will to power touches him; that the most idealistic of men, Kurtz, can become a sadistic murderer; that the dirty work of this world is carried out by men whose reputations are preserved by lies. Conrad's moral tale becomes, in several respects, our story, the only way we can read history and each other. Hannah Arendt's definition of the "banality of evil," the nihilism of the average man, is fully relevant. It is a terrible story.

In commenting upon their collaboration, Ford Madox Ford said that Conrad was experimenting with blank verse in the late nineties and used it in "Heart of Darkness." Ford even tries to scan some of the lines. However, nearly all of Conrad's work, strongly influenced as it was by the cadences of the English Bible and Shakespeare's plays, has its own robust rhythms which began with *Almayer's Folly* and extended through *The Rover*, rhythms which only fortuitously fall into blank verse. Conrad's important advance in "Heart of Darkness" was not his poetic prose but his way of conceiving his material through images which, seemingly disconnected and tangential, relate to further aspects of general experience beyond the narrative. This is one of Conrad's major contributions to the development of the English novel.

To go from "Heart of Darkness" to "The End of the Tether" is to proceed from a universally tragic experience to a rather tepid personal one. Old Captain Whalley, who for personal reasons must return to the sea, like Kurtz enters into a pact with the devil by separating himself from the solidarity of mankind. Whalley's transgression is that he continues as a captain long after his vision has failed and he is unable to rely on his own faculties in guiding the ship. In attempting deception, Whalley's position becomes self-destructive once the forces he has activated begin to surround and crush him.

Whalley is one of that long list of Conrad "heroes"—a Lord Jim grown up and become gray and respectable—who are stanch and intrepid, although tending toward tediousness and sentimentality. Within the format of a short story, Whalley's plight is carried to the attenuated length of 174 pages, and even Conrad admitted in the Author's Note to *Youth* that he was not too deeply interested in the captain or the story.

As a minor figure in a minor tragedy Whalley might have commanded attention, but Conrad tried to invest him with the whale-like qualities that his name implies. Whalley, consequently, is described as an Old Testament deity, a chivalrous knight, a blinded Samson, and an incarnation of wisdom itself. As a whale of a man caught in the circumstances of a trapped bulldog, the old captain becomes tiresome.

III

Typhoon and Other Stories[8] appeared the year after the *Youth* volume, but despite the various laudatory opinions of many readers, the four stories in this volume are not among Conrad's best either in form or content. Even the celebrated titular story[9] becomes as dull as its hero, MacWhirr, whose sublime stupidity has often been generously translated by critics into a happy stolidity and heroic persistence. As possessor of many of the solid virtues, MacWhirr's personality simply cannot engage us; with his lack of imagination, his one-track mind, his ignorance of life, his blind sense of mission and orderliness, he is more a symbol than a person. MacWhirr's fidelity to duty surely

[8] 1903, published by William Heinemann, London.
[9] *Pall Mall*, XXVI (January-March 1902).

bulked large in Conrad's view of a responsible universe, but the struggle of man versus nature in this story is an adventure pure and simple. Magnificent though the adventure may be, it loses stature by its very particularity. *Typhoon* is personal experience *per se*, without that forging of fact and fiction into an art form. Forgoing the story as a whole, we must finally return to the storm scene itself as one of the finest examples of sustained writing in sea literature.

Perhaps one of the difficulties with the story is its lack of surprise, either of word or structure. The form, as though following the central character, is simplicity itself —except for the last twelve pages which are a Browning-like presentation of various points of view as they bear on MacWhirr and his ship. In this rapid recapitulation which ends the story we have:

(1) *The revengeful second mate paid off and fired from the ship.*
(2) *Respectable Mrs. MacWhirr, far from the storm, living in boredom with her children and her daily emptiness.*
(3) *Mrs. Rout, wife of the chief engineer Solomon Rout.*
(4) *The mother of Solomon Rout.*
(5) *A friend of Jukes, the chief mate.*
(6) *Jukes' letter to his friend.*

These six short scenes provide an ironical contrast between the heroism on board the *Nan-Shan* and the complacency and placidity of life ashore. Furthermore, these scenes are presented through a sequence that is structurally sound—an attempt to suggest simultaneity of action and observation with a minimum of discourse.

Of the three remaining stories in *Typhoon*, "Amy Foster," [10] "Falk," [11] and "Tomorrow," [12] only "Amy Foster"

[10] *The Illustrated London News*, CXIX (December 14, 21, 28, 1901).

warrants comment. This short story, with its Polish exile in England, has drawn from its critics several comparisons with Conrad's own feelings as an exile in England. The story itself, once the biographical likenesses are put aside, is, nevertheless, far from being among Conrad's best. Its pretentiousness is manifest in the narrator, Kennedy, whose "wisdom" is often more suffocating than Marlow's. The too frequent classical allusions add ponderous weight to the thin trappings, while the excess of rhetoric inundates an essentially simple story of the heart. It happened frequently in his minor works that Conrad, recognizing or subconsciously suspecting their lack of stature, tried to bestow a gratuitous verbal magnificence and merely unintentionally underscored the basic insignificance of theme. "Amy Foster" is not of course insignificant, but its combination of poignancy and cruelty is only important on a small scale.[13]

---

11 "Falk," 1903.

12 *Pall Mall*, XXVII (August, 1902). Called "The Son" in MS.

13 In his perceptive psychoanalytic study of Conrad, Dr. Bernard Meyer examines in detail the language and imagery of "Amy Foster," finding significant correspondence with Grimm's fairy tales, "The Twelve Brothers" and "The Six Swans." Of particular interest, Meyer finds, is Conrad's use of images, recalling Grimm, of castration, cannibalism, and child envy. Such an analysis turns the story from its usual biographical interpretation toward far broader meanings relevant to Conrad's entire canon.

There are, moreover, several sides to Conrad's expressions of fear and anxiety. He had, for example, many more solid sources for his novels than he revealed to his friends. In the Author's Note to *Nostromo*, for instance, he talks vaguely of a man who singlehanded had stolen a whole lighterful of silver. The source for this, discovered by Mr. John Halverson and Professor Ian Watt, is *On Many Seas: The Life and Exploits of a Yankee Sailor* by Frederick Benton Williams (pseudonym of Herbert Elliot Hamblen), 1897. From George Frederick Masterman's *Seven Eventful Years in Paraguay* (1869), Conrad drew the names of most of his characters—Decoud, Mitchell, Gould, Fidanza, Antonia, Monygham, Barrios— as well as many of his situations and details. From Edward B. Eastwick's

In what I have called Conrad's early period, there are three works, *The Nigger of the "Narcissus," Lord Jim,* and "Heart of Darkness," which demonstrate his growing mastery over his raw materials. Conrad came to follow successfully James' advice in "The Art of Fiction" to catch the "very note and trick, the strange irregular rhythm of life," which is the work of those "whose strenuous force keeps Fiction upon her feet." James addressed the young novelist [Conrad]: "Remember that your first duty is to be as complete as possible—to make as perfect a work. Be generous and delicate and pursue the prize."

Conrad discovered that to be "as complete as possible" meant to suggest aspects of experience through coalescence of technique, tone, and subject, a combination of idea and form that James called "the needle and thread" of the story. Beginning with *Nostromo* (1904) and continuing through the publication of *Victory* (1915), we find Conrad at his most mature and his most ingenious. It is striking that in his fiction after *Victory* there is no work worthy of a major novelist. His effective period of writing lasted twenty years (*Almayer,* 1895—*Victory,* 1915), nine of which were preparation intermixed with sporadic achievement, and the rest fruition.

Throughout his early fiction, we see Conrad struggling to find a form for his work, especially in a work like "Heart of Darkness" in which experience tended at times to force itself out as subjective comment. The object was to isolate and dramatize, to gain "aesthetic distance" between the material and the creator. Marlow, or an equiva-

---

Venezuela (1868), Conrad found descriptions which he applied to the topography of Sulaco, including the gulf, cape, customs house, and lighthouse. There was, evidently, a psychological compulsion in Conrad, here and elsewhere, to hide his tracks and, masochistically, to make his every situation or condition appear worse than it actually was. It is difficult, at times, to draw the line between his paranoia and his romanticism.

lent narrator, was important but not sufficient; all explanations of Marlow—his presence for purposes of dramatization, for the collaboration of narrator and listener, for the entrance of the reader into the creative process, or for getting the story started—all these ways of explaining Marlow only define one part of Conrad's method of creating. The process of objectifying is more subtle.

When we reach *Nostromo,* we see that all the early lessons have been learned. The novel comes to us as the very stuff of human experience, with an intensity of impression that shows Conrad to be "one of the people on whom nothing is lost."

chapter 5

Nostromo

Gestaltung, Umgestaltung,
Des ew'gen Sinnes ew'ge Unterhaltung.
Goethe

Shaping, re-shaping,
The eternal mind's eternal occupation.

Writing to Major E. Dawson less than one month before beginning *Nostromo,* Conrad said he doubted whether greatness could be attained at that time in imaginative prose work. He commented that when such a work does come, ". . . it will be in a new form; in a form for which we are not ripe yet." Aware of the possibilities of new forms in the novel and now approaching full literary maturity, Conrad, nevertheless, began *Nostromo* with serious misgivings, gaining confidence only as he went deeper into the work. Without doubt this novel was to be a grand and capacious work, and the discomforts it caused were not unusual in the light of Conrad's aims. He wrote dubiously to H. G. Wells that he was going on "as one would cycle over a precipice along a 14-inch plank. If I falter I am lost." Shortly afterwards, to Cunninghame Graham he claimed that he was "dying over that curst *Nostromo* thing." Then candidly recognizing his frail source material, he deplored his situation, admitting: "All my memories of Central America seem to slip away. I just had a glimpse 25 years ago,—a short glance. That is not enough *pour bâtir un roman dessus.*"[1]

Nostromo was begun almost casually.[2] In 1903, Conrad was persuaded by friends to come up to London to meet an American financier who was a staunch admirer of his early novels. The American upon meeting Conrad almost immediately asked: " 'When are you going to spin some more yarns about the sea?' "—a question which infuriated the finely-tempered Conrad who had always considered himself anything but a sea writer. Conrad's rage was finally quieted and his feelings soothed, and in the ensuing discussion a contract was signed whereby the American promised to commission a 100,000 word novel which would be serialized in *Harper's Magazine.* This novel was *Nostromo.* Harper's subsequently broke the contract and paid a forfeit to Conrad, who then published the novel in weekly installments in *T.P.'s Weekly.*[3]

In his depression over the breaking of the Harper's contract and though he was deeply involved in the novel it-

[1] Writing to Richard Curle, Conrad revealed his summary view of Venezuela: "As to No.[stromo]. If I ever mentioned 12 hours it must relate to P[orto] Cabello where I was ashore about that time. In La Guayra [sic] as I went up the hill and had a distant view of Caracas I must have been 2½ to 3 days. It's such a long time ago! And there were a few hours in a few other places on that dreary coast of Ven'la." Reprinted by Curle in *Caravansary and Conversation*, p. 214.

[2] Jean-Aubry says that *Nostromo* was begun at Pent Farm in early 1903 and completed on September 3, 1904, a period of twenty months. There is, however, a slight discrepancy between Jean-Aubry's dating and Conrad's own. In a letter to Galsworthy (Jean-Aubry, I, 332, September 1, 1904), Conrad says he finished his most ambitious novel on August 30th in the Stanford house of G. F. W. Hope in Essex. The last page of the first draft of *Nostromo* is also dated August, 1904. Jean-Aubry perhaps mistakenly dated the novel from a letter Conrad had written to William Rothenstein (Jean-Aubry, I, 336) on September 3, 1904 in which he said that *Nostromo* had just been completed. Baines repeats August 30.

[3] Serialized in numbers III and IV (January 29 to October 7, 1904). Published by Harper and Brothers, London and New York, in 1904.

self, Conrad was still anxious, so his friend Hugh Clifford asserted, to return to sea even at this late date. He was, however, under certain strong pressures to continue his literary career. By 1903, besides being deep in his own work, he was at the height of his collaboration with Ford Madox Ford. Their work on *Romance* was at its most distressing point, for both were trying to put into practice many theories they had hitherto valued only verbally. Mrs. Conrad's lengthy and often exasperated comments on Conrad's work with Ford demonstrate the difficulties both writers had in trying to attain a *modus vivendi* for the novel. In so far as *Romance* was almost contemporaneous with *Nostromo* and does manifest some influence on the structure and conception of that book, it is necessary to spend some time on this their most ambitious collaboration.

In a holograph note in T. J. Wise's copy of *Romance,* 1923, Conrad said:

> The tale as it stands here is based on Ford Madox Hueffer's MS. of "Seraphina," a much shorter work and quite different in tone. On this we went to work together, developing the action and adding some new characters. We collaborated right through, but it may be said that the middle part of the book is mainly mine with bits of F.M.H.—while the first part is wholly out of "Seraphina": the second part is almost wholly so. The last part is certainly three quarters MS. F.M.H. with here and there a par. by me.

Ford, in the appendix to *The Nature of a Crime* (1924), the last of their collaborations, remarked that parts one, two, three, and five of *Romance* are a mosaic of alternately written passages while part four is entirely Conrad's work.

The surface of *Romance*, then, shows a close working

agreement between Ford and Conrad, and demonstrates
an awareness of method that almost inevitably carried
into *Nostromo,* which had been eight months in the writing while Conrad was still reading and altering the proofs
of *Romance.* There are scenes and characters in *Romance*
that clearly overlap with those of *Nostromo,* although the
collaboration evidently falls far short of the stature of
the Conrad work. *Romance,* it should be recognized at
once, is a light book of small accomplishment, lacking the
seriousness, the breadth of vision, and the variety that are
found in *Nostromo.* But despite its obvious shortcomings,
Conrad was nevertheless influenced in some significant
ways by the earlier work and showed that he put the collaboration to good use.

Central to both books are scenes which occur in the
foggy silence of the bay in *Romance* and in the dead calm
of the gulf in *Nostromo.* In the one, the treasure is Seraphina, the beautiful Spanish girl; in the latter, it is the
protean silver. In *Romance,* John Kemp and Tomas Castro
—the rescuers of Seraphina—dip noiselessly into the fog-
hidden waters of the bay as they endeavor to save their
treasure, like the stealthy Nostromo and Decoud, the
would-be rescuers of the silver. The artful Castro with his
silent ability and instinctive sense of what to do and how
to do it is a worthy forerunner of the ingenious Nostromo.
Despite his predatory fierceness, he has, like Nostromo, an
element of integrity that sustains his reputation for faith-
fulness. When his courage is tested, he is true to character
and shows he can sustain his heroic pose under duress.
But these superficial and obvious comparisons would afford in themselves only a weak and dubious relationship
between the two books. It is, rather, Conrad's peculiar
feeling for the material in each book, his particular way

of visualizing character and scene, that calls for special comment. Richard Curle once remarked in passing that Conrad had learned how to write mob scenes from Flaubert's *Salammbô;* but Curle did not have to look further than *Romance* to find a sharp prefiguration of those ragged and disorganized mob scenes in *Nostromo.* The *Lugareños* (village riff-raff) of *Romance* are a disorderly, shouting mob at once awed by and disdainful of the very things they are attacking. In their clamorous and unrestrained emotionalism, they represent everything Conrad feared and hated; their vehemence is dictated by a passing situation they fail to understand, and their violence is subject to the tyrannical whims of their amoral masters. Conrad's disdain is obvious as he ironically treats their self-seeking and naïveté:

> For a time that motley group of bandits stood in the light, as if intimidated by the great dignity of the house, by the mysterious prestige of the Casa whose interior, probably, none of them had ever seen before. They gazed about silently, as if surprised to find themselves there.

These rabble followers of O'Brien in *Romance* become the village riff-raff who follow the dictators and petty tyrants of *Nostromo.* Either Ford or Conrad wrote in *Romance:*

> Some of the *Lugareños* carried torches, others had pikes; most of them, however, had nothing but their long knives. They came in a disorderly, shouting mob along the beach, intending this not for an attack, but as a simple demonstration.

In *Nostromo* this scene was speeded up and became:

Knots of men ran headlong; others made a stand; and the irregular rattle of firearms came rippling to his ears in the fiery, still air. Single figures on foot raced desperately. Horsemen galloped towards each other, wheeled round together, separated at speed.

In conveying the sweeping and disorganized movement of the attacking populace, Conrad, whether in collaboration or alone, momentarily caught in sharp relief the forms of the mob as it wavered between the superficial dictates of its own emotions and the demands of its corrupt leaders.

In the shallow *Romance*, the mob scenes are almost always incidental events, merely colorful pageants of descriptive writing; while in *Nostromo*, the mob is the very stuff of Nostromo's genius, who is himself only once removed from it by passion and ambition. In this latter novel, the actions of the mob, taken together with the towering and isolating range of mountains and the silence of the foggy gulf, are part of the tempos of the book and help to define what Nostromo is and where his strength lies. The mob, the water of the gulf, the overhanging and brooding natural surroundings—all in combination with the silver itself—provide that distinctive movement which results from the fusion of scene and character.

In language as well, the two books have a common sense of richness, for both contain an awareness of words in their double role as atmosphere and texture. In *Romance*, as we know from Ford's comments, Conrad decorated basic sentences with adjectives and adverbs while Ford was trying to tone down the rhetoric to more natural speech. Nevertheless, Conrad evidently prevailed, for in one short paragraph there appear the adjectival qualifications of "desperate," "silent," "cloaked," "evil," "enchanted," "sordid," and others; or from a paragraph on the following page: "enveloping," "vague," "dim," "impenetrable," "luminous," "endless," and others. There is a distinction, however, which must be made between the adjectival excesses found in Conrad's Malayan works and those found in *Romance*, which looks ahead to *Nostromo* rather than back to *Almayer's Folly* and *An Outcast*. In the early work, language seemed to exist for itself, filling out and padding while erecting a rather static barrier of verbiage. But here, and particularly in *Nostromo*, the language is more closely wedded to other elements in the book—to character and basic theme, to natural surroundings—elements that through interaction simulate a rhythm which is central to the novel.

The expository beginning of *Nostromo*, for example, is a brilliant natural setting for the situation in Sulaco. In six pages, Conrad suggests most of the novel's major themes and creates a background that gives inevitability to the story and conveys a significant part of its sub-surface movement:

> Sulaco had found an inviolable sanctuary from the temptations of a trading world in the solemn hush of the deep Golfo Placido as if within an enormous semi-circular and unroofed temple open to the ocean, with its walls of lofty mountains hung with the mourning draperies of cloud.

And then Sulaco itself is described:

> The town of Sulaco itself—tops of walls, a great cupola, gleams of white miradors in a vast grove of orange trees—lies between the mountains and the plain, at some little distance from its harbour and out of the direct line of sight from the sea.

In *Romance* the Casa Riego in Rio Medio is similarly described:

The Casa Riego raised its buttressed and loopholed bulk near the shore, resembling a defensive outwork; on my other hand the shallow bay, vast, placid, and shining itself behind the strip of coast like an enormous lagoon. The fronds of palm-clusters dotted the beach over the glassy shimmer of the far distance. The dark and wooded slopes of the hills closed the view inland on every side.

Too often in viewing a major work, we tend to minimize or dismiss its inconsequential precedents. In this case, however, it is possible to see that Conrad learned a great deal from *Romance*, a novel that was a forerunner of *Nostromo* as much in language and arrangement of scene as in certain parallels of character and situation. *Romance* was a rather unsuccessful experiment that nevertheless provided a trial ground for Conrad's best novel.

I I

It is interesting to speculate what constituted Conrad's mental version of *Nostromo;* for in two letters written on August 22, 1903, one to his agent J. B. Pinker and the other to John Galsworthy, he said he had written about 42,000 words, what he at this time thought would be one-half of the projected novel. This number of words is, in fact, less than one-quarter of the completed book, which in the Collected Edition comprises a volume of approximately 175,000 words. The manuscript itself cannot provide any idea of initial conception, for it stops short exactly where any significant differences in length might be noted; and in parts that are extant, the manuscript shows differences more of quality than quantity. We also find that the first published version, serialized in *T.P.'s Weekly*, is of little help in judging the mental version; the serial is but slightly shorter than the Collected Edition, with differences in length mainly occurring near its end.[4]

If we remember that Conrad misjudged the length of four of his novels—*An Outcast, Lord Jim, The Nigger,* and *The Rover*—all of which were conceived as short stories, then we can see that in the case of *Nostromo* as well Conrad had planned a much shorter novel, a book perhaps the length of *An Outcast* and surely shorter than *Lord Jim.* As it frequently happened, Conrad watched with dismay as the novel grew, and then rather than re-work his material to suit greater length, he unnaturally clipped short the ending. The serial of *Nostromo,* with its hastily tacked on ending, is an excellent indication of his lack of staying power; a more fully developed ending was subsequently written for the first edition in 1904.

This shortcoming aside, however, *Nostromo* displays a large number of significant qualities, for with this novel, Conrad became a major author and entered a period of production that saw *The Secret Agent,* "Il Conde," *Under Western Eyes,* "The Secret Sharer," *Chance* and *Victory* all appear within ten years. In *Nostromo,* as in his other novels, it was not Conrad's ability to achieve new and original techniques that makes his work distinctive, but rather his resourcefulness in organizing and revamping the conventional matter of the novel. Most of all, we find Conrad learning from himself, growing larger and more varied as he progressed in his craft. In the intervening years since 1895, he had come to exercise a more acute critical intelligence, the same type of self-directed criticism we find operating in his major work between *Nostromo* and *Victory.* Possibly *Victory* rather than

---

[4] The extant typescript, probably the only one between the manuscript and serial, is too fragmentary to permit any comment on its possible length.

Nostromo is his best "constructed" book, but *Nostromo* is his broadest and most profound novel. *Nostromo* is the high point of Conrad's literary maturity, although maturity, as Chesterton once astutely pointed out, is not necessarily commensurate with perfection. With the exception of its melodramatic ending, *Victory* is perhaps the least spoiled of Conrad's major novels; while *Nostromo*, on the contrary, is perhaps one of the most spoiled, one of the most imperfect. Notwithstanding, in its awareness of human possibilities and in its ability to catch the semblance of historical reality, *Nostromo* joins the list of great novels which transform the matter of the world into artistic forms. *Nostromo*, in the company of those other novels, has sufficient strength to suggest its own terms which eventually make insignificant the numerous moments of failure.

To get at the bold rhythms of a Conrad novel, particularly one as complex as *Nostromo*, it is necessary to look beneath the scaffolding in order to identify individual elements of structure. But to dissect a novel, especially a modern novel with its difficulties of order and point of view, is to lose many of its potentialities. Every worthwhile literary work, as we have often been reminded, evades total dissection. The critic can only point to the constituent parts and demonstrate their relevance while recognizing that, finally, the reader must put the elements together for himself and literally reconstruct the book according to his own experience. *Nostromo* is one of the first of the "difficult" modern novels, requiring, as the early magazine and newspaper reviewers recognized, a close attention to word and scene.

III

Matters of order, of choice of word, of psychology of scene, and of point of view contribute to that elusive thing we call rhythm in a novel. *Nostromo*, for instance, possesses a rhythm that is as much of spoken words as it is of transitions between words and scenes. A Spanish critic in reviewing Conrad's work said that, "Como Maeterlinck, [Conrad] interpreta elocuentements los silencios"[5]; by which he meant that Conrad gains cumulative rhythms through special awareness of both the sounds and silences inherent in language, rhythms which grow in significance and intensity as the novel progresses. The *progression d'effet* which Conrad and Ford strove to reach through careful selection of word and phrase is conveyed in *Nostromo* through ever-increasing sub-surface rhythms. It is Conrad's delving into these subconscious rhythms, as much as his "underground" scenes and characters, which makes *Nostromo* intrinsically significant as well as important in the history of the novel.

Not the least important element in the rhythm of *Nostromo* is the ever-present silver mine. It has often been remarked, and correctly, that the silver of the mine provides a focus for the plot, and that many of the other elements are chiefly appendages to the mine. The silver, in short, provides the same center for *Nostromo* as the ivory for "Heart of Darkness." Conrad himself was anxious to point out the significance of silver in a long letter to Ernst Bendz, an early admirer and critic of his work:

I will take the liberty to point out that *Nostromo* [sic] has never been intended for the hero of the Tale of the Seaboard. Silver is the pivot of the moral and material events,

[5] "Like Maeterlinck, Conrad eloquently interprets the silent pauses."

affecting the lives of everybody in the tale. That this was my deliberate purpose there can be no doubt. I struck the first note of intention in the unusual form which I gave to the title of the First Part, by calling it "The Silver of the Mine," and by telling the story of the enchanted treasure on Azuera, which, strictly speaking, has nothing to do with the rest of the novel. The word "silver" occurs almost at the very beginning of the story proper, and I took care to introduce it in the very last paragraph, which would perhaps have been better without the phrase which contains the key word. (March 7, 1923)

The dramatis personae of *Nostromo* are many and varied, representing numerous social classes as well as different nations and races (American, English, Spanish, Italian, Jewish); but the nature of each character—no matter what his position—is defined in terms of his reaction to the mine. Early in the book, Conrad described the mine as a way of life in which "its [the mine's] working must be made a serious and moral success." One can well analyze *Nostromo* in terms of what the mine means to character and theme, and how it becomes a structural motif as it attains psychological and political significance. The mine is Conrad's most persistent symbol; pervading the novel from the first chapter to the last paragraph, almost indeed to the last word, it increasingly acquires meanings which themselves enlarge in succeeding circumstances. The mine, godlike in its omniscience, goes on, said Conrad, "as if neither the war nor its consequences could ever affect the ancient Occidental State secluded beyond its high barrier of the Cordillera."

The idea of treasure first enters in the third paragraph in the legend of gringos who perished while searching for "heaps of shining gold." This short account of their disaster presages the central tale of the silver mine. For the mine—from which, as Conrad said in the Preface, "there is no escape in this world"—literally becomes one of the Furies of the world. A testing ground for man's ideals as well as for his ability to handle reality, it is a symbol of progress for Charles Gould, who apart from it would have no existence; it causes loss of family for Mrs. Gould; it creates diversion for Holroyd, the American who backs the enterprise; it provides a way of gaining Antonia Avellanos's love for the disenchanted Martin Decoud and a means to reputation for the swaggering Nostromo; it is ever a source of greed and power for the Central American politicians; and, finally, it becomes, paradoxically, the means of regeneration for Dr. Monygham. The mine is the public symbol of each private failure; as cause and effect, instigator and outcome, it is the symbolic embodiment of personal neuroses.

At its most literal, the mine represents a handy means to personal wealth and materialistic power. Like the ivory in "Heart of Darkness," it partakes of man's selfishness and pays tribute in dubious rewards. As Kurtz had an ivory head, so Gould has a silver heart. Strictly speaking, the silver is metallic, crass, and vulgar, although it can force heroic, even spiritual, responses. Psychologically, the mine reaches into the subconscious of each character. Surrounded by material interests, all except Mrs. Gould have little self-control. While Gould and his cohorts deal with the solidity of the mine and its various compensations, she is concerned with human problems, with feelings that perforce run counter to the mine. It is no accident in the psychological make-up of the novel that she becomes sole repository of Nostromo's admission of greed for the silver. The silver is, in addition, a political and economic force, for its possession is the key to control of Costaguana. Conrad recognized that material wealth meant political power, and that personal ambition could be translated into political terms.

In his relation to the mine, Gould, despite his obvious materialistic interests, is an idealist, while his wife, on the contrary, is a realist. Her anti-materialistic humanity is opposed to Gould's philosophy of "I make use of what I see." Gould naïvely believed material interests themselves would eventually create stable conditions in which they could thrive, and that the result in time would be better justice for all. Psychologically, this belief is a necessity for him, for he would surely be nothing, would have no prop, without his idea. This eagerness for attachment—a typical nineteenth-century identification with progress of a sort—is his desire to assert what he considers best in himself and to strip away any encroaching uncertainties. An artist only in his sedulous devotion to his work, Gould possesses an imagination that is as prosaic as the silver itself; his reactions are no less basic then MacWhirr's (*Typhoon*), Powell's (*Chance*), or Inspector Heat's (*The Secret Agent*). Mrs. Gould, on the contrary, is first in a line of sensitive and feeling twentieth-century women who are the opposites of their materialistic husbands; she foreruns, for example, Mrs. Ramsay (*To The Lighthouse*), Lady Chatterley, Mrs. Dalloway, Mrs. Moore (*A Passage to India*), and Mrs. Wilcox (*Howards End*), without manifesting their non-intellectual smugness. In her hands Gould becomes a child; she treats him, Conrad points out, "as if he were a little boy."

Nostromo's reaction to the silver is more complex than Gould's, and therefore more fraught with doubt. For the latter, the mine is both means of existence and way of life; but for Nostromo, the mine is only one of any number of possibilities for building his reputation. Because he is not closely involved with the success or failure of Gould's mission to continue the flow of silver, his goals are quite different and the silver can corrupt him with small inner struggle. Nostromo, with the possible exception of Decoud, is least fixed, least rooted, of all the characters—both float, as it were, beyond the confines of any given situation. Not being dedicated to the mine and its functions, each in his way is more liable to deviation than Gould, Dr. Monygham, Don Jose Avellanos, or Captain Mitchell.

Dr. Monygham's relation to the mine is relatively simple, although he is surely one of Conrad's most interesting minor figures. In his devotion to the mine, Monygham, next to Gould, is perhaps the most selfish; for the only way he can expiate his past is through saving the silver and this by outwitting the piratical Sotillo. His motives remain simple and clear—if he is to survive psychologically, he must relate himself to the effort to save the silver. To Dr. Monygham, the mine is Mrs. Gould; to regain his dignity, he must feel accepted by her, and the mine is his only agent. He has the full sense of being, as he admits to himself, the "only one fit for dirty work," but emasculated by his past he sees his weakness recurring in every action. Fully aware of what Conrad calls "the crushing paralyzing sense of human littleness," Monygham recognizes that his attempt to attain psychological stability means participating in the very type of action he disdains. In his reaction to Nostromo's heroics—which he can view only with contempt—Monygham demonstrates his own limitations, the result of his morbid past. What is a means to reputation for Nostromo is a psychological necessity for Monygham.

Decoud is caught by the silver in a situation where he must write and print what he does not believe, what with his skepticism and intelligence he could not possibly believe. The silver has corrupted his sense of indifference; confounded by the illusion of love, Decoud must play the game of silver. For him, he says, "life is not . . . a moral romance derived from the tradition of a pretty fairy tale," as it is, for instance, for Charles Gould. The reality of his own situation can cause only banter; the seriousness of the mine is fit sport for his irony. Yet Decoud is caught more firmly perhaps than the others, for unlike Gould, Nostromo, and even Dr. Monygham, he cannot hide the actual situation from himself by disguising his true motives and interests. The mine, as *he* knows, is a farce; yet because of Antonia he finds himself committed to something he can only scorn. Mocking the idealists and contemptuous of the realists, Decoud must still admit that his actions, like those of the others, are also "clothed in the fair robes of an idea"—his love for Antonia Avellanos.

Important as the mine may be, rhythm in a novel is not achieved solely through a central symbol, even though character is directly related to that symbol. Using as theme the silver mine which involves all the characters in the novel, Conrad gave otherwise different personalities certain psychological affinities. Through the use of character complements and doubles, Conrad tried to create a dimension that is beyond verbalization. Perhaps it is these rhythms and half hints that caused Edward Crankshaw to comment: "Before the hundredth page is reached the reader is aware of infinitely more than he actually knows and is free to watch the psychology of the innumerable characters as they are revealed."

The most important pair of doubles is the complementary Nostromo and Decoud: Decoud, a nihilist, who denies even the value of his own feelings, and Nostromo, an egoist, who denies the existence of others except as their opinions increase his own sense of worth. Nostromo realizes that his finest moment—the moment when he had saved the silver—means nothing to the others; "Betrayed! Betrayed!" he cries and with great loss of confidence admits that "No one cared" about his great deed. Similarly, Decoud, after admitting his devotion to Antonia, cannot believe seriously even in his own being and destroys himself while silently mocking his attachment, exactly as Nostromo was later to mock his own reputation. As Conrad comments, Decoud in recognizing only intelligence had "erected passions into duties"; in like manner, Nostromo had believed so strongly in his emotions that when he found even they had failed him he was easily corrupted. Feeling the weight of solitude which follows upon dishonesty, Nostromo is engulfed by the same fears that had destroyed Decoud. As much as Decoud, the brilliant boulevardier who, "weighted by the bars of San Tomé silver, disappeared without a trace," Nostromo, the slave of San Tomé silver, "felt the weight as of chains upon his limbs. . . ." The two men, despite their many differences, combine, with the silver never far from either. Disbelief, nihilism, and reputation all fall victim to the voracious silver, which as fast as it draws victims destroys them physically and spiritually.

Even in death, Nostromo and Decoud are brought together through the silver. When old Viola mistakenly shoots Nostromo, the spirit of Decoud still lives in the air, conscious, as it were, that the Italian Capataz should perish in the same spot for almost the same reason. Conrad writes: "The tree under which Martin Decoud spent his last days, beholding life like a succession of senseless images, threw a large blotch of black shade upon the grass." Destroyed by silver, Nostromo joins Decoud, Mrs. Gould, and the hapless businessman Hirsch, all victims of the power of the mine. Only Dr. Monygham and

Gould are benefited by the silver, and they stand alone, straddling the smashed remains of a past which will nurture, Monygham is sure, an even more destructive future. "It'll [the mine will] weigh as heavily, and provoke resentment, bloodshed, and vengeance," says Dr. Monygham, "because the men have grown different." A cynic like Dr. Monygham can see the mine's true course, and only a fool like Captain Mitchell can believe that it will be a force for good. In corrupting the "incorruptible Capataz," the silver has shown that its possibilities for contamination are limitless. Victimized by four missing ingots of silver and by a world that is too busy to praise his cleverness in spiriting away the treasure, Nostromo worships at the altar of silver: "And the spirits of good and evil that hover about a forbidden treasure understood well that the silver of San Tomé was provided now with a faithful and lifelong slave." By reducing to nonsense Nostromo's one fixed idea, his reputation, and by forcing Decoud into actions completely contrary to his temperament and design, the silver has turned everything finally to its own shape. The epitaph for the silver can be no more final than Conrad's epitaph for Decoud, a part of which was quoted above:

> A victim of the disillusioned weariness which is the retribution meted out to intellectual audacity, the brilliant Don Martin Decoud, weighted by the bars of San Tomé silver, disappeared without a trace, swallowed up in the immense indifference of things.

In an essay on *Nostromo*, Dorothy Brewster and Angus Burrell remarked that Decoud signifies thought and Nostromo action; that when, however, they reverse their roles they ruin themselves. Although this is a partial simplification of their qualities, both characters are evidently incomplete, in the way that Jim and Heyst are incomplete. Decoud lacks the belief in illusions which maintains Nostromo, destroying himself when he realizes brain is not sufficient; while Nostromo literally destroys himself when he realizes his illusions are no longer real. After the loss of illusions for both, there follows a quick loss of life —Stein's warning to Marlow is repeated.

Dr. Monygham, on the other hand, is a realist among the illusionists; he understands by mind what Mrs. Gould knows through feeling. Sentient, sympathetic, and knowing, she is the doctor's idea of perfect woman, one who would buttress a man's loneliness and sense of duty with understanding tenderness. Similarly, Monygham's own nature, says Conrad, consisted of "his capacity for passion and . . . the sensitiveness of his temperament . . . [lacking] the polished callousness of men of the world. . . ." These qualities find appreciation in Mrs. Gould, who becomes sole repository of Dr. Monygham's faith. Isolated by the mine and by her husband's dedication to its success, she is as alone as Monygham, whose past puts him psychologically beyond human companionship. Treading the fringes of lonely lives, they reach across to each other in a moment of common commiseration.

Mrs. Gould's role as comforter affects even Nostromo. When he wants to divulge his deception, it is she whom he wants; the ever-sympathetic woman, "cloaked and monastically hooded over her evening costume," assumes a priestly role in the confessional, and like a priest maintains the secrecy of her oath. When the dying Nostromo says the silver has killed him, she recognizes that it has as well killed her, and her note of compassion takes the form of a similar confession: " 'I, too, have hated the idea of that silver from the bottom of my heart.' " Then she adds about the lost silver: " 'No one misses it now. Let it be lost for ever.'" Later, while commenting on Nostromo's relationship to Giselle Viola, Mrs. Gould says that as she herself was forgotten by Gould, so too Nostromo would have forgotten the girl for treasure. Across the pitiless and soulless mine, arms reach in condolence and understanding, while many of the characters join psychologically in similar wants and needs.

Even Dr. Monygham and Decoud—otherwise unlike in many ways—meet in their awareness "of the crushing, paralyzing sense of human littleness." But while the doctor at least believes in Mrs. Gould, Decoud can believe in nothing, not even in his own emotions. On a lesser scale, many of the minor characters play complementary roles: the figure of heroic Viola with his antiquated principles is placed, for example, against "heroic" Gould with his "modern" ideas; the terrified Hirsch in the foreground suggests Monygham's own terror at the hands of Guzman Bento; as a barely suggested double, the charming Decoud is now and then in mind as supplement to the priggish Gould.

All these characters, through either partial or complete identification, create the meanings as well as the rhythms of *Nostromo*. But the meanings of this novel, as of every major novel, are numerous. Conrad believed in the far-reaching power of evil, although he also believed that evil, even more than virtue, could not be simplified or explained. If the silver was evil, it also brought prosperity; if Nostromo became corrupt, it was because he lived among self-seekers who lacked courage to probe the motives of their inner convictions; and if Decoud could only banter when inner conviction was needed, it was because he recognized that each conviction contains the seeds of an almost equally convincing counter-conviction. No one is to blame for evil; it is a condition of life, a part of the rhythmic flow which Conrad tried to catch in the novel.

As a political institution, the mine forms a documented allegory of the cyclical rise and fall of a Central American republic. Gould's naïve belief that the flow of silver would create a stable economy, one in which resulting prosperity would make possible conditions under which the mine could continue to flourish, comes under serious attack in Conrad's ironic arrangement of material in the latter third of the book. Not unintentionally, Conrad has the triumph of Sulaco narrated by Captain Mitchell, a dullard whose own accomplishments are a pompous display of the English colonial mind at its worst. In his almost senile report, the success of the silver mine becomes an ironic tale with two sides. The civilization it has brought Sulaco is prosperity tempered with inherent vulgarity which portends an even worse future. Only Dr. Monygham fully understands the cycle of events and foresees what the mine will come to mean; material interests, he says to Mrs. Gould,

> have their law and their justice. But it is founded on expediency, and is inhuman, it is without rectitude, without the continuity and the force that can be found only in moral principles . . . the time approaches when all that the Gould Concession stands for shall weigh as heavily upon the people as the barbarism, cruelty, and misrule of a few years back.

When Gould dies, as Dr. Monygham realizes, all semblance of moral principle, no matter how righteous and short-sighted it really is, will die with him, and anarchy will once more disrupt Sulaco.

Mitchell's narrative, then, relates the triumph of self-righteous bourgeois mediocrity. In the new Sulaco, Mitchell is official guide, the parvenu Don Juste Lopez is Chief of State (Mitchell calls him "a very sagacious man

. . . a first-rate intellect"), and Hernandez, the ex-bandit, is Minister of War. Sulaco is rapidly being modernized —a café has replaced the sale of wine on street-corners, while wealthy tourists are increasingly drawn to the American bar. And presiding over all is the local bishop. As a final irony, in claiming that Nostromo was originally his protégé—"The sailor whom I discovered and, I may say, made, sir."—Mitchell wants full recognition for this depressing triumph to fall on himself. Perhaps society at the end of *Nostromo* is preferable to that at the beginning —order has been restored to a lawless land, and poverty has been replaced by at least a façade of prosperity. But as Robert Penn Warren shrewdly commented, materiality can work two ways; it is only a phase and not an end. The sky is still foul at the end of *Nostromo,* and the foulness will without doubt persist.

The San Tomé mine, then, has manifold possibilities which depend upon the point of view of the person involved; the mine gains new aspects each time it appears. In its psychological and political connotations, the mine suggests at least two sides of Conrad's belief in moral principle; it demonstrates that sustained moral principle can work toward bettering man while also containing, paradoxically, the seeds of its own destruction. If *Nostromo* is a view of human destiny at a certain historical moment, then the mine is one of those half-forgotten forces which form society into what it is and help define the individual as well as the collective nature of man.

IV

As already suggested, it was Conrad's ability to combine different elements in *Nostromo*—symbol and character, for example—that gives the book its distinctive rhythm. Working together with the mine and with character is setting, comprising those natural forces which seem to define man's psychology as much as the silver itself. The setting of the novel gives both the limitations and possibilities of Sulaco, of man lost in nature while trying to attain a *modus vivendi* in what he cannot possibly understand and surely cannot control. The great difficulty Conrad had in writing the early pages on the Golfo Placido, which extends from Punta Mala to Azuera, and in describing "The Isabels," which rest in the calm of the Gulf, testifies to his concern about this particular setting.

Conrad attempted four versions of this important early passage; for the spirit of "The Isabels" is to brood over the entire novel, and Decoud, the would-be Parisian *boulevardier,* is to find his will destroyed by the silence of the Gulf. Conrad realized that the terms of Decoud's suicide, which comes much later, must be presented from the first artistically and cogently.

My investigations of the Rosenbach Manuscript of the novel show this part crossed out, with passages deleted or intercrossed and words added or changed; the corrections are often more numerous than the original statements. In MS, Conrad wrote two versions describing Hermosa, the smallest of "The Isabels," neither version appearing in the first edition. This is how the MS looks:

That last [Hermosa] is a mere naked top of
                                awash in
a grey rock which would have been

perpetually awash in more turbulent waters;
the Little Isabel has   strange palm-
                    a tall

```
tree grows      on the cen                tall
          has                 sprung up
straight in the [?]. [sic]
```

Conrad completely rewrote this passage below the first version:

```
          a foot high
That last            would have been per-
petually awash in more turbulent waters; it
is the mere flat top of a grey rock which
smokes like a wetted hot cinder after a
          on which                would
shower; and        no prudent man
care to land barefoot
          would care to trust a
naked sole to it much before sunset. On
                    has sprung
the little Isabel a tall palmtree
up perfectly perfectly straight growing there
perfectly straight
          growing in the grace of a
perfect straightness undisturbed by the gentle,
irresolute airs of the hot gulf sends the low
          on all sides
rustling of its leafy head        beyond
the narrow circle of the shore.
```

The corrections in typescript concerning Hermosa more closely approximate the book, but the part on the Little Isabel is still far from that of the first edition. The TS follows:

```
          a foot high would have been
That last,
perpetually awash in more turbulent waters,
it
   no more than a foot high and about seven
```

paces across, is the mere flat top of a grey
                              wetted
rock which smokes like a   hot cinder
                   no
after a shower, and   where no prudent man
                   trust his
would care to   venture a naked sole
to it
        much before sunset. On the Little
        a tall   growing
Isabel   an old palm tree,

immobile in the grace of a perfect straight-
        undistinguished
ness   amongst the gentle,
irresolute airs of the hot gulf sends
                                tremu-

lous sighs passing over the gulf, sends out

the low rustling of its leafy head on all
                                the shore
sides beyond the narrow circle of

yellow sand.

In the serial and first edition, the verbiage was pruned considerably, and the resultant concrete description is more effective:

That last [Hermosa], no more than a foot high and about seven paces across, is the mere flat top of a grey rock which smokes like a hot cinder after a shower and where no prudent man would care to venture a naked sole before sunset. On the Little Isabel an old ragged palm, with a thick bulging trunk rough with spines, a very old witch amongst palm trees, rustles a dismal bunch of dead leaves above the coarse sand.

The developing image, for example, of the palm tree, which rustles its dead leaves above a bare rock, foreshadows Decoud's own bare existence on the Great Isabel. In the first MS passage, the tree hardly appears; in the second, it is passive and undefined; then in the TS, it becomes the weak agent of a gentle wind, while in the serial its very witchery creates a distinctive and precise image, that image of desolation and forlornness which will recur in different forms throughout the narrative.

One passage from the manuscript, typescript, and serial was completely deleted in the book; it follows:

> They ["The Isabels"] are insignificant bits of land with sides so sheer that if the water were withdrawn they would
> of
> appear rising from the bottom   like enormous columns on the floor of the vast ampitheatre of the coast.

Following the description of the Gulf, Conrad leads from the Great Isabel to Sulaco itself and, then, the story begins. The MS, here criss-crossed with revisions, shows the awkwardness of Conrad's first version of this passage, which in its rhythm should sweep in upon Sulaco like the Gulf itself.

> It is that end of the Great Isabel that faces
>
> the harbour of Sulaco. From the piece of
>   shore   right into
> sandy   beach the eye plunges
>   of the coast
> through an opening   two miles
>   as if it was   out
> away as abrupt as if   chopped
>   in
> with an axe   of the regular sweep of the

[?] coast, right into the bay; for the har-

                                  bay a
bour of Sulaco is in reality an oblong,

lake-like piece of water with one of its sides
          against   undulations **of**
close   under the wooded
                              undulating in
spurs of the mountains   rolling
                              waves
away regularly like the long   swell of **a**
          [?]
dark green sea,   and on the other with an
                              made
open view of the great Sulaco plain

passing into the opal mystery of a thin [?]

dry haze clinging to the levels of grass.

The same passage in the serial shows Conrad's marked concern with movement, with pushing the novel forward through words as well as through action. The following passage *reads,* its images plastic and vivid; whereas the movement in the MS was jerky and wordy, the imagery unsure.

From that end of the Great Isabel the eye plunges through an opening two miles away, as abrupt as if chopped with an axe out of the regular sweep of the coast, right into the harbour of Sulaco. It is an oblong, lake-like piece of water. On one side the short wooded spurs and valleys of the Cordillera come down at right angles to the very strand; on the other the open view of the great Sulaco plain passes into the opal mystery of great distances overhung by dry haze.

Even an earlier section on Higuerota, part of the Cordillera mountain range that dominates the mainland as much as "The Isabels" do the Gulf, gave Conrad a great deal of trouble in MS and TS. The TS follows (the deleted portion appearing in parenthesis):

> (But soon the clouds begin to roll out of the
> Then as the ascending sun withdraws from the
> (lower valley stream out of chaos, float amongst
> gulf the shades of the mountains the clouds
> (the peaks, drift in smoky trails over the fields
> begin to roll out of the lower valleys. They
> (of snow. They rise from the slopes wrap
> swathe in sombre tatters the naked crags of
> (up the crags swathe in sombre tatters the
> precipices above the wooded slopes, hide the
> (inclined expanses of tree tops mingle into
> peaks, smoke in stormy trails across the snows
> (a solid mass that hides all that looms over
> of Higuerota.
> (the shore.)

The corrected version is in substance the same as that of the first edition.

The passages on the Gulf and "The Isabels," as well as the description of the Cordillera range and the "white head of Higuerota [which] rises majestically upon the blue," are an organic part of the novel; for nature is implacable, and its ruthlessness helps to define, like the silver, each character it touches. The Gulf provides an appropriate background for Decoud's suicide, Nostromo's deception, Dr. Monygham's near martyrdom, and the collective greed of the local diplomats. In the central scene of the novel, the omnipresent and silent Gulf generates an overpowering darkness that swallows the lighter on which Nostromo and Decoud are trying to save the silver. The oppressive darkness fits the spirit of negation in De-

coud's own mind, and the stillness of his natural surroundings is a public sign of his inner failure. Its deathly
calmness, "like a wall," drives Decoud back into himself,
isolates him as much as it has isolated Sulaco from the
rest of Costaguana. The blackness of the Gulf is most suitable for this "imaginative materialist," as Conrad called
him, who inexplicably is caught in a situation that demands idealism and selflessness.

The TS of this scene is heavily worked over, and an
entire passage was struck out in favor of the version appearing in the book. This passage is at the very beginning
of the scene on the Gulf. The book follows:

> Decoud did not move; the effect was that of being launched
> into space. After a splash or two there was not a sound but
> the thud of Nostromo's feet leaping about the boat. He
> hoisted the big sail; a breath of wind fanned Decoud's cheek.
> Everything had vanished but the light of the lantern Cap-
> tain Mitchell had hoisted upon the post at the end of the
> jetty to guide Nostromo out of the harbour.

In the earlier TS, the same passage was written:

> A narrow belt of vague shimmering grey surrounded the
> lighter and that was all that Martin could see of the whole
> harbour. He sat on the pile of treasure boxes filling the
> middle of the undecked hold. A breath of wind fanned his
> cheek. Nostromo hoisted the sail and flitted past him back
> to the tiller. Suddenly a small spark of light glimmered in
> the vast void increased into a flame and on the head of the
> jetty made visible for a moment quite near overhanging the
> stern of the boat Captain Mitchell in his white waistcoat and
> in shirt sleeves.

Besides demonstrating a better use of punctuation, the
later version is less inflated and imparts more dramatically
the immediacy of scene.

Nature conveys the loneliness of the characters, with the mountains on one side and the Gulf on the other crying "Separate" to the area and its inhabitants. Sulaco, as its inhabitants, is truly "distinct and separated," isolated, Conrad said, "as if within an enormous semi-circular and unroofed temple open to the ocean, with its walls of lofty mountains hung with the mourning draperies of clouds." The bare face of the Cordillera range, "immense and motionless, emerging from the billows of the lower forests like the barren coast of a land of giants," combined with hovering clouds and bands of silent water on the Golfo Placido to reduce man's existence to that of an animal. Against this setting, Nostromo is manifest as part of nature itself, an Adam "as natural and free from evil in the moment of waking as a magnificent and unconscious wild beast."

Conrad, however, used more than the symbolic presence of nature as a means of illuminating his major themes; he was also able to rely on man-made circumstances—a seemingly irrelevant scene, a few words of comment, even a gesture—to suggest new aspects of the situation. Certain instances immediately present themselves. In the description, for example, of the desolate Custom House, deserted except for Hirsch's tortured and twisted body, we have the dismal solitude of a "man struggling with natural forces, alone, far from the eyes of his fellows." The House, reminiscent in itself of Almayer's abandoned office, is full of weird clicks of doors and latches, the rustling of torn papers, and gusts of wind passing under the high roof. Here is the entire desolation of the Sulacan situation, an epitome especially of the mental processes of Decoud, Nostromo, and Dr. Monygham. Hirsch, having died tortured and disregarded, is a reminder to the Doctor of his own fears; while the lonely house emphasizes Nostromo's change of attitude, his realization that he is applauded only because he is needed. Off in the background is the deserted Decoud, who had "lost all belief in the reality of his actions past and to come."

In the latter part of the book, the lighthouse serves an ironic as well as strictly functional purpose. It becomes a symbol of disclosure, lighting up Nostromo's secret fears and his inner disgrace. That Nostromo, who had once lived in the light of the "admiring eyes of men," should now be afraid of light, bespeaks the ironical position in which materialism has placed him. He has now become a self-admitted pariah, outwardly honest, but inwardly marked by the dark of his secret. As a sexual symbol, the white lighthouse—"[which], livid against the background of clouds filling the head of the gulf, bore the lantern red and glowing, like live embers kindled by the fire of the sky"—comments most ironically on Nostromo's choice of Linda, who controls the light, and his rejection of Giselle, whom he really loves. The lighthouse literally and symbolically searches out every detail of Nostromo's corruption, affecting even his choice of a wife and inevitably leading to his death.

One further example suggests Conrad's use of a nondiscursive technique to illuminate the plot. In the scene around Mitchell's "sixty-guinea gold half-chronometer," which so absorbs Sotillo and his followers that they forget the silver, we have a fleeting insight into the processes of predatory politics, whether in Costaguana or elsewhere. Once more, Conrad dramatized his themes and represented scenically what had largely been presented discursively in the Victorian novel. Through the mine, natural setting, and chance objects, he cast new light on his subject and created a distinctive rhythm in *Nostromo.*

But the question of scenic presentation cannot be separated from narrative method, and that in turn is connected with the entire range of Conrad's artistic purposes.

V

It can be granted that in *Nostromo* the narration of the story by different commentators is a deliberate way of shaping subject matter which is itself based on the disruption of society. It can then be argued that the differences in technique between the two parts of the novel—the long part on the revolution and the shorter section devoted to Nostromo's activities—were consciously emphasized, and that the short section on Nostromo's fortune was *designed* as an ironic coda on the results of the revolution. It could, perhaps, also be argued that here, as well as in *Under Western Eyes* and *Victory*, the swift ending results not from a loss of staying power or failure of conceptualization but is a deliberate way of comment through authorial intervention. We could possibly prove that the brevity of the second section was part of a formal plan in which insufficient development was aesthetically necessary. This line of argument, however, must eventually be withdrawn in face of contrary evidence in the early versions of *Nostromo*.

If we examine at first the serial, we find that the part after the ending of the revolution is *even sketchier* than in the first edition. The serial ends abruptly; two pages of serial (perhaps ten or eleven regularly printed pages) sum up what takes thirty-seven pages to develop in the book. This shortened part is related by Dr. Monygham, and except for essentials is unlike the later form. In the twenty pages preceding this part, the book shows a marked attempt to expand the meager details of the serial.

The parts that Conrad subsequently developed after the serial was published were those concerning Nostromo's relationship with the Viola girls and the introduction of the cargador Ramirez; particularly stressed were the parts showing Giselle's love for Nostromo and his preference for her sister, Linda. In the book, then, Conrad tried to emphasize a new Nostromo, one who as a "civilized" man develops into a successful business man and lover. Now, if Conrad's original aim had been to use deliberately the shortened second part of the novel as ironic comment, why, then, in the book would he have tried to reconstruct this section so that it could balance the longer and more intricate first part? The manuscript is useless here, for the latter part is completely missing; this is also true of the extant typescript. However, it is possible to conjecture that the manuscript and typescript—similar in *essentials* to the serial where comparisons *can* be made— were in their now missing parts likewise similar to the serial; and that in all three of the earliest versions (MS, TS, and serial), we have an even more abrupt version of the second part than we now have in the final form of the Collected Edition. All changes toward a more developed second part were evidently made by the time of the first American and English editions in 1904; this means that in the few months between the serial and first edition Conrad was already rewriting the latter part of the novel.

With this evidence before us, it is possible to remark that the very uncertain second part of *Nostromo* is more a breakdown of original conception than a deliberate attempt to comment aesthetically through the foreshortened ending of the novel. I believe this is also so with *Under Western Eyes* and *Victory*, that their abrupt endings are artistic failures and not designed as ironic comments on the earlier parts of the novels. Following these lines, Ford

Madox Ford remarked late in life that Conrad finished his books with contrived endings because of despair and panic; that the grandiose fabrics of *Nostromo, Under Western Eyes, Chance,* and even *The Secret Agent* are never fully realized in development; and that the unimpressive end pages of these novels display an artistic reversal of their earlier parts. For all its wealth of incident and character, *Nostromo* is too short for its scope; its insufficiency of ending, which at first may seem like design, is in reality an aesthetic failure. What in Gide's "incomplete" and "undeveloped" *Les Faux-Monnayeurs* is an artistic means of letting form intertwine with subject matter, is in Conrad's novel a lack of staying power and adequate conception.

V I

Richard Curle commented that the different versions of *Nostromo*—from manuscript to the Collected Edition—show more variations, with the possible exception of *The Rescue*, than any other of Conrad's novels. But one thing is striking: that the original manuscript and Collected Edition twenty years later are close despite verbal variations. Furthermore, the differences between the serial in *T.P.'s Weekly* and the first edition are also only verbal, once more exclusive of the ending.

I remarked above that Conrad's mental version of *Nostromo* was for a short novel of fewer than 100,000 words, but it is significant that by the time of the MS he had projected most of the bulk of the first edition. The Rosenbach MS is only about fifty per cent complete, but the extant parts, except for verbal changes and paraphrases, are the same in essentials as the serial and subsequent versions. What happened between the mental version and the MS will perhaps never be known, but what happened between the MS and the Collected Edition can be analyzed in part and conjectured in part. In this analysis, my materials are: the Rosenbach MS, about fifty per cent of the entire version; the fragmentary TS owned by Yale and Huntington; the serialization in *T.P.'s Weekly;* the first English and American editions published by Harper and Brothers in 1904; and the Collected Edition published by Doubleday in 1925.

In the first hundred pages of MS, we find Conrad using far more pages of revised MS for each page of printed text than he did further on. As he progressed, the alterations became fewer, and the MS page more closely resembles the book. The beginning of the novel, as I said above, gave Conrad difficulty and demonstrated the importance of natural description as an introduction to the theme. Consequently, the paragraphs on "The Isabels" contain more than the usual number of deleted passages, transposed words, and various shades of meanings tried and retried.

Nevertheless, even in those passages most assiduously reworked, it is uncommon to find Conrad completely deleting a passage; frequently, he would eliminate a passage, a phrase, or even a single word only to use it in succeeding paragraphs or pages. Only rarely did he waste anything. On p. 11 of the MS of Part III and IV, for example, Conrad wrote about Nostromo's state of mind when he thinks of Teresa, old Giorgio's wife; for in his superstition Nostromo remembers her dying curse which now hangs over him: "Was she dead he asked himself," which under revision became, "He wondered whether she was dead were dead in her anger with him or still alive." In the Collected Edition this sentence became: "He wondered

whether she was dead in her anger with him or still alive."
Even in the small matter of a simple phrase, Conrad
was niggardly about deleting a word or two. In the same
passage of the MS—a continuation of the one quoted
above—there appears a paragraph that was subsequently
reworked and revised for the Collected Edition:

> In the downfall of all the realities that
> was ready
>   made his force he was affected by
>   of
> the superstition [?]   and shuddered slight-
>   dead
> ly. Signora Teresa must have   died then.
> Another shred of his betrayed individuality
>
> was gone. It could mean nothing else.
>   It
>
> could mean nothing else.

Which became in the book:

> . . . a big owl, whose appalling cry: "Ya-acabo! Ya-acabo!—
> it is finished; it is finished"—announces calamity and death
> in the popular belief, drifted vaguely like a dark ball across
> his path. In the downfall of all the realities that made his
> force, he was affected by the superstition, and shuddered
> slightly. Signora Teresa must have died, then. It could mean
> nothing else. The cry of the ill-omened bird, the first sound
> he was to hear on his return, was a fitting welcome for his
> betrayed individuality.

Almost every word of the MS passage was relocated and
utilized to gain fluency in the book. The revised version
also limns sharply that shadow of personal foreboding

which will follow Nostromo until he meets ignominious death at Giorgio's hand. The owl's lament and Teresa's death are clear omens of Nostromo's fall and trenchant symbols suggesting what happens to nearly everyone in Sulaco who comes into contact with the silver.

Many times in the MS and TS, Conrad's changes, simple though they seem in their finished version, helped him gain more idiomatic and fluent English. In the MS, for instance, Conrad wrote: "And would have don Carlos been content————" which became "And would Don Carlos have been content————?" Or at the beginning of the MS: "The common folk of the neighborhood believe that lumps of virgin gold lie at the bottom of the awful precipice [fissuring] the stony levels of Azuera." This became: "The common folk of the neighborhood . . . are well aware that heaps of shining gold lie in the gloom of the deep precipices cleaving the stony levels of Azuera."

Certain crucial passages that we should expect Conrad to have found troublesome often show few or no revisions. Decoud's important soliloquy on the island, in which he debates life or death, contains almost no vacillations in composition and appears except for minor verbal changes nearly identical in an incomplete portion of the MS and in the book. The interview between Nostromo and Dr. Monygham, which is of great psychological import to both characters, also contains almost clean MS pages, the revisions amounting to no more than a few shifted words. In this section, there appears one of the few passages which were not in the book: Dr. Monygham has just told Nostromo that the best thing for him is to disappear. "'————Me! Disappear!' exclaimed the Capataz with the incredulity of a man for whom life consists in a perpetual appearance before the public eye."

The MS provides, then, nearly a complete prefiguration of the later versions, for the emphasis and development are essentially the same. All of *Nostromo*, exclusive of the more expanded ending, is in the extant parts of the MS, and when we come to the TS we find only further efforts to gain fluency.

In commenting on the Huntington Library TS, George W. Whiting showed that Conrad's main purpose in revising was to clarify and revitalize his narrative. He pointed out that the TS "broadly speaking created the text of the tale," just as the MS, broadly speaking, created the text of all succeeding versions. Even though a photograph of pp. 327-328 of the TS shows many lengthy revisions which amount to a complete rewriting of the page, these revisions do not by any means signify a break from the MS. My own examination of the Yale TS shows a continuity of text that runs directly from the MS through the TS into the first and succeeding editions.

The fragmentary nature of the TS precludes any sustained comparison with the MS before it or with the serial after it, although one can draw some general conclusions. The corrected TS, not unnaturally, approximates the serial more closely than it does the MS; for if this is the only extant TS of these passages, then the Yale TS is the sole version directly before the serial itself. Except for the difficult beginning of the novel, the TS is remarkably close to the serial, and the written corrections are those that stood through the Collected Edition twenty years later. The extensive verbal changes notwithstanding, many passages, at times whole pages, remained the same in the MS, TS, and book.

Some passages in TS nevertheless were subsequently eliminated from the first edition. The one that follows on Dr. Monygham exists only in TS:

He could hear the shots of the executions
everyday in the main court of the Castle.

was

On one occasion the sound of the firing
had been so heavy that he asked the soldier
who came in then with a jar of water and a
piece of scorched meat on a stick whether
there had been a revolution in town and the
Castle was being attacked. But the man in
subdued   's voice said "No
his soft   Indian
answered that no, it was nothing but some
prisoners being shot. . . . "It will be your

his

turn tomorrow senor" he had added in   a
sad quiet tone, going out and leaving Dr.
Monygham comforted in the fungus-grown,
lightless dripping dungeon, with the spiders
running about busily on his motionless
skeleton limbs.

Wholesale excisions of this sort, however, were rare. Often, changes were only verbal, and altered parts would recur later under different circumstances. The general import of the TS was toward smoother copy, toward sharpening what already existed rather than altering essentials. When we read the fragments of the TS, as when we read the MS before it, we meet the novel of the Collected Edition.

The serial is less interesting than the MS and TS, for it of course contains none of Conrad's handwritten notes. The most notable thing about the serial is that several of its long descriptive passages were somewhat diminished in the first edition. Some of these passages are full of fine and relevant writing that Conrad nonetheless deleted.

One passage that does not appear in the book concerns the possible benefits of the mine as envisaged by Gould:

> . . . skinny, dreadful old hags, ragged men, women with hopeless faces, and then, naked children. . . . Those were the very poor, the starving fringe outside the body of the people that worked in towns and upon the estancias; and the great empty vastness of the landscapes made their existence incredible and their state appear hopeless, for this was not a question of room to live in. Was the remedy for that, too, in the development of material interests? Charles seemed to hug that belief in his taciturn and observing reserve.

In describing the gulf scene, Conrad emphasized Nostromo's vanity in the serial to a greater extent than in the Collected Edition:

> In the still blackness of the gulf obliterating the land and the sea, and even the very memory of events whose weariness still weighed on his limbs, the overweening vanity of the man, which had many times amused him [Decoud] in their former intercourse, seemed to take a concrete and fateful shape.

Perhaps the tendency to overwrite in the serial is best shown in the following passage which was deleted from later versions. Again the scene is on the gulf; the book follows:

> And the fate of Senor Hirsch remained suspended in the darkness of the gulf at the mercy of events which could not be foreseen.

To which the serial added:

> . . . [foreseen], as the light of the candle burning on the strengthening beam was at the mercy of the first wandering

puff of wind in the black, death-like stillness of the night, the image of the impenetrable and secret destiny in which each man's life is kindled and extinguished mysteriously like a precarious flame.

As the serial continues more deeply into the narrative, however, we find that its overly rhetorical passages occur less frequently; that it becomes in fact less expanded than the later book; and that there is a steady de-emphasis, ever so slight, of character and scenic description. Page after page of the serial lacks two or three sentences of the Collected Edition. Most differences now between the two versions are lines added to the book rather than verbal variations, additions of a descriptive nature which fill out and pace the novel. From p. 351 to p. 359 of the Collected Edition, for example, there are included eleven sentences that did not appear in the serial, a total of about three hundred additional words. This pattern, having begun in the second half of the novel, continues almost to its end. The long rhetorical passages in the first chapters of the serial that were later eliminated are more than compensated by these extensive additions to the book. Approximately five thousand more words appear in the first edition than in the serial, not counting the long rewritten passage which expands Nostromo's personal relationships near the end of the book. If we include that part as well, the book exceeds the serial by ten to fifteen thousand words, being seven to ten per cent longer. No such tabulation can be made with the MS, which is only fifty per cent complete, or with the TS, which is altogether too fragmentary for comparison.

What does all this rearrangement mean? The expansive element of the book would seem to point to Conrad's weariness in the serial. We know that *Nostromo* was not finished until August 30th, 1904, also that the serialization had already been begun on January 29th and was to appear until October 7th, which was only five weeks after the completion of the novel. There is good reason to believe Conrad felt anxiety about finishing the book, and that the shortened ending of the serial is a direct result of the need to forgo artistic considerations in favor of expediency. Conrad's letters do not make definite reference to anxieties about completing the necessary installments on time, but he does frequently remark the drain the book was making on his energy: to Cunninghame Graham he wrote, ". . . my mind, jaded with a sort of hopeless overwork"; to Galsworthy, ". . . I feel half dead and wholly imbecile"; to J. B. Pinker, "I have never worked so hard before—with so much anxiety"; to William Rothenstein, "I am not myself and shall not be myself till I am born again after *Nostromo* is finished"; to Galsworthy, "[*Nostromo*] Finished! finished! on the 30th in [G.F.W.] Hope's house in Stanford in Essex, where I have to take off my brain that seemed to turn to water"; to Edward Garnett, "I drop you these lines just to say that *Nostromo* is finished; a fact upon which my friends may congratulate me as upon a recovery from a dangerous illness." It is, however, in another letter to William Rothenstein that Conrad seemed to sum up his feelings while writing *Nostromo* (Sept. 3, 1904, Houghton Library, Harvard):

> The book is finished; it has been finished for a couple of days now, but I have been too tired, too flat to write you at once. The last month I worked practically night and day, going to bed at three and sitting down again at nine. All the time at it, with the tenacity of despair.

> What the book is like, I don't know. I don't suppose it'll damage me: but I do know that it is open to much intelligent criticism. For the other sort I don't care. Personally I am not

satisfied. It is something—but not *the* thing I tried for. There is no exultation, none of that temporary sense of achievement which is so soothing. Even the mere feeling of relief at having done with it is wanting. The strain has been too great, has lasted too long.

But I am ready for more. I don't feel empty, exhausted. I am simply joyless—like most men of little faith.

The nervous pressures on Conrad to finish the novel are evident in these comments, and they no doubt contributed to the hasty ending of the serial.

It was during the composition of *Nostromo* that Conrad gave his impression of the writing process to H. G. Wells as "just simply the conversion of nervous force into phrases"; and, he continued, "when the nervous force is exhausted the phrases don't come—and no tension of will can help." This loss of nervous force, Conrad's phrase for the creative power of the imagination, usually occurred near the end of his novels, especially in *Nostromo*, *Under Western Eyes*, *Victory*, and *Chance*. The grandiose beginnings, conceived as they were on a huge scale, are not sufficiently developed to avoid that characteristic Victorian ending, a quick summary, which, while tying together numerous threads in an expository narrative, loses along the way nearly all sense of tragic inevitability. Even in *Nostromo*, expanded though it was for the first edition, Conrad's nervous energy was too soon exhausted, and the novel for all its 566 pages is still of insufficient length.

In any examination of the early versions of an author's work, especially when the author is an exacting craftsman, one's expectation of discovery is unusually high. Even here, however, we find little that is startling. Conrad's conception in the MS was his conception of the published

volume, and the main faults of the novel remained
through the Collected Edition. If we could know his original mental version, either from notes or letters, then we
should have more likely material for comment. That Conrad worked hard over his first version, the MS and TS
bear out; but that he radically changed his ideas between
the MS and book is not borne out by my investigations.

John Dozier Gordan, whose examination of Conrad's
early manuscripts and typescripts makes his a definitive
book on this subject, concluded that Conrad's revisions
were toward greater fluidity in his use of English idiom,
toward clarity, and toward dramatization of character
and scene. Gordan points out that when we do find Conrad groping toward a new way of handling his material,
he revised only on a minor scale through an accumulation
of detail rather than by shifting his point of view. The
early pages of his manuscripts, it is true, are full of
"cancellations, new attempts, economies, incoherence, and
. . . perplexities," as Gordan says, but by the time the
MSS were corrected Conrad had the details substantially
in hand. What Gordan showed to be true in the early
MSS and succeeding versions is essentially true for
Nostromo. It is worth remarking that Conrad was often
unsure of his material and, to quote Gordan, "felt his way
towards the plot of his stories and towards the best presentation of his material," but by the time the manuscript was ready for typing his arrangement of his basic
material was sure. Later attempts at revision rarely departed far from the original conception, although it is
evident that Conrad himself by the time of the serial and
book often recognized shortcomings in the development
of his plot.

chapter 6

Middle Conrad

A public is not to be found in a class, caste, clique or type. The public is (or are?) individuals. *Le public introuvable* is only *introuvable* simply because it is all humanity. And no artist can give it what it wants because humanity doesn't know what it wants. But it will swallow everything. It will swallow Hall Caine and John Galsworthy, Victor Hugo and Martin Tupper. It is an ostrich, a clown, a giant, a bottomless sack. It is sublime. It has apparently no eyes and no entrails, like a slug, and yet it can weep and suffer. It has swallowed Christianity, Buddhism, Mahomedanism [sic] and the Gospel of Mrs. Eddy. And it is perfectly capable, from the height of its secular stability, of looking down upon the artist as a mere windlestraw.

> Letter from Conrad to Galsworthy,
> Birmingham (England) U. Libr.
> November 1, 1910.

From *Nostromo* to *Victory*, we find Conrad in his most political period; no fewer than five works, two of them major novels, are concerned directly or indirectly with political man: *The Secret Agent, Under Western Eyes,* "Il Conde," "The Informer," and "An Anarchist." One other, "The Secret Sharer," also has certain political implications—as if the Captain by honoring his secret has to atone for Razumov who betrayed his.

The first book that Conrad published after *Nostromo,* however, was anything but political, *The Mirror of the Sea,* a book of essays on various aspects of the sea. These essays reveal a great deal about Conrad's other love and not a little about Conrad the writer. They make clear that whether in loading a ship's hold, in sailing a craft, or in writing a book, he always looked to craftsmanship. In an essay on sailing, called "The Fine Art," Conrad stressed the art itself, not solely the results of the effort. He wrote:

> Such skill, the skill of technique, is more than honesty; it is something wider, embracing honesty and grace and rule in an elevated and clear sentiment, not altogether utilitarian, which may be called the honour of labour. It is made up of accumulated tradition, kept alive by individual pride, rendered exact by professional opinion, and, like the higher arts, it is spurred on and sustained by discriminating praise.

He continued:

> Efficiency of a practically flawless kind may be reached naturally in the struggle for bread. But there is something beyond—a higher point, a subtle and unmistakable touch of love and pride beyond mere skill; almost an inspiration which gives to all work that finish which is almost art— which *is* art.

Even the loading of a ship—once a craft in itself—is now betrayed by the "filling up," the "dumping" of cargo into a modern steamship. "Stevedoring," says Conrad, "which had been a skilled labour, is fast becoming a labour without the skill." The coming of the steamship has replaced the art of the sailing vessel with the brute force of the machine. "A modern fleet of ships," he says, "does not so much make use of the sea as exploit a highway." A ship should be the object of the "pride of skill, the pride of responsibility, the pride of endurance. . . ." Like William Morris and John Ruskin before him, Conrad deplored the passing of the dignified worker into an industrialized nonentity. His constant protest against steam, against the disappearance of the sailing vessel, and against the mechanization of shipping is all part of his support for a craftsman-centered universe. Conrad's apprenticeship to the sea, then, while he learned the art of seamanship, also inspired in him literary values.

II

The Secret Agent[1] is at once one of Conrad's simplest and most elusive works. With a surface that betrays little complexity, the unpretentious story encompasses the ideas of a major novel. The exotic settings of *Almayer's Folly, An Outcast, Lord Jim,* and *Nostromo* have been subtly transformed into the city settings of London, and in their ramifications these city images are even more mysteriously suggestive than the jungle backgrounds of the Malayan novels. *The Secret Agent* was described by Conrad as "A simple Tale," but its simplicity is surely only of the surface.

Certain remarks of Conrad's in the Author's Note convey hints of the novel's true subject matter, intimating that political anarchism is not the theme. After pointing out that a friend had given him the idea for anarchists, the idiot boy, and his sister, and after revealing his familiarity with the Greenwich Observatory bomb outrage, Conrad tells how all these seemingly disparate items coalesced when he came upon a little known volume of recollections by an Assistant Commissioner of Police. He says:

[1] London: Methuen, 1907; New York: Harper's, 1907. Originally called *Verloc, The Secret Agent* was first serialized in *Ridgeway's Militant Weekly,* I (October 6 to December 15, 1906). The book was conceived immediately after Conrad finished *Nostromo* and *The Mirror of the Sea.* See Author's Note, 1920.

And then ensued in my mind what a student of chemistry would best understand from the analogy of the addition of the tiniest little drop of the right kind, precipitating the process of crystallization in a test tube containing some colourless material.

Of course, the tale that would be *The Secret Agent* was as yet imperfectly apprehended and not sharply focused in any particularized setting. Then came the idea of the city, Conrad's first big city background.

Then the vision of an enormous town presented itself, of a monstrous town more populous than some continents and in its man-made might as if indifferent to heaven's frowns and smiles; a cruel devourer of the world's light. There was room enough there to place any story, depth enough there for any passion, variety enough there for any setting, darkness enough to bury five millions of lives.

Against this city background, Winnie Verloc's story—and Conrad emphasizes that her plight is the center of the novel—stands out in bold relief. Her story is one of "utter desolation, madness and despair," and it is conveyed by and through the presence of the city. The horror of Kurtz, the fears of Jim, the interior loneliness of De-coud and Heyst, and the negation of Donkin and Wait all come together in the inhumanity of grimy London. Precisely as "Heart of Darkness," *Nostromo,* and *Victory* are central among Conrad's non-European works, so *The Secret Agent* and *Under Western Eyes* are keys to his European views; taken together, they convey the Conradian world of brutality, loneliness, fear, and human sympathy. The troubled skies of Costaguana are now the cloudy skies of London, the symbol of silver has become the symbol of city streets. London is described as dismal, gloomy, and dirty, full of the mud of the streets, soiled paper, gas-jets turned low, fatigued and hungry people, and dreary shadows. The people are desolate city dwellers: Winnie feels no love for her husband; her brother, Stevie, is a hopeless idiot; Verloc himself is a mysterious figure who can know only insecurity; Mrs. Verloc, Winnie's mother, is crippled, "staggering on swollen legs." Conrad, as he stated in the Author's Note, earnestly believed that ironic treatment alone would enable him to say all he felt in scorn as well as in pity. The irony, as we shall discover, is not solely of the word, but also, as in every good novel, an irony of scenic conception.

The city and their ironic position in it are the twin aspects of the ungracious existence of Adolf and Winnie Verloc. Every element of Verloc's existence partakes of the desolation of a modern city. He is an organic part of its grubbiness, and through him the city lives. A seller of shady wares, he is of fatty build and unprepossessing in appearance; married by Winnie not for love but for security, he is an ineffectual Prufrock, who in anarchistic circles possesses not even a name but a designated mark, $\triangle$. Nameless, loveless, and unable to function effectually as a counter agent, Verloc is as impotent as the gloomy city which enfolds his activities. We first meet him issuing from the back of his store with "eyes naturally heavy" and "an air of having wallowed, fully dressed, all day on an unmade bed." From here we shortly see him pass along the street, with its rattling milk carts and its vast assortment of matter indifferent to man's fate, a bloodless man walking mechanically to the Embassy where Vladimir berates his lack of activity and makes fun of his pretensions to anarchy. An isolated counter agent who can turn to no one, Verloc is a lost figure in a heartless city which rejects even its most gifted sons.

It soon becomes apparent that Conrad's London is a direct outgrowth of Dickens', with perhaps overtones of the Paris of Baudelaire. In regard to Dickens, I have in mind a book like *Our Mutual Friend,* in which the scrubby side of London is the very stuff of the story, and the waste-bearing Thames flows through the lives of the chief characters; or a novel like *Little Dorrit,* in which the Marshalsea becomes the equivalent of prison-London in *The Secret Agent.* Even Conrad's eccentrics are not far removed from the character creations of Dickens—the Professor, for instance, is obviously a caricature of an idea. Further, the scene between the Assistant Commissioner and Sir Ethelred, the "Great Presence," whose interest is in Fisheries rather than in the affairs of people, is Dickensian humor; and the scenes involving Winnie's mother and brother have Dickensian grotesqueness. In this connection, while writing about the stage version of *The Secret Agent,* Conrad said that the subject "is all a matter of feeling, without which the existence of Mrs. Verloc's mother as a personage . . . could not very well be justified. For after all what is that old woman doing there?" In matters of London city background, irony of word and scene, and attitude toward character, Conrad in this novel approached the work of that greatest of all English city novelists.

As part of city life, the central scene of the book—the lugubrious cab ride of Winnie, Stevie, and their mother to the charity home—is first and foremost a symbol of complete desolation. In its implications, the cab ride is as much a symbol of desperate faith as the silver in *Nostromo.* The ride conveys the hopelessness of spirit in a modern city and creates a sense of "impending chaos," although the chaos is not that of political anarchism or anarchists. *The Secret Agent* possesses only superficial resemblance to a police story. Its chronology defeats the main elements of the detective novel, for the very arrangement of the book destroys suspense. We can reason that if the police are aware of who planted the bomb almost as soon as the reader, then the chase or the activity of anarchists is evidently not of primary importance. The theme, like that of *Nostromo* and "Heart of Darkness," is surely a presentation of moral corruption as it spreads back and forth from city to character. Conrad's aim is the ironic castigation of modern life, particularly the middle-class worship of science and materialism and the drab world it has built for itself. If *Victory* presents a dialectic of the forces that created the First World War, then no less does *The Secret Agent* convey a view of spiritual despair haunting a world which looks only toward its own materialism. But while Conrad disclaimed any social or philosophical intentions in this novel—he said it "is *purely a work of imagination*"—he did admit its moral significance.

These implications are a big order for a cab ride that takes only sixteen pages in a novel of more than three hundred, but Conrad has prepared the way for the scene. The old cab as it rattles and jolts and jingles along the London streets is barely able to maintain the precarious position of its riders, and for each it assumes the violence of a torture chamber. The cab, says Conrad, "was so profoundly lamentable, with such a perfection of grotesque misery and weirdness of macabre detail, as if it were the Cab of Death itself," that even the horse pulling it appears as a figure of doom. For Stevie, who is pathologically helpless, the horse becomes an immediate object of sympathy; as the butt of man's inhumanity and lack of sympathy, the animal is the poignant equivalent of all the idiot Stevies in the world:

Stevie was staring at the horse, whose hind quarters appeared unduly elevated by the effect of emaciation. The little stiff tail seemed to have been fitted in for a heartless joke; and at the other end the thin, flat neck, like a plank covered with old horsehide, drooped to the ground under the weight of an enormous bony head. The ears hung at different angles, negligently; and the macabre figure of that mute dweller on the earth steamed straight up from the ribs and backbone in the muggy stillness of the air.

Driven by a maimed driver and a maimed horse, the ancient and wobbly coach rattles its way across ". . . the early dirty night, the sinister, noisy, hopeless, and rowdy night of South London. . . ." Within are the idiot boy, his yellow and bilious mother, and his devoted sister who has married solely for her family's security. The coach, the animal, the driver, and the riders are all in a state of disequilibrium as they pass Brett Street across St. Stephen's on their way through the back-alleys of London to the charity home. When Stevie implores the driver not to whip the horse, the humanity of the idiot is ironically pitted against the gross realities of city life; for the driver answers: "'Ard on 'osses, but dam' sight 'arder on poor chaps like me.'" Stevie, however, can say nothing, "for the tenderness to all pain and misery, the desire to make the horse happy and the cabman happy, had reached the point of a bizarre longing to take them to bed with him."

If the theme of *The Secret Agent* is moral corruption or the lack of moral sanity, then this scene is a symbolic embodiment of all the major threads of the novel. Its irony is implicit in its central figure, Stevie, who ineffectually tries to substitute love for man's inhumanity. The necessity for survival, expressed in the cabman's words—"'I've got my missus and four kids at 'ome. . . . This ain't an easy world.'"—becomes the cry of a grimy city which perpetuates crime in the name of self-survival. Stevie's plea for humanity, as the innumerable circles he draws, is lost among the rejoinders of cruel and expedient adults.

Stevie's penchant for—

> . . . innumerable circles, concentric, eccentric, a coruscating whirl of circles that by their tangled multitude of repeated curves, uniformity of form, and confusion of intersecting lines suggested a rendering of cosmic chaos, the symbolism of a mad art attempting the inconceivable.

symbolizes an inner perfection made manifest by his drawings. The circle, a geometric form of perfection, clashes ironically with Stevie's outward imperfection. More than his few words, the circles express sympathy and compassion for all the downtrodden, and also, as Thomas Mann has pointed out in *Past Masters*, display an artistic sensibility. His beauty of soul, like Myshkin's in *The Idiot* of Dostoyevsky, places him at an immediate disadvantage amidst a materialistic world of realities. That his idiocy contains deep sensitivity is summarily dismissed early in the novel when Ossipon, the anarchist, remarks that Stevie's circles represent a typical form of degeneracy. To back his statement, Ossipon "scientifically" points to Lombroso's study of degeneracy, and by so doing demonstrates the inability of scientific materialism to deal with human emotions. This is, says Conrad, the theme of the novel.

Conrad held in the Author's Note that this was a novel about Winnie Verloc, and so far she seems to have little or no role in the development of the book. Winnie's story, however, is carefully presented in the novel; for through Verloc's own dreary existence and through the insensibility of the anarchists, the scene is aptly prepared for Winnie with her day-to-day existence, devoid as it is of any illusions or ideals. Winnie's end is a fitting close to the desolation and despair that have marked her life with the counter agent Verloc and the anarchists. Her view that things "do not stand much looking into" is an indication of her moral superficiality, a lack of substance that is as manifest in her gas-lit surroundings as in her relations with her husband. By the time we meet Winnie in her own right, we recognize that she too will act from a surface morality, that she too will never ask the right questions at the right time.

Coming as she does so late in the story—not until p. 190 does Winnie come to the fore—her sudden strong position may seem to impair the novel structurally. In Conrad's later stage version of *The Secret Agent,* for example, she is quickly presented as a strong personality who, through her physical attraction for Verloc, can confidently make him acquiesce in her demands. But returning to the novel proper: by means of Winnie's marked identification with Stevie and through a personal spiritual bankruptcy that is the result of dismal surroundings, her ultimate despair and death become an integral part of the novel—the story is surely her decline and fall.

Conrad's emphasis on the doubling of Winnie and Stevie is not fortuitous. From the very beginning of her marriage to Verloc, she has been her brother's defender; and when Verloc's plot inadvertently leads to Stevie's death, she avenges his death by killing her husband. In that scene of grotesque irony—while Verloc expects forgiveness Winnie contemplates murder—it is really the idiot Stevie, now resurrected, who in Winnie's form kills Verloc; it is the fallen artist who rejects his oppressors and strikes for freedom. Conrad describes the scene:

He [Verloc] waited. Mrs. Verloc was coming. As if the homeless soul of Stevie had flown for shelter straight to the breast of his sister, guardian, and protector, the resemblance of her face with that of her brother grew at every step, even to the droop of the lower lips, even to the slight divergence of the eyes.

Shortly after, Ossipon remarks the likeness: " 'It's almost incredible the resemblance there was between you two . . . yes, he resembled you.' " By making Winnie a physical double of Stevie, Conrad related her firmly to the preceding sections of the book and technically made allowance for what otherwise might have seemed an almost arbitrary shift. Literally veiled from Verloc by her intentions—she sat, says Conrad, "like a masked and mysterious visitor of impenetrable intentions"—Winnie gains revenge for Stevie on the sordid world of which both are "sick" products. The role, then, that Winnie plays can be fully explained only if we see her as an inadequate human being surrounded by moral anarchy and spiritual decay.

The sense of moral despair that is conveyed through Verloc and Winnie, through Stevie and his surroundings, and through London city is found at its fullest single expression in the activities of anarchists like Ossipon, the Professor, Karl Yundt, and Michaelis, whose implicit belief in the overall efficacy of science can evoke only ironic comment from the author. As part of the desolation pervading a modern city, the anarchists "fit" perfectly; that is, their lack of humanity is a significant complement to those other elements of inhumanity in London. Nevertheless, as anarchists in the political world, they are, as Irving Howe has pointed out, no more than shams. Their ideas and methods of working can only make them objects of ridicule and not forces to be taken seriously.

In pursuing this role of the anarchists, Howe attacks Conrad's aesthetic and political failure to describe what "really happens in the world of anarchism." If one is, like Howe, searching solely for the "political reality" of *The Secret Agent,* then one's conclusion can be no other than that of castigation of the anarchists. If, however, one recognizes that the anarchists are only part of a larger scene, part of the general immorality of the time, then one can see them in a more reasonable perspective. No doubt, Conrad could have depicted the anarchists differently—obviously, as he himself recognized, they are politically ridiculous—but a more realistic presentation of anarchy rather than adding to the aesthetic truth of the novel might have shifted the theme to something that was never intended, to something more topical but less significant.

Howe, in pursuing his point, further remarks that Conrad constantly presented the anarchists in their weakness rather than in their strength. His argument runs that if the anarchists are to have any weight dramatically, they must be of sufficient significance to engage us seriously, and that, he claims, the anarchists of *The Secret Agent,* as well as those of *Under Western Eyes,* fail to do. By becoming solely objects of ridicule, Howe contends, they fail to provide the tension for Verloc's moral emptiness, or Razumov's confession of guilt. If the anarchists are contemptible, he continues, then Conrad's political prejudices have invalidated his dramatic denouement and precluded any serious heroic gesture. Howe's position, when adapted to the political question alone, can hardly be disputed, but seen in the entire perspective of *The Secret Agent* it seems a simplification. For Conrad to have emphasized the anarchists would be tantamount to making anarchy in its strictly political sense the theme of the novel, something he explicitly denied in a letter to Galsworthy in 1906. To do this would be to detract from the main theme of the book, the pervading sense of moral corruption that touches everyone as it extends back and forth from city to inhabitants, infecting the anarchists, the police, the Verlocs, even the pitiful draft horse itself. This is the theme toward which all other elements must conform, as Conrad suggested in the Author's Note. When Howe argues that anarchy in *The Princess Casamassima* is presented in its strength, he forgets or fails to recognize the difference in theme between the James book and *The Secret Agent*. James deliberately presented the anarchists in their power, for Hyacinth's problem is to choose a course of action that would mean dedication either to anarchistic activity or to an equally "attractive" life of art and contemplation. Under these conditions, the presentation of anarchy in a favorable, or at least strong, light was an artistic necessity. Under Conrad's conditions in *The Secret Agent*, a similar presentation would surely have been disastrous. Even if we grant that Conrad's politics were conservative and orderly, perhaps quite aristocratic, and that he extended this bias to his presentation of anarchy and anarchists, even if this is granted, the anarchists of *The Secret Agent* are still aesthetically valid when they are seen against that larger theme of moral corruption which had engaged Conrad since *Almayer's Folly*.

I have thus far only barely suggested the widespread use of irony in *The Secret Agent*.[2] In the Author's Note, Conrad pointed out that only an ironic treatment could

[2] Richard Gordon Lillard, in an article on "Irony in Hardy and Conrad" [*PMLA*, L (March 1935), 316-22], illustrates the three basic types of irony that are found in Conrad's work. These are: (1) Dramatic irony, or Sophoclean irony, in which the character is unconscious of what the reader is aware; (2) Rhetorical or Socratic irony, in which there is a disparity between the surface and the underlying meaning; and (3) The

give him the point of view needed to say all he felt "in scorn as well as in pity." He was aware that his approach was successful: "It is one of the minor satisfactions of my writing life [he wrote in the Author's Note] that having taken that resolve I did manage, it seems to me, to carry it through to the end." The ironic method gave Conrad one of his prime requisites—that sense of distance from his material which was tantamount to mental security. Irony, though, can be a double-edged weapon: it can destroy the characters while also giving the author an authentic instrument of attack. Conrad, however, managed to maintain the shaky balance between constructive irony and destructive ridicule; for the ironic method here is another important way of suggesting the theme.

Conrad's attitude toward the police in their relation to criminal elements in society is part of the irony implicit in the book; the police, no less than the anarchists, are morally corrupt. Each needs the other to exist, for anarchy without an opposition from order is as unthinkable as order existing without elements of anarchy. The Professor—whose ideal is the perfect detonator—is, ironically, a slave to human order and justice. He himself, in comment to Ossipon, unknowingly defines his own position while castigating his fellow revolutionary: " 'You revolutionists . . . are the slaves of the social convention, which is afraid of you; slaves of it as much as the very police that stands [sic] up in the defence of that convention. Clearly you are, since you want to revolutionize it. . . . The terrorist and the policeman both come from the same basket.' " It is only because of Inspector Heat's organized world that the Professor can have an existence; in a world lacking in order, the Professor would obviously

---

irony of Fate, in which an entire group is unaware of the course of events. *The Secret Agent* partakes of all three possibilities.

have nobody and nothing to threaten. Heat, for his part, recognizes that the common type of criminal is "of the same kind as the mind and the instincts of a police officer," but the psychopathic Professor creates problems beyond his understanding. For the Professor intends to upset the very conditions which maintain both criminals and police. At the end of the novel, it is, ironically, the Professor who remains, "frail, insignificant, shabby, miserable," who in his madness wants to regenerate the world through destruction.

In his attachment to anarchy as a form of aggression that masks a personal neurosis, the Professor is an outgrowth of the grumbling Donkin (*The Nigger*) and the perverted Sotillo and Pedro Montero (*Nostromo*), and in many ways is a forerunner of the villainous Jones (*Victory*). By advocating a society wherein the weak would be exterminated, the Professor is expressing a psychopathic personality that has since been transmuted into the grotesque realities of modern political life. He says:

> "First the great multitude of the weak must go, then the only relatively strong. You see? First the blind, then the deaf and the dumb, then the halt and the lame—and so on. Every taint, every vice, every prejudice, every convention must meet its doom."

After all the weak and the sick have been exterminated, what remains, he is asked, and he answers, " 'I remain —if I am strong enough.' " The Professor is a political prophet.

Not only is Conrad's irony directed toward law and disorder, but also toward nearly every relationship and situation in the novel. The motivating idea—the proposed bombing of Greenwich Observatory—is plotted in ironic terms: that the bourgeoisie could only be infuriated by an attack on science, which in its eyes is untouchable. The Embassy agent Vladimir comments:

> A bomb in the National Gallery would make some noise. But it would not be serious enough. Art has never been their fetish. . . . What do you think of having a go at astronomy? . . . Such an outrage combines the greatest possible regard for humanity with the most alarming display of ferocious imbecility. . . . And there are other advantages. The whole civilized world has heard of Greenwich. The very bootblacks in the basement of Charing Cross Station know something of it. See?

That entire scene in the Embassy between the testy Vladimir and the muttering Verloc partakes of Conrad's most devastating irony. Without becoming ridiculous, Verloc is, in fact, a natural object of irony in every scene in which he appears, and even after his grotesque death he becomes an ironically conceived source of confusion to Winnie and Ossipon. In that latter scene, Winnie is telling of her murder of Verloc while trying to gain affirmation of her deed from Ossipon, who himself thinks that Verloc died long before in the attempted bombing of the Observatory; and when she goes on hysterically about her dead brother, though without naming him, Ossipon inevitably thinks she means Verloc. Ossipon says:

> "Ah, but he is dead now," was the best he could do. And he put a remarkable amount of animosity into his gnarled explanation. Mrs. Verloc caught at his arm with a sort of frenzy. "You guessed then he was dead," she murmured, as if beside herself. "You! You guessed what I had to do. Had to!"

Verloc of course is dead to both, but through their misunderstanding of motives and remarks and their distance from each other as human beings, the sublime stupidity of their lives is epitomized in these few words.

This type of misunderstanding, which occurs frequently in Conrad's work, becomes a symbolic way of suggesting an underlying idea. The ironic situation—based as it is on a misunderstanding of which the reader but not the character is aware—comes to support the major theme of the novel. In *The Secret Agent*, the inability of Winnie and Ossipon to communicate with each other is the inability of science to come to terms with human emotions, the inability of one person to enter into another's tragedy, and, finally, the inability of human beings to be honest even in their relation to each other's feelings. Conrad is forcefully suggesting that a failure in understanding is a concomitant of a failure in morality, and to communicate effectively with each other, human beings must have not only minds and feelings but also a sense of ethical conduct that can rise above immediate needs.

III

A consistent irony runs through Conrad's work of this period, an irony that began with *Nostromo* and will continue through *Victory*. The influence of Flaubert, whose characters have little or no belief in themselves or society, was never stronger and is now supplemented by a fuller recognition of James' use of irony. Typical Jamesian characters, particularly those in his later novels, suffer self-distrust while still maintaining moral belief, and by creating a tension between principles and the ability to live up to them, the novelist has a situation which is pregnant with ironic possibilities. Conrad's works contain

a long line of such characters, none perhaps in *The Secret Agent*, but the list includes Nostromo, Razumov,
Heyst, Kurtz, perhaps Jim, among others. By equating
individual moral necessity with the realm of social and
political facts, Conrad in this period of his work was dealing with material that is central to man's existence, what
Thomas Mann meant when he suggested that every major novel is in some way political. Furthermore, in presenting this material, Conrad showed his keen awareness of
the aesthetic problems that he had tried to define in his
essays and letters and in the Preface to *The Nigger* ten
years earlier. For the reader to go from *The Secret Agent*
to "Il Conde" and then to *Under Western Eyes* and *Victory* is to travel the road of the modern mind.

A Set of Six,[3] published in 1908, consists of six short
stories, of which one, "The Duel," is of sufficient length
to be called a novella. These stories were conceived and
written while Conrad was still working on *The Secret
Agent*. The most considerable of the stories is "Il Conde,"
which has been almost entirely neglected by Conrad's
critics, although its numerous potentialities certainly warrant further analysis. "Il Conde" contains the basic theme
of his other major stories and novels: the recognition
that humanity and ethical responsibility must precede ac-
quisitive self-seeking. The story, which took Conrad only
a few days to write, is based on a tale related to him by a
fellow Pole, Count Szembek. Although Conrad rarely even
mentions "Il Conde" in his letters, it is surely one of

[3] London: Methuen; New York: McClure, Phillips.
"Gaspar Ruiz," *Pall Mall Magazine*, July-October 1906; "The Informer," *Harper's Magazine*, December 1906; "The Brute," *The Daily
Chronicle*, December 5, 1906; "An Anarchist," *Harper's Monthly*, August
1906; "The Duel," *Pall Mall Magazine*, January-May, 1908 (Called "A
Point of Honor" in the serial); "Il Conde," *Cassell's Magazine*, August
1908.

his finest stories and looks ahead to his last major novel, *Victory*. There is a curious affinity between Heyst of the later novel and the dignified and art-loving old Count of the story. In their respective lives, they symbolize, to some extent, what was happening to Europe on the eve of the First World War.

It is not fortuitous that the climax of the story—the encounter in the park between the Count and the predatory young *Cavaliere*—should occur to the accompaniment of classical music. For in the *Cavaliere's* invasion of the Count's privacy and dignity, we have a vast symbol of modern violence as it clashes with the timeless aesthetic taste of the Count. The new generation is grotesquely represented by the stiletto of the young *Cavaliere*, while the music and peaceful surroundings represent the complacency and dignity of the old man. There is some temptation to point to the gardens where the encounter occurs as a worldly paradise from which the Count is forcibly expelled into the wilderness where he must fall ill and die. But such an allegorical interpretation must surely run counter to Conrad's subtitle of "A Pathetic Tale," which is more applicable to a human story than to Biblical allegory. If further meanings are to be sought, one must look toward Conrad's own themes as he developed them from book to book.

In his inability to face the more vulgar realities of life, the Count is Heyst grown older and mellower, more appreciative of his surroundings and consequently more hedonistic. Heyst's choice to withdraw from reality, according to Conrad, was equivalent to suicide, but the Count's withdrawal is of a different kind, and perhaps more tragic. As a devotee of leisurely and self-indulgent living, he necessarily found himself apart from most of his fellow men, although he was neither a dilettante nor a connoisseur. He was in most ways an intelligent man of the world in the best sense—not garrulous, nor verbose, Conrad says, "but distinctly communicative" —a fortunate man whose financial security allowed him a restful retirement from the affairs of the world. He is unimportant to anyone except possibly his married daughter; excelling in no art and productive in no way, he enjoys music, books, and the small pleasures of an uninvolved life. Conrad makes him a representative of the slow, leisurely life that had meaning before the World War when self-indulgence was possible and attractive. He is thoroughly civilized, cultured in a gentlemanly and gracious way, and his idleness is not to be confused with indolence. The Count is Conrad's conception of a European gentleman, perhaps the prototype of some of Conrad's own family in Poland, particularly of his uncle, Thaddeus Bobrowski, easy, generous with his time and sympathy, and human in his relationships. The Count is, really, the best a cultured society can produce, and the sudden violence that overtakes him is symbolic of the violence that was to overtake all Europe in 1914.

Without forcing unduly the relationship between the fate of the Count and the course of pre-war European culture—a relationship in which the young *Cavaliere* is a new type of political gangster—it is possible to see from Conrad's own works the background of the coming struggle for power. Unlike Heyst, whose desire for withdrawal is neurotically compulsive, the Count wants to live in the world but cannot. Within the framework of his tragedy, his fate is worse than Heyst's, for the reticent Swede actively courted disaster by the very terms of his existence; but the Count is forced into what amounts to suicide through no personal defect. He is innocent, and it is the innocent who must suffer contempt; the life of the civilized gentleman has been effaced.

If we follow the themes from "Heart of Darkness" and *Nostromo* through *The Secret Agent* to "Il Conde" and then on to *Under Western Eyes* and *Victory,* we find Conrad ranging back and forth through the major problems of the twentieth century—colonialism, the condition of European culture, the expediency of modern capitalism, the nature of political man, the ethical laxity of contemporary civilization, the decline of the individual, the growth of the bureaucratic state, et al. He suggests the tensions of historical and social tragedy in the form of symbolic characters and scenes. The political novel of our time, especially the work of Graham Greene, Arthur Koestler and George Orwell, is a phenomenon that in fact began with Dostoyevsky's and Conrad's insights into the modern political mind. Conrad's way of working, however, was not to make a frontal assault on a particular issue, but to allude to, and suggest through symbols, the generic situation of which a particular issue would be only part. "Il Conde" is just such a work. Its surface is always human, and its dramatic climax is resolved in human terms, but the political meanings of the story are now common coinage to the contemporary intelligence.

Continuing in *A Set of Six:* "Gaspar Ruiz," whose Latin-American setting might suggest *Nostromo,* is only a hasty magazine piece of minor Conrad. "The Brute," a tale of a destructive ship which kills on every trip, was among those stories Conrad wrote to fill out the volume and then referred to as "mere trifling." Included in the "trifling" category is "An Anarchist," a mere pretense of a story which can be immediately passed by. "The Informer," on the other hand, is a political piece of some interest, for it manifests Conrad's persistent theme of anarchy and revolution; no fewer than four of the stories in the volume are of this kind. Conrad's chief political insight in this story—which, technically, is a simple narrative directed by the omniscient author—is his presentation of a respectable and graceful revolutionary who possesses the same good taste in food and clothes as his middle-class critics. In recognizing the respectability and middle-class values of the revolutionary movement, Conrad was evincing the same social and political foresight that James displayed in *The Princess Casamassima*. Notwithstanding, this story, frequently gauche and absurd, contains only cardboard characters whose activities warrant no further attention.

"The Duel" is a slight piece of fiction in which Conrad found it possible to reduce excessive honor and faith to ridiculous terms. He was very pleased with the novella as an example of light, humorous writing, and there is no reason to make more of the piece than that. Perhaps "The Duel" only attains stature in its final meaning: that with the illusion and the struggle gone, life loses significance. For after their numerous personal duels, when D'Hubert finally has Feraud's life at his disposal, the former recognizes the emptiness of his life now that the years of challenge have passed. Stylistically, "The Duel" is direct and simple, but its subject matter repeats Stein's injunction in *Lord Jim*, that only immersion in the illusions of life can give existence meaning.

Razumov in *Under Western Eyes*[4] tries to pry him-

[4] London: Methuen, 1911; New York: Harper's, 1911. Started at the beginning of 1908 and finished in January 1910 (Jean-Aubry, II, 5-6), the novel was published serially in the *English Review*, VII, VIII, IX (December 1910-October 1911). First known as *Razumov*, this novel underwent many changes in development and conception before Conrad pub-

self from human solidarity in order to go his own way, a decision that inevitably proves self-destructive. Conrad, we remember, rarely equated self-imposed isolation with independence or individualism. Freedom from others is burdensome, an incubus and not a release, which in most cases leads to personal catastrophe. Conrad's conception of the individual is, ironically, a person who, once thrown out of society, must recognize the terms of his existence and then try to re-enter or else be overcome by a hostile world. His way of re-entry, in so far as he has a choice, can be through conquest or renunciation. Razumov makes the latter choice, and paradoxically his renunciation leads to both his destruction and acceptance, in each case by the same people.

But this overt theme is surely not the sole importance of *Under Western Eyes,* for Conrad not only pioneered the

---

lished it serially as *Under Western Eyes.* In early 1908, Conrad wrote to John Galsworthy that he was planning a story which would capture "the very soul of things Russian." He then outlined the theme, which in its first part—the surrender of Haldin to the police by Razumov—was later followed in the final version. But then the resemblance ends. Razumov, after the episode with Haldin, goes abroad to meet the mother and sister of the betrayed conspirator, and subsequently marries the sister. When their child shows a resemblance to Haldin, Razumov confesses to her the part he played in the arrest of her brother. Conrad said that the psychological developments leading to Haldin's betrayal and to Razumov's confession were to form the real subject of the story. The early version was evidently concerned solely with personal psychology, without the political overtones of anarchy and revolution.

Conrad did not have a particular source for *Under Western Eyes.* He did, however, have sources of information about revolutionaries, from the Garnetts, and followed newspaper stories of anarchists and assassination attempts in Russia. Conrad explained to Galsworthy that a certain de Plehve, assassinated in 1904, was the basis for Haldin's crime. Some characters appear to have been, at least partially, modeled on real people: Peter Ivanovich is a burlesqued version of Tolstoy and Prince Peter Kropotkin, while Mikulin is based on Lopuhin, the head of Russian police, eventually sent to Siberia.

political detective novel in English, but he also knew how to provide effective psychological drama. *Under Western Eyes* is full of subtle devices which by appearing at nearly every turn in the novel replace a direct narrative line and provide psychological depth for otherwise superficial political and social activity. As in "Heart of Darkness," *Nostromo,* and *The Secret Agent,* Conrad in *Under Western Eyes* attained psychological depth through certain professional touches: the placement of a crucial image, the sudden shift of narrative, the use of a large symbolic scene which draws together various elements of the plot, or simply an ironic comment which cogently suggests another dimension. Before enlarging, however, on these aspects of the book, one should note Conrad's debt to Dostoyevsky for this particular novel.

It is difficult to believe that Conrad could have written *Under Western Eyes* without Dostoyevsky's *Crime and Punishment* before him as a model. While differing obviously in ideology and political ideas, Conrad and Dostoyevsky often meet on common ground: for example, the Mikulin-Razumov and the General-Razumov interviews can be compared to the Porfiry-Raskolnikov interviews in *Crime and Punishment;* Razumov's mental playing with his secret is similar to Raskolnikov's temptation to divulge his crime; the need for spiritual cleansing is common to both "sinners"; the tensions of a pathological condition affect the sanity of both men; and there finally remains the fact, curious in the light of Conrad's hatred for Dostoyevsky's ideology, that both Razumov and Raskolnikov consider themselves superior to other men and destined for some calling in which their worth will be realized. Each tries to conduct himself apart from the solidarity of mankind, and each as a result has part of himself destroyed. The transformations that Conrad made between the initial version of *Razumov* and the final version of *Under Western Eyes* show great reliance on Dostoyevsky with his emphasis on social and political overtones. The initial version grew from a sentimental novel, in which Razumov's child resembles Haldin, to a dramatic tragedy told with irony and sensitivity.

Despite a narrative that is only occasionally intricate and a group of characters that lacks the variety and range of his other major novels, Conrad was able to give *Under Western Eyes* the elements of literary greatness. There are a thickness and density of tragic event and an awareness of the complex things of this world which we usually find only in great literature. The conclusive element in *Under Western Eyes* is perhaps its irony—not the pervading ironic comment of *The Secret Agent*—but an irony, rather, that is evoked through the juxtaposition of people and objects, an irony less of word than of scene. I have in mind, for instance, the scene in which Razumov retires to the islet guarded by the statue of Rousseau, and while sitting under the enthroned author of *The Social Contract* meditates his position and begins his diary.

For this scene, however, to possess more than momentary interest, the whole unfavorable position of Razumov must first be examined. When he is taken into Haldin's confidence, his world of security is suddenly shattered, and he must deal nakedly with all the forces he had hitherto chosen to ignore. He becomes a helpless man exposed upon a craft which is at everyone's mercy, and because of his realization of guilt, a man unable to function for himself. The everyday world is left behind—food, clothes, marriage, the niceties of societal intercourse, even the leisurely and relaxed moments a person intermittently allows himself—all these necessities of sane living are pushed into the background. Razumov recognizes himself as a Sisyphus who, morally speaking, can never escape his burden. Lacking roots and with nothing to fall back upon but himself, he is perforce isolated and introspective. Agonizingly, he feels the necessity of moral support; as Conrad says, "No human being could bear a steady view of moral solitude without going mad." Decoud, Renouard ("The Planter of Malata"), and Heyst to some extent all feel the want of human encouragement and recognize the "naked terror . . . of true loneliness" which destroys the will to live. Sensing this terror, Razumov, at the very moment of betraying Haldin, feels the need to embrace the revolutionary "in an incredible fellowship of souls," a feeling of hysterical insecurity in which he momentarily wants to embrace the personification of everything he fears, in which he momentarily wants to assume the form and character of another person. As Razumov later points out to Haldin, the latter has family connections to fall back upon, while he, Razumov, has no one; he is just "a man with a mind." He says: " 'I have no domestic tradition. I have nothing to think against. My tradition is historical . . . You [Haldin] come from your province, but all this land is mine—or I have nothing.' " After Haldin leaves, to fall into the police trap, Razumov again identifies with the now equally isolated revolutionary, and in their common rootlessness they become spiritual brothers; "After a moment he [Razumov] thought, 'I am lying here like that man. I wonder if he slept while I was struggling with the blizzard in the streets. No, he did not sleep. But why should I not sleep?' " Razumov truly has nothing but himself; his "solitary and laborious existence had been destroyed" by Haldin's intervention, and wherever he goes he must go alone. " 'Where to?' " asks Mikulin, for Razumov, as the State Councillor realizes, has lost his direction in life.

Two hundred pages later, Conrad answers the rhetorical question, and we find Razumov in Geneva sitting under the statue of Rousseau. The irony of the scene on the islet can perhaps be seen now in a clearer perspective, for the exiled Russian eventually finds peace only on that isolated islet which is the home of the "exiled" Frenchman. Watched over by this exponent of human freedom, Razumov, alone and morbid in spirit, writes his own diary, a virtual record of conformity, an anti-social contract. The companionship of the two is made even more ironical by the physical parallel: both sit near the bridge looking for possible passers-by; both are ready to greet visitors, Rousseau in honor, Razumov to dispel suspicion. The Russian student has found the perfect place to write his diary, to explain his own desolation while sitting in the loneliness of this small piece of land as the current breaks against the corner of the islet. All his hopes and dreams are centered here—"'Extraordinary occupation I am giving myself up to,' he murmured." Like Decoud, his brother in gloom and wretchedness on the Great Isabel, Razumov is cut off from all human intercourse; his only companion is a bronze statue, and his only concern is himself and his own safety. After hours of introspection, he finally leaves the island, confident that "there is no longer anything in the way of [his] being completely accepted." Later that night he confesses to the revolutionaries and is hopelessly crippled for life.

Why should Conrad, one may ask, have chosen Rousseau as a companion for Razumov? Surely, the choice was not fortuitous or solely for verisimilitude or even to impart historical depth to the novel. The reason, we may speculate, was more intimate, was posed more in terms of irony and feeling than for reasons of historical or philosophical magnitude. Conrad was, as he always claimed, a writer of feeling, interested more in colors and tones than in a strictly intellectual appeal. Razumov, on the other hand, has been a faithful believer in the intellectual life and has always tried to regulate his activities in accordance with a strict logic of profit and loss. Now in his decline, when intellectuality, as he realizes, cannot even begin to sustain him, he turns to the image of Rousseau, that lifelong exponent of the emotional and the sentimental, and within his shadow finds temporary peace. The spirit of Rousseau, manifest in the bronze statue, spurs Razumov to conduct himself with other than intellectual assumptions. Once Razumov recognizes that a pact with logic is a pact with the devil, he becomes spiritually cleansed, and his confessions, first to Miss Haldin and then to the revolutionaries, are the fruits of his conversion.

The scene on the islet, meaningful as it is, does not, however, exist in isolation, for Conrad worked through reduplicating situations; and this present scene between Razumov and Rousseau harks back to an earlier one that related Razumov to another statue, and more directly to Haldin himself. In that earlier scene, Razumov has gone to see his patron, the Prince, and has told him that Haldin is hiding secretly in his room. The two then go to the General's palace, one corner of which is filled by a bronze on a pedestal, a quarter-life-size statue of a running adolescent figure, Spontini's "Flight of Youth." As the Prince comments upon its lines, Razumov stares semi-hysterically at the statue, transfixed by its resemblance to the "running adolescent" Haldin, now in his room. Conrad writes: "He [Razumov] was worried by a sensation resembling the gnawing of hunger." When Razumov finally returns to his own room, he sees Haldin, "already at the door, tall and straight as an arrow, with his pale face and hand raised attentively, [who] might have posed for the statue of a daring youth listening to an inner voice." When Haldin becomes identified with the "Flight of Youth," he is forever fixed in Razumov's mind as a personal Fury that can never be exorcised, a Fury that bedevils him until his repenting confession before Miss Haldin.

The recurring scenes of the statues bring together in sharper identification Razumov and Haldin themselves and through this acute psychological doubling enrich the narrative. Conrad very subtly developed the identity of these two whose psychologies at first would seem to be completely divergent. The revolutionary Haldin initially enters Razumov's life at the moment the latter has decided to enter an essay contest, the psychological moment when he is ready to strike for fame. Thus Razumov is even more than usually interested in self, while Haldin, on the contrary, has just committed his most selfless act for the revolutionary cause. Each one, at first meeting, has been pushed to the limits of his particular personality; yet such is their reaction upon each other that they approach similar psychological conditions. In a moment of desperation Razumov is tempted to embrace his opposite, but instead embraces the police, as logic tells him to do. Then he almost at once recognizes that Haldin is sincere and that the police and the General are despicable—he senses that Haldin's sympathies should have been his. He realizes that life without happiness is impossible, and that his own way leads not to personal happiness but only to a tainted success. When he suspects that Haldin, in his way of life, was happy, he reaches to him as to his double. Razumov's logical program of "History not Theory, Patriotism not Internationalism, Evolution not Revolution, Direction not Destruction, Unity not Disruption" fulfills only the public and not the private man.

From Razumov's initial meeting with Haldin until his confessions in Geneva, he acts always in the shadow of Haldin. His betrayal of his fellow student destroys himself rather than the revolutionary, for Razumov's existence is never his own henceforth. He exists only because of Haldin's memory, only because Haldin exists for the people in Geneva. Rather than gaining self, Razumov has completely lost whatever personality he once had. He still has no life of his own; once an exile in his own country with only an historical tradition to look to, now he has forfeited even that prop. Completely rootless, completely exiled from the niceties of life, he must assume Haldin's family as his own. He is an extension, a physical corollary of Haldin's spirit and idealism. As he eventually comes to realize, *he* is the victim, not Haldin; the great Cosmic Joke, as Conrad called man's destiny, had been using him as its butt. In betraying Haldin, as he suggests himself in his confession to Miss Haldin, he has most basely betrayed himself. Conrad's juxtaposition of Haldin and Razumov, first through the recurrence of the statues and then as spiritual brothers in conflict, gives thickness to the novel through incidents and characters that recall antecedents from other contexts. This is a key part of Conrad's novelistic art.

On still another level, Razumov is doubled by the hapless Tekla, whose existence in isolation parallels his. Her only use is to help others, and still she is shunned; a virtual pariah, she says: " 'No one talks to me, no one writes to me. . . . I have no use for a name. . . .' " Earlier in her life she had nursed another crushed and tortured spirit, a revolutionary, Andrei, who during a beating had let out some information. Only Tekla would assist Andrei, as only Tekla would take care of the crippled Razumov after his confession. Nameless, sexless, treated like a beast,

Tekla is Razumov's fate; in her idiotic slavishness, she becomes the sole means of survival for this ex-student with intellectual pretensions.

Closed in by Haldin on one side and by Tekla on a second side, Razumov is still far from being defined. There remains a third side, the drunken driver, Ziemianitch, who is incapable of action when he is most needed and who commits suicide, it is thought, because of inconsolable remorse for having failed Haldin. Razumov, who likewise is incapable of an audacious decision, believes that Russia must decide between two basic types: the Ziemianitches, drunken and unable to perform their duties, and the Haldins, who have the dream-intoxication of the idealist and are unable, in Razumov's view, to perceive the true character of either men or the world. Razumov, ironically, flatters himself that he falls into neither category. But there is a third category which Razumov cannot, fails to, or does not want to see—that is, his own fluctuating and indeterminate position. In his way similar to all three—a failure like Ziemianitch, a nameless and homeless cipher like Tekla, and an idealist like Haldin—Razumov fits neatly into no category and consequently must forfeit any hope for personal status. In the eyes of society, a Haldin, a Ziemianitch, even a Tekla, have status of a sort, no matter how low; but Razumov is a nonentity because he is unidentifiable. His confessions to Miss Haldin and to the revolutionaries, when he finds peace is unobtainable, are, then, ways of identifying with Haldin and with the drunken sled driver as victims. For in this world, the ex-student realizes, even the victims are a class with status. To attain this is, for Razumov, a way of success.

In discussing Conrad's method in *Under Western Eyes,* it is important to remember his injunction in the Author's

Note written in 1920. He said: ". . . [it is] my primary conviction that truth alone is the justification of any fiction which makes the least claim to the quality of art. . . . I have never been called before to a greater effort of detachment: detachment from all passions, prejudices and even from personal memories." He said his chief problem was to gain a view of the characters as they appeared to the western eyes of the old language teacher. The teacher himself is a Marlow-like character who remains more or less static during the course of the novel, but is useful as a chorus, as a confidant to Miss Haldin, and, most of all, for providing the practical mechanics of the narrative.

The narrative, without possessing the complicated chronology of *Nostromo* or *Chance,* is unfolded amidst what we now identify as typical Conradian involutions of time. The novel comes to the reader as the very stuff of history and contains besides the omniscient author two additional sources, Razumov's personal diary and the narrative of the language teacher. Conrad perhaps tried to construct the plot entirely on these two sources, but certain scenes do not fit easily into either and must be ascribed to the author's own direction of the novel. However, by interchanging all three possible means of information, Conrad was evidently able to juggle the narrative to his artistic satisfaction. He was chiefly concerned with providing ready and plausible sources for his information: the confession scene, for example, is reported by Laspara, one of the revolutionaries present, and it is he, Conrad is careful to point out, who originally chronicled Razumov's startling move. The full story of Razumov's confession, however, is later told to the narrator by Sophia Antonovna, who had heard it from Razumov himself; the rest of the narrator's information comes from the diary.

By using Razumov's diary to provide the principal facts of the story, Conrad was of course employing a device as old as the novel itself. Earlier, in *Nostromo,* he had used Decoud's long letter to his sister to bolster the narrative at a crucial point, and later, in *Chance,* he was to throw together all the traditional devices of the novel—Conrad evidently did not forsake a novelistic trick solely because of its traditional utility. Casting the narrative of *Under Western Eyes* in a characteristically involved time sequence, he brought invigorating freshness to well-worn material and conveyed an irony of form and content. By ending Part One with the sardonic question, " 'Where to?' " and then shifting to Geneva to sketch the group that is waiting for Razumov as Haldin's friend, Conrad created the situation neatly and tersely. A technical comment like this informs a scene that most previous novelists, Flaubert excepted, would have verbalized to their own detriment.

Another, and more significant, example of trenchant technical comment comes toward the end of Part Three, when Razumov is sitting in anxiety and meditation on the islet containing Rousseau's statue. Having placed Razumov on the islet, Conrad suddenly shifts to his motives for coming to Geneva and for the first time recreates his plight immediately after Haldin's capture and execution. The ironic juxtaposition of the Geneva location with the detailed circumstances leading to Razumov's activity as a counter-agent heightens the absurdity of his position and the absurdity of all people involved in conscious or unconscious duplicity. Everyone literally becomes a fool: Mikulin with his short-sighted wisdom, Haldin with his savage energy, Razumov's princely patron with his aristocratic complacency, the red-nosed student who is willing to starve for a misconceived ideal, the playboy Kirylo who is anxious to steal from his own father to aid the revolutionary cause—all become less than human in Razumov's eyes, all become ridiculous buffoons who are "always dazzled by the base glitter of mixed motives." The biggest fool of all is of course Razumov himself, who must play out the game with deadly seriousness, while realizing, as he communes with Rousseau, that he is dealing with dangling puppets in matters of life and death. This is the stuff of Conrad's irony, and it is attained here succinctly through a structural framework.

Structure, however, can break down even in major novels, and any discussion of the narrative in *Under Western Eyes* inevitably brings one to the climax and then to the eleven-page coda which ends the novel. Leading up to this coda is a series of episodic events that make up half of the novel although they last only one day. The events themselves are in the form of a number of linked scenes between Razumov and several individuals, events that, having been strung together one after the other, are broken only by the episode on the Rousseau islet and the short flashback to Russia. Part of the narrative is intermittently shifted to the language teacher, but always in relation to Razumov's activities in the past and present. Yet such is the episodic nature of the book that it involved Conrad in a number of false moves which considerably reduced the seriousness of the novel. Keeping in mind Conrad's difficulties with other endings (in *Nostromo*, *Victory*, and *Chance*), one can see that the conclusion of *Under Western Eyes* also lacks proportion and fails to make sense dramatically. After the close of the action proper—that is, after Razumov confesses to the revolutionaries—ten distinct fragments of information are presented that account for everyone while tying together all loose ends.

Many of these events are incredible if the story is to maintain its artistic realism. That Sophia Antonovna, an ardent revolutionary, and her comrades would visit the counter-agent Razumov after he has admitted betraying Haldin and spying on them, is, in the sequence of the novel, impossible to believe. When she goes on to praise Razumov's character in glowing terms, she destroys the illusion of the revolutionaries as a serious group and reduces them to ridiculous actors in a make-believe drama. If Conrad has succeeded in making his revolutionaries seem ridiculous, then Razumov's feelings of guilt, along with his dramatic self-effacement in their presence, all become meaningless. If they are contemptible, one may ask how can they be Haldin's heritage? But if we do grant that the revolutionaries have, up to the present point, stayed just this side of sanity, then we can see that in this hasty summation they and their activities become meaningless. For it is incredible that in the meeting between Mikulin and Peter Ivanovitch the former should divulge Nikita's true identity. This makes a farce of Razumov's inner tensions as he fluctuates between Mikulin, who represents Russian power, and Peter Ivanovitch, who is the revolutionary guide. Then to be told further that Peter Ivanovitch is now living in Russia, is to be outraged by what Conrad had done to the novel. The latter part of the story clearly works to the loss of dramatic intensity in the entire narrative.

Irving Howe, who has many cogent things to say about Conrad's anarchists, believes that Conrad's political prejudices (his inability to see anarchy and revolution at their strength) invalidated the dramatic denouement in which Razumov and the reader must take the revolutionary world seriously. The faultiness of the latter part of the novel, however, is not so much a result of Conrad's political prejudices as it is an aesthetic flaw in which he seriously misjudged the true climax of his story. If Razumov's confession to Miss Haldin and *not* to the revolutionaries is seen as the dramatic climax, then all the later business at Laspara's house becomes superfluous. It is Miss Haldin who causes Razumov's confession; his love for her and not his feeling of guilt toward the revolutionaries leads to his inner conflict. If we return for a minute to *Razumov*, that early version of *Under Western Eyes*, it is evident that Razumov's confession to Miss Haldin, in that version his wife, is the climax of a severe psychological struggle. Without the direct evidence of the *Razumov* MS before me, it is impossible to be certain that Conrad simply grafted the elements of conspiracy onto the manuscript without revising the psychological center of the plot. Of course, in the earlier version, the private lives of the characters were emphasized—Razumov marries Miss Haldin and has a child by her—all of which leads away from any stress on revolutionary activities. In the book, the most telling passages are those in which Razumov's personal struggle engages us, and the least convincing are those concerning the conspirators. Conrad had always disclaimed both the ability and the desire to create a realistic revolutionary world, and if we take him at his word then the personal elements in the novel must remain paramount.

But even so, the conspirators, while obviously neither heroic nor savory, can be granted some credibility. In their lack of organization and in their mixed motives, they seem the very group that Razumov could effectively deceive. Give them efficiency—for instance, the organization of a modern bureaucratic spy system—and Razumov's dissembling would have been impossible. Their utter pigheaded egoism and lack of cohesiveness make plausible Razumov's movement among them. The very looseness of their activity would also seem to bolster my speculation that Conrad beyond a token effort did not try to develop their role in the novel. The conspirators are sufficient, however, as background for Razumov's conflict with regard to Miss Haldin; it is only when Conrad attempted to give importance to their hold upon Razumov that he went wrong aesthetically, and showed that as a political writer he was not Dostoyevsky's peer.

Conrad himself seemed to recognize the shortcomings of the novel. In a relatively little-quoted letter to John Galsworthy, which Jean-Aubry prints, Conrad answered his friend's criticism of Part Two of *Under Western Eyes;* while defending this part as the residue of many revised and now destroyed pages, he admitted that good work takes more time than he was able to give: ". . . to invent an action, a march for the story, which would have dispensed with Part II as it stands, was a matter of meditation, of trying and retrying for goodness knows how long. This I could not afford to do." Then Conrad wrote a passage which is, I believe, the clue to what I have called his lack of staying power, the one element that prevented his development of *Nostromo* along its grand early lines and that partially destroyed the aesthetic truth of *Victory* and the present novel. Conrad said:

I went on the obvious lines and on these lines I developed my narrative to give it some sort of verisimilitude. In other words, I offered to sell my soul for half a crown, and now I have neither the soul nor the coin. . . . at my age [51] such passages embitter and discourage one beyond expression. I have no heart to think of compressing anything, for I have no illusion as to the quality of the stuff. . . . It should not be there at all. (Nov. 30, 1908, Birm. [Engl.] U. Libr.)

It is not Conrad's political inconsistency that makes hash of the conclusion to *Under Western Eyes*. It is once again a matter of conceptualization. After Razumov's confession to Miss Haldin, everything also is anti-climactic. Given this development, even a more cogent ending could not have retrieved the novel aesthetically, for Razumov's devotion is clearly to her and through her love he realizes he must spiritually cleanse himself; only then can he be worthy of her and only then can he gain forgiveness. Not unlike Raskolnikov, who finds that his crime is doubly abhorrent when faced by Sonya's love, Razumov recognizes his own impurity confronted by Miss Haldin's trust. Through love and trust, Razumov attains self-knowledge and realizes that in betraying Haldin he has most basely betrayed himself. His contempt for others, a sense of scorn which now extends even to himself, has become a viper in his soul which can only be exorcised by confession. After Razumov recognizes this point and abases himself before Miss Haldin, the rest is explanatory and not dramatic necessity. When Conrad failed to develop this change in Razumov as the *sole* climax of the plot, as *the* psychological inevitability of Razumov's story, then he committed many grievous errors aesthetically, the worst of which is the ending.

From Conrad's failure to conceive the story along its own inevitable lines, there ensued many awkward and obvious touches, all of which to some extent detract from the novel's effectiveness. All these defects, significantly, are connected with Razumov's relation to the conspirators; none relates to his feeling for Miss Haldin. For example, the storm symbolism of *Under Western Eyes* occurs at two distinct times, both of which are crucial in Razumov's development: initially, during the snow storm in Russia, he decides to betray Haldin, and later, during the rain storm in Geneva, he decides to confess. These acts are the twin nodes of Razumov's behavior, and both are carried out to the violent accompaniment of the elements. Yet the second is that kind of evident device which adds nothing at all to the novel and what is more likely becomes an affront to the reader. As Razumov's resolution to confess becomes stronger, the rain increases in intensity; as the storm cleanses him physically, so his confession is to cleanse him spiritually; as he nears Laspara's house where the revolutionaries are meeting, a single clap of thunder heralds his arrival; and after he is deafened by Nikita and thrown into the street, the violence of the outer world can no longer touch him—his confession has truly led to serenity of mind and spirit. As a psychological comment the storm is senseless, for Razumov's own conflict must be powerful enough by now to give his decision sufficient thrust of its own, and as a physical medium of expression, the storm forces the obvious.

Another weak attempt at the obvious parallelism of situations concerns the stoppage of a watch. When Haldin leaves Razumov's room to go to his doom, the latter's watch stops at midnight; time literally stops for Razumov at this point. It is at midnight in Geneva, then, that he goes forth to confess, to make his absolution an exact duplication of Haldin's martyrdom. Once again, Conrad seemed afraid to let Razumov's conflict speak for itself without those unnecessary decorations which inevitably cheapen the novel.

The ending itself, as I have suggested, is a concomitant of this need to "dress up" the novel, to give completion to the various personages introduced in the course of the story. By forcing Razumov into a second confession, a clear breach of the dramatic inevitability of the plot,

Conrad flawed the book and forced himself into a succession of false steps. The incredible last eleven pages have almost nothing to do with Razumov; if he is the central figure of the book, these pages are evidently superfluous. So much of *Under Western Eyes* is powerful and compelling, intuitively driving to the heart of serious moral problems, that one is dismayed to see Conrad frustrating the dramatic force of his theme with irrelevancies and encumbrances. This was his way, however, in nearly all his major novels, and when we come to *Victory* we are faced by a similar aesthetic defect.

IV

In *Some Reminiscences*[5] (called *A Personal Record* in the Collected Edition), Conrad attempts, as he said, to treat "the literary life and the sea life on parallel lines, with a running reference to . . . [his] early years." He began this series of reminiscences at Ford's request and temporarily put aside *Under Western Eyes* and the already advanced *Chance* in order to devote himself entirely to the volume, in which he dealt loosely with his early memories of Poland, his life at Marseilles in the French merchant fleet, and his beginnings as an English sailor and as a man of letters. *Some Reminiscences*, along with *The Mirror of the Sea* and *Notes on Life and Letters*, constitutes Conrad's attempt at autobiography.

In earlier chapters, many of the salient points in *Some Reminiscences* have already been suggested, particularly Conrad's ideas on literature as he revealed himself in these pages. In the Author's Note, Conrad attempted to

[5] Serialized in Ford's *English Review*, I, II (December 1908-June 1909). Published in London by Nash, 1912, and in New York by Harper's, 1912, under the title, *A Personal Record*.

clear up any misunderstandings about his use of the English language in his books. He claimed that a distinct choice of a language in which to write never entered his mind; that English more or less adopted him; and that, he added, if he "had not written in English [he] would not have written at all." On many occasions Conrad cursed the English language for its numerous ambiguities and manifold connotations, but he also revealed to Hugh Clifford during a conversation that he was afraid "to attempt expression in a language as perfectly 'crystallized' as French." Given Conrad's temperament, he seems, as a romantic prose stylist, more closely fitted to English than to the traditional purity and spareness of an ironic French prose. One further point is worth mentioning before returning to Conrad's fiction: it is remarkable even in this volume, a book of memories, that Conrad's method approximates the same shifting focus and liberty with narrative sequences that are found in his novels. For, following his fictional method, Conrad wrote: "Could I begin with the sacramental words, 'I was born on such a date in such a place?'" In those pages Conrad makes clear that his way of thinking of himself was like his way of seeing and organizing his literary material; that the Polish patriot, the English seaman, and the literary artist were all of the same stuff; and that that oft-used expression "The style is the man" truly conveys Conrad's personality and work. Conrad treated his own memories as he did those of his fictional heroes, and in defining his artistic aims he wrote what could have been his epitaph:

And least of all can you condemn an artist pursuing, however humbly and imperfectly, a creative aim. In that anterior world where his thought and his emotions go seeking for the experience of imagined adventures, there are no policemen, no law, no pressure of circumstances or dread of opinion to keep him within bounds. . . . All intellectual and artistic ambitions are permissible, up to and beyond the limit of prudent sanity. . . . If they are mad, then so much the worse for the artist.

In his willingness to have artistic considerations alone justify a given subject, Conrad was in step with common modern ideas on aesthetics. He repeated that it is not the Why that matters so much as the How—for always "there is the manner . . . for those who know how to look at their kind."

The years from 1908 to 1911 were a period of great activity for Conrad. Having finished *Some Reminiscences,* he returned to work on *Under Western Eyes,* while also writing "The Secret Sharer" [6] and correcting proofs of the French translation of *The Nigger of the "Narcissus."* He had also been holding *Chance* in abeyance (since 1906) and about five months after finishing *Under Western Eyes* he sat down to modify and conclude that novel, which began to appear in the early part of 1912. During the summer of 1910, while still busy with *Chance,* he wrote "A Smile of Fortune" [7] and shortly afterward, "Freya of the Seven Isles." [8] These two stories, along with "The Secret Sharer," appeared in the volume *'Twixt Land and Sea,* which was published in 1912.[9]

Of the three stories in the volume, only "The Secret Sharer" need command our attention. The other two are self-explanatory magazine pieces which in their themes and settings signal a return to Conrad's early fiction about

[6] Written in November 1909 and published in *Harper's Magazine,* August-September 1910.
[7] *The London Magazine,* February 1911.
[8] *The Metropolitan,* New York, April 1912.
[9] London: Dent, 1912; New York: Doran, 1912.

the Malayan Archipelago. "The Secret Sharer," though surely not so profound and far-reaching as "Heart of Darkness," is for several reasons one of Conrad's major stories. Writing to Garnett, Conrad revealed his own feelings about the tale:

> I dare say Freya is pretty rotten. On the other hand "The Secret Sharer," between you and me, is *it*. Eh? Every word fits and there's not a single uncertain note. Luck my boy. Pure luck. I knew you would spot the thing at sight. But I repeat: mere luck. (Nov. 5, 1912)

"The Secret Sharer" has been the target of more many-sided interpretations than any other Conrad work with the possible exception of "Heart of Darkness." Rather than repeat the literal, ethical, psychological, and aesthetic meanings of the story, I should prefer to examine "The Secret Sharer" in a context that partakes of all the other possibilities and still remains true to Conrad's work as a whole. "The Secret Sharer" deals principally and simply with the theme of apprenticeship-to-life, which is the same theme of growing up and maturing that Conrad treated in many other stories and novels. Placed in this large category, the story can then be seen, as necessary, in its various subdivisions of ethical, psychological, and aesthetic development.

Excessive emphasis on the psychological phenomenon of the alter ego belabors what is the most obvious and perhaps the weakest part of the story. If Conrad stressed any one thing, he stressed the resemblance, both physically and psychologically, between the Captain and the fugitive Leggatt. The constant parallel descriptions of the two men, the use of doubles, doubling, second self, secret self, other self, and so on, are tedious. The repetition is as evident in this story as Marlow's use of qualifying adjectives in "Heart of Darkness." In both stories, of course, much still remains after we have put the obvious behind us.

"The Secret Sharer" is the other side of *Under Western Eyes:* the Captain is a Razumov who does not betray his trust, and Leggatt is a Haldin who escapes his oppressors. The two works taken together pose a double question and show the consequences leading from both answers: what happens when you betray a trust? and what happens when under duress you remain true to your secret? It is the Captain's recognition of these points that sustains the dramatic interest of the story.

Professor Zabel, in his well-known essay "Joseph Conrad: Chance and Recognition," remarked that the crisis in every one of Conrad's novels and stories arrives when by accident, decision, or error a man finds himself abruptly committed to his destiny. This recognition, Zabel says, occurs through a series of steps: isolation of the character from society; his recognition of his situation in a hostile world; and then, once self-knowledge is attained, his way, as we saw with Razumov, of either solving or succumbing to his problem. This is also the problem of the artist; and Conrad through his particular way of developing "The Secret Sharer" was able to relate the psychological and moral contradictions in human nature to the ambivalence of reality as art embodies it, and finally to a searching analysis of value itself. Commensurate with this search for value in life, another way of looking at "Heart of Darkness" suggests itself (with "The Secret Sharer" also in mind): the journey of Marlow-Conrad into the Congo is a means to self-knowledge in which the crucial experience is a process of maturation into both adulthood and artistry; once the journey into this turmoil of experience has been resolved, the survivor is able to proceed to live and create. The experiences of Marlow-Conrad in the Congo, together with the Captain's experience on his ship, are forms of initiation which all must undergo, but which only the true artist in life or fiction can successfully sustain.

Self-knowledge is as much a key to survival as it is to artistic creation; and self-knowledge is one of the chief ingredients in the apprenticeship novel. Jim's personal tragedy is that he unconsciously continues to romanticize a situation that can be alleviated only by a stancher view of reality, a view impossible, perhaps, for one as self-destructive as Jim. As a "successful" Jim, the Captain in "The Secret Sharer" is faced by the stern materials of his salvation and is courageous enough to act on his problem once he has intuitively formulated its substance. This story, then, becomes a microcosm of Conrad's major themes; but for all its suggestiveness, it is, paradoxically, one of his most straightforward and obvious works. Its narrative is a model of clarity, like those uncomplicated narratives "Youth" and *The Shadow Line* (1917).

In giving the terms of initiation into maturity and/or art, Conrad was traveling very familiar and sure ground; in failing, however, to wrap the story in artistic form, he made every point a stated point and every psychological-ethical commentary a labored verbal explanation. In fact, when Conrad continues to force the obvious physical parallels between the two men, the story often loses its thrust in a welter of amateur behaviorism.

Even R. W. Stallman's interpretation of the story's aesthetic level (according to this view, the story objectified a particular crisis in Conrad's life as an artist, a crisis in which he had to come to final terms with his aims as a creator) is purely speculative, depending as it does on broad critical extension of objective correlatives in the narrative. The scenes and images of "Heart of Darkness," for example, are of a variety which permits extension, and an almost limitless number of references are possible. But "The Secret Sharer" is notable for its lack of variety, for the sameness of its images, for its failure to conceptualize the material in less direct form. This is surely not to denigrate the story, but only to show where analysis is possible and where excessive probing may go wrong. I want to emphasize that even though "The Secret Sharer" does not contain cosmic significance, it is, concerning matters of doctrine as well as intrinsically, among Conrad's more important works. The surface in this case *is* the story, and the surface is the arrival of the Captain at a degree of maturity in which he gains self-respect and confidence. This is the obvious fact of "The Secret Sharer," and it must remain of the greatest import.

As an initiate, the Captain has the recognizable qualities of Conrad's isolated individuals who must demonstrate responsibility in the face of challenge. As a stranger to his ship as well as to himself, he is insecure and untried. But he is a realist, and therefore he can recognize the challenge when it comes. In order to dramatize the demand that is made upon the Captain, an analogy was necessary, and it is here that Conrad forced the obvious. If the symbol of threat is a fugitive (Leggatt) who has killed, then a similar "fugitive" quality must be found in the Captain. Conrad quickly established the Captain's insecurity as his strangeness on board ship (the crew had been together for eighteen months or so), his youth (second youngest aboard), and, most of all, his desire to be faithful to an ideal conception of his personality. Clearly, then, like the knights of old, he must go through an ordeal. His ordeal is simply to protect Leggatt, and this forms the narrative of the story. As doubles in secrecy, they are of common size, common origin, common age, and even wear common clothes. This close identity between the two was of course necessary for realism, for without it the Captain's attachment to Leggatt, except perhaps on some sexual basis, would contain no substantiation. But once this rapport is clear, then the two become interchangeable, and the success of one depends upon the success of the other. Yet how Conrad labored the point, and how the critics have jumped on the obvious and praised his astute recognition of psychological phenomena, his grasp of the alter ego, of man's secret self, of the dark elements in man's character! There is no doubt that Conrad intuited many psychological problems, but how much more subtly and artistically he proceeded in *Victory* and *Under Western Eyes* and *The Secret Agent* than in this story; and in those works how much more dramatically he used his special insights into the psychology of guilt as part of a larger point of view! Nevertheless, even when one recognizes that "The Secret Sharer" is psychologically shallow, there still remains its importance as the case history of a typical Conradian hero.

One point deserves further comment: the meaning attached to the floppy white hat which the Captain almost desperately thrusts upon Leggatt (what Stallman identifies as a symbol of the Captain's fidelity to selfhood and to the dictates of his conscience). The hat is given fortuitously, and yet it is this very object which provides the marker that saves the ship from grounding. If the Captain's entire previous efforts were to have been wasted without the last minute gift of the hat, and if his daring attempt to meet a personal challenge was all in vain unless the hat had found Leggatt's head in the dark, what then is Conrad's point? Seen in this light, the meaning of the story can go many ways: is it that personal courage

means relatively little in a world in which chance rules
heavily, and that to meet a challenge successfully one
must combine personal fortitude with cosmic luck? or is
it Conrad's point that in giving the hat, the Captain was
really following a logical turn of mind derived from his
original decision to hide Leggatt? If the latter, then the
fortuitous giving of the hat only *seems* fortuitous, but is
indeed an integral part of the Captain's complete identification with and giving of himself to Leggatt. These two
possibilities, while not necessarily opposing each other,
become the chief ambiguity of the story and lead directly
into Conrad's next novel, *Chance*.

V

In the summer of 1910, Conrad, while still known only to
a coterie of admirers, moved to Capel House, Orlestone,
near Ashford, Kent, and recommenced work on *Chance*,
which he had put aside since 1906. The impetus to pick
up the partly-completed novel was provided by an offer
from *The New York Herald* to buy his work in advance.
Between June, 1911 and March 26, 1912, Conrad finished
the novel which was at last to bring him before a popular
audience, and *The Herald* began the serial on January 21,
1912, fully two months before the book was finished.[10]

Chance, as Conrad's most elaborately designed novel,
Nostromo and *Victory* notwithstanding, was for him a
radical departure in subject matter. This is substantially
the only time (if we discount the early story, "The Return," which is of little import) that Conrad treated the
state of marriage as of importance in itself. This is, in
fact, the only time that Conrad wrote about married love,

[10] *The New York Herald*, January 21, 1912-June 30, 1912. Published in
London by Methuen, 1914, and in New York by Doubleday, 1914.

complete with a troublesome (father) in-law and neurotic childhoods. Even though the elopement and honeymoon are remote from the ordinary, the problems of land —such as the struggle for supremacy between the sexes and the whole range of familial relationships—dominate the life at sea; for Conrad in this novel, it was truly a woman- and man-centered universe.

Chance is also Conrad's only novel of the maturing of a girl to a young lady; all his other novels of growing-up are concerned with the apprenticeship of men. Flora de Barral has to overcome all the frustrations and barriers facing Jim, George (*The Arrow of Gold*), the Captain ("The Secret Sharer"), John Kemp (*Romance*), et al., but because of her sex, she lacks their mobility. Her role is necessarily more passive, and her first important decision is the only one she really ever must make, the choice of Anthony rather than her father. But despite her passivity, Flora is the center of a situation that suggests widespread social changes.

Typical of the problem of growing-up is the relation between parents and children: between the isolated Flora and her swindler father, between Captain Anthony and his poet father. Despite riches, position, a name, and a personal governess, Flora was, says Conrad, "the captive of the meanest conceivable fate." She fiddles in innocence while her fortune burns away, and then must watch in silence as all her illusions are destroyed. Thrown out by society because of the nature of her father's past, Flora is as cursed as Jim and Razumov. Yet original sin is not hers; she is faultless, and perhaps for this reason her sanity prevails, and instead of being forced into self-destruction she endures her tormentors. When she and Anthony come together—he, the isolated son of an unsympathetic poet who is in his way a verbal swindler—they are, like

Heyst and Lena in *Victory,* "the only two people on the wide earth," rootless and helpless.

Common outcasts, they are, Conrad says, "untrammeled in a sense as the first man and the first woman." One critic sees them as Adam and Eve persecuted "in a society increasingly menaced by outbreaks of unreason and violence." Anthony, however, is an outcast through choice. Despite his evident nobility, he rarely gains our affections because he is *too* intoxicated "with the pity and tenderness of his part," *too* aware of his knightly character in saving Flora. Flora, on the contrary, clearly is an outcast through circumstances beyond her control: she is hated by her governess and turned out by everyone with whom she goes to live, suspected by the Fynes of having deceitful motives, fearful that Anthony does not care for her, and tied to a father who sees in her his only prop, a father whose insanity infects nearly everyone he touches. The salvation of Flora's well-being, then, becomes a major job of character reconstruction, and to remake her into a functioning individual suggests a large scheme.

If we look ahead to *Victory,* we can see that the reconstruction of Heyst—the injection of feeling into his intellectual attitude—takes on historic significance. His gaining of heart and his realization of wholeness become the attainments of an age maturing to a recognition of its problems. While we cannot make the same claims for Flora, we must mark her successful repudiation of her imprisoning background and her realization of self in a fruitful attachment as directly antecedent to the situation in *Victory* and as expressing in their way Conrad's interpretation of what man must attain to survive.

Conrad used as epigraph to the novel a quotation from Sir Thomas Browne: "Those that hold that all things are governed by Fortune had not erred, had they not persisted there," illustrating the point that though chance is "a mighty force . . . absolutely irresistible yet manifesting itself often in delicate forms," it is still not all of human existence; but that man's option often determines what chance cannot effect. While chance is a large constituent of life, it is, nevertheless, human choice that is of paramount interest. It is this point which has characterized all of Conrad's work, from *Almayer's Folly* to *Chance,* and will continue through *The Rover,* his last completed novel.

If human relationships are the center of the novel,[11] then they are relationships responsible only to the consciences of individuals, never to the dictates of God. Conrad's atomic view of sin and salvation, the necessity for the individual to be aware of his rights and wrongs, makes each person accountable only to himself. There is no squaring of accounts with heaven. Rewards are on this earth, and hell exists solely as a conscience in each man's heart. In *Under Western Eyes,* Razumov's sin and salvation are secular; his are never considered sins against God; they are not even in their strict sense religious sins. Similarly, Nostromo's remorse of conscience is connected with his fears for his reputation; and Heyst's dilemma is purely one of personal decision. Jim, also, must get back into normal society through self-discovery and not

[11] Writing to the publisher Alfred A. Knopf a year after the serial publication of *Chance* (Jean-Aubry, II, 147, July 20, 1913), Conrad stressed what he considered his popular and human themes: "When it comes to popularity I stand much nearer the public mind than Stevenson, who was super-literary, a conscious virtuoso of style; whereas the average mind does not care much for virtuosity. My point of view, which is purely human, my subjects, which are not too specialized as to the class of people or kind of events, my style, which may be clumsy here and there, but is perfectly straight-forward and tending toward the colloquial, cannot possibly stand in the way of a large public. As to what I have to say —you know it is never outrageous to mind or feeling."

through prayer; his salvation, which is of this world, can come only when he redeems his sins of omission through self-sacrifice. If God exists, as Conrad (who received a Catholic burial) never denied, then He exists in the individual and not as an ambiguous force Whose ways man can never ascertain.

Despite his Catholic rearing, Conrad presents a view of man that is entirely secular;[12] for him, the universe was man-directed. Earlier in his work, nature had been paramount and its mysterious workings conveyed some of the qualities of an inscrutable God; but in this, his middle period, Conrad's emphasis was clearly on man as center, directing his own affairs and assuming final responsibility for his decisions. Man is, in a sense, autonomous; society does not make decisions for Razumov, Winnie Verloc, or the Captain ("The Secret Sharer"). Similarly, in their secularity, Flora can fall back only on herself; Captain Anthony is an egoistic knight, not a Christian gentleman; de Barral fails to ask for and receives no forgiveness—rather his bourgeois sense of invincibility hovers over the entire scene: "I am," he says, "the great Mr. de Barral"; the governess is motivated by selfishness with no

---

[12] Conrad was not vague about his feelings, for while writing to Edward Garnett about Tolstoy (*Letters,* pp. 244-5, February 23, 1914), he said: "Moreover, the base from which he starts—Christianity—is distasteful to me. I am not blind to its services but the absurd oriental fable from which it starts irritates me. Great, improving, softening, compassionate it may be but it has lent itself with amazing facility to cruel distortions and is the only religion which, with its impossible standards, has brought an infinity of anguish to innumerable souls—on this earth."

In another letter to Garnett (*Letters,* p. 185, December 22, 1902), he wrote: "It's strange how I always, from the age of fourteen, disliked the Christian religion, its doctrines, ceremonies, and festivals. . . . And the most galling feature is that nobody—not a single Bishop of them—believes in it. The business in the stable isn't convincing; whereas my atmosphere (vide reviews) can be positively breathed."

thought of heavenly retribution; and the Fynes live the good life in the sight of earthly rewards. Even Marlow, who assumes a large role as narrator and commentator, is completely a secular philosopher speculating, "between jest and earnest," about feminism, suicide, and the loneliness of individuals, while voicing the whole range of general ideas involved in mundane human relationships. By secularizing the matter of the novel, Conrad was carrying into English the freedom of the French novel. Along with James, he de-emphasized that amorphous sense of religious morality that had marked the nineteenth-century novel, a morality that was in essence a Christian morality responsible to a Christian God.

Carleon Anthony, the deceased poet of *Chance,* wrote voluminously of chivalrous Christian love; but his son, Captain Anthony, transformed chivalry into a compulsive "need for a woman"; and his daughter, Mrs. Fyne, advocated, as if in rebellion against her father's doctrine of womanly acquiescence, "that no consideration, no delicacy, no tenderness, no scruples should stand in the way of a woman. . . ." This view of course indicates self-reliance and independence. Consequently, although Marlow sardonically scorns this kind of feminism and pours contempt on female insincerity, Conrad has nevertheless broken from the idea of women placed according to a strict Christian morality. Flora's decision must be made from the standpoint of personal happiness and personal salvation. By choosing Anthony she selects sanity; the way of her father, she recognizes, is self-destructive. The very fact that she can embrace her husband while rejecting her father shows the cracks in the traditional family structure based on Christian precept. Each individual, Conrad stresses, must choose his own salvation.

Despite the conscious formalism of *Chance,* with its involved construction that seems strikingly contemporary, it is, rather, Conrad's humanization of his subject matter that marks a precedent for the secularity of several major contemporary novelists. By de-emphasizing the relation between man and some murky God or between men and an organized Christian morality, Conrad subscribed to an atomistic view of morality in which self-responsibility determines individual action. Not only does this view of personal morality cut deeply into twentieth-century literary ideas, but it is also close in its general notions to the philosophic existentialism theorized by Sartre and Camus. Conrad's ideas also in their way both parallel Gide's insistence on human liberty, leading into the latter's notion of the gratuitous act in which the individual is at his zenith of freedom, and give background to the work of Proust in which the individual with his recurring past is the very center of the only universe that counts.

Chance is surely not the sole novel for illustrating Conrad's secularity, but its heroine, Flora, is the best example of a completely helpless person turning inward, and not upward, for help. As a woman in a masculine world, she is far more helpless and isolated than a Jim or a Razumov; yet she finds the strength and the power within herself to salvage what remains of her life. Her moral conflicts are a matter of personal conscience.

Chance is, for all its trappings, thematically one of Conrad's most straightforward novels. As I have suggested before, the vast scaffolding of method is perhaps more distracting than edifying, more detrimental than constructive. Unlike, for example, the winding method of Faulkner's *Absalom, Absalom!*, the involutions of this Conrad novel often seem more like clutter than amplification. The only rationale for complicated construction is the inevitability of material that cannot be shaped another way. In parts of *Under Western Eyes* and *The Secret Agent*, the shape is the very stuff of the story, and the material allows no other method. *Chance*, on the other hand, ostensibly gains little from its tortured sequences. The structure often shows more difficulty than substance.

Illustrations of awkward and even miscalculated formal arrangements abound in this novel. Frequently, Conrad had to produce a witness for each scene, for *Chance* is told almost solely by its participants; but in order to maintain verisimilitude, it was necessary for a key figure to be present at all times, someone who could subsequently narrate what had passed. Halfway through the book there occurs that crucial scene between Flora and Captain Anthony in his hotel room, a scene at which no third person was present and, consequently, one that could not at this time be dramatized. Conrad could only speculate: "We may well wonder what happened when, after Fyne had left him [Anthony], the hesitating girl went up at last. . . ." Or, "It is conceivable he might have cried at her in the first moment of humiliation, of exasperation, 'Oh, it's you! Why are you here?'" Or, "And perhaps nothing was said." Although at a later time, Conrad did reproduce the scene through Marlow, the dramatic moment has been forever lost, and one of the fine climaxes of the story becomes part of a case history. The drama of the story in this case is secondary to the logical niceties of structure.

The reader is consequently more often preoccupied with the How and What of the novel—"How did Marlow know this? what is his source?"—than with the novel itself. The scene, for example, between de Barral and Anthony, in which the latter says he has willed everything to Flora, has no evident source. How does Marlow know of this? Certainly not from Anthony, and surely not from

Flora herself. Too often, a character like Franklin, the chief mate of the *Ferndale,* seems no more than a means of achieving the complicated apparatus; in this case, Franklin is necessary to give the relevant information about the first trip of the *Ferndale,* the voyage before Powell has joined the ship. Even the narrator Powell must be used for a further purpose, based on his sentimental attachment to the widowed Flora Anthony. Compare, on this point, the organic role of Mitchell, a narrator in *Nostromo;* as a survivor of the revolution he is its typically commonplace heir, and his complacency becomes an integral part of Conrad's irony. The various narrators of *Chance,* Marlow excepted, fulfill no such role, for in their hands the novel's machinery becomes oppressive. One is tempted to suggest that Conrad was coming close to a satire of the Conradian method.

The close designing of *Chance* and its melodramatic aspects are, as Paul Wiley has pointed out, in a direct line from Wilkie Collins and Dickens, perhaps closer to Dickens than has been sufficiently stressed. Consider, for example, the scene in which de Barral tries to poison Anthony; or Flora's recounting of her suicide attempt; or de Barral's somber exit from prison. The latter is described:

> Prisons are wonderful contrivances. Open-shut. Very neat. Shut-open. And out comes some sort of corpse, to wander awfully in a world in which it has no possible connections and carrying with it the appalling tainted atmosphere of its silent abode. Marvellous arrangement. It works automatically, and, when you look at it, the perfection makes you sick; which for a mere mechanism is no mean triumph.

Even Conrad's sense of caricature is often Dickensian, as in the following passage:

A gas bracket hung from the middle of the ceiling over a dark, shabby writing-desk covered with a litter of yellowish dusty documents. Under the flame of the single burner which made the place ablaze with light, a plump, little man was writing hard, his nose very near the desk. His head was perfectly bald and about the same drab tint as the papers. He appeared pretty dusty too.

With the confidence man de Barral hovering in the foreground and prison-like surroundings ever present in the background, this novel strongly reminds us of the gloomy scenes of *Little Dorrit*. The city background of *Chance*, as well as that of the earlier *The Secret Agent*, is in its grubby aspects never far from the London of Dickens' novels. Similarly, in his theme of the imprisoned heart which may either free itself or be broken, Conrad was following closely one of Dickens' favorite themes. After *Chance*, Conrad turned to another type of imprisoned heart, that of Axel Heyst, and in *Victory* wrote perhaps the best novel of his middle period.

chapter 7

Victory

O God, God,
How weary, stale, flat, and unprofitable
Seem to me all the uses of this world!
Fie on't, ah fie, 'tis an unweeded garden
That grows to seed, things rank and gross in nature
Possess it merely.

Hamlet, I, 2, 11. 132-37

With *Nostromo* and *Victory*,[1] Conrad felt he must stand or fall as a major novelist, as his remarks about the latter novel to Henry Seidel Canby bear out. While *Nostromo* for many years did not receive its just critical praise, *Victory* was from the beginning one of the critics' favorites, but rarely for those reasons we would now applaud. Hailing Conrad's power, his imagination, and his insight into the bizarre and the eccentric, the contemporary reviewers failed to see in *Victory* those social and political implications which give it major stature. Together with Mann's *The Magic Mountain*—a more fully wrought work which Conrad's novel resembles in many

[1] *Victory* was finished on May 29, 1914, according to Conrad, Preface, viii; on June 28, 1914, according to Jean-Aubry (II, 7). It was serialized in *Munsey's Magazine*, New York, LIV (February 1915), pp. 112-240, and reprinted in the *London Star*, August 24, 1915-November 9, 1915. *Victory* was dramatized by R. Macdonald Hastings and presented at the Globe Theatre. It has also been produced in the moving pictures. The first edition in 1915 appeared with this epigraph from *Comus*:
  "Calling shapes and beckoning shadows dire
  And airy tongues that syllable men's names
  On sands and shores and desert wilderness."

246

significant ways—*Victory* interprets several of the events
that foreshadowed the First World War. But lest *Victory*
become too closely identified with matters of war and
peace, we should point to its aesthetic significance and its
poetic nature, to its quality as "pure art," which harks
back to Shakespeare's *The Tempest*. It is not accidental
that Conrad's interest in Shakespeare's plays never appeared stronger than at this time.

Conrad's Note to the volume in the Collected Edition
gives few clues to its subject. Only in one respect does he
suggest a major theme, and that in his discussion of the
personality of Axel Heyst. Heyst, he says, "in his fine detachment had lost the habit of asserting himself"; Conrad
then continues in a general statement: "The habit of profound reflection, I am compelled to say, is the most per-
nicious of all the habits formed by the civilized man. . . ."
Heyst's flaw is his penchant for reflection, an "unbalance"
which, as in Greek tragedy, must lead to his undoing.
Heyst's attitude is a clear indication of certain late nine-
teenth- and early twentieth-century ideas, which strongly
imply that before 1914 man could make a pretense of detachment, but that, eventually, everyone must become involved in life. In Conrad's prophetic novel, Heyst's trouble
on the island amid the violence of the predatory Jones
and Ricardo is, so to speak, his own world war.

To bring together all the diverse elements of *Victory*,
Conrad used, in the figure of Axel Heyst, a human symbol
of large dimensions; analogously, in the novel's setting, in
its shifting chronology of narrative, and in its various
subsidiary symbols of sight and sound, Conrad has made
the book a model of arrangement and suggested meanings.

The problems entailed in the construction of both *Victory* and *Nostromo* were similar, and the beginning of **one**

recalls that of the other: each starts with a description that is organic and meaningful; each comes to its main figure indirectly and through the eyes of others; and in each the major themes of the novel are summed up in the first five or six pages. Such is the first chapter of *Victory,* which ends with the words, ". . . there was no reason to think that Heyst was in any way a fighting man." Then, the smoking volcano, ironically juxtaposed to Heyst in these pages, prefigures the sudden violence that is to engulf him and Lena. Beginning *in medias res,* the reader comes to Heyst in the same way that reality catches up with this "Hamlet of the South Seas."

From the hints thrown out in the first chapter, Conrad moves in ever larger concentric circles while developing his main character and introducing episodically the derelict Morrison, the innkeeper Schomberg and his wife, the omnipresent Davidson, and, through recurring references, the much-persecuted Lena. For the first sixty-two pages— Part One of the novel—we see Heyst only indirectly. Built up and filled in by seemingly scattered details, Heyst comes to the reader just as Nostromo earlier, but with this difference: Heyst's activities *are* the center of a book which directly or indirectly he dominates in a way that Nostromo does not dominate *Nostromo.* What Heyst does and thinks determines *Victory* on all its levels at once. He is the central figure as well as the central symbol. *Victory,* therefore, seems a more unified book. With a single basic situation—capable though it is of great extension—*Victory* has none of the problematical development of the more diverse *Nostromo.* In four hundred pages, Conrad was able to develop the novel fully. Its melodramatic coda aside, *Victory* ends when it must, with Heyst's recognition of the active role he should have played in the human scene. There amid the wreckage that he has helped create, he finally recognizes Lena's triumph as the victory that has regenerated even while destroying him. The rest is truly silence.

I I

Part One of *Victory* provides the sources and materials of the novel, Part Two, so to speak, the novel itself. In the first part Conrad was careful to account for his sources, while in the second and succeeding parts he assumed the role of omniscient narrator. The chapters, like those in the long *Anna Karenina,* are short and deceptively convey the sense of a less lengthy novel. Conrad, despite continued verbal opposition to Russian writers, had their method of elaboration—a delving into attendant and antecedent circumstances to produce the effect of power, not speed. This is, in fact, one of Conrad's major developments from *Almayer's Folly* through *Nostromo* and *Victory.* The images themselves take on a precise and calculated effect, as Conrad shows his ability to work imaginatively within a tightly-knit frame of reference. Entirely applicable to *Victory* are his later remarks on matters of form:

> I am a man of formed character. Certain conclusions remain immovably fixed in my mind, but I am no slave to prejudices and formulas, and I shall never be. My attitude to subjects and expressions, the angles of vision, my methods of composition will, within limits, be always changing—not because I am unstable or unprincipled but because I am free. Or perhaps it may be more exact to say, because I am always trying for freedom—within my limits.

"Within limits" describes the form of *Victory,* for it is by means of a strict formal arrangement that Conrad was able to shift the novel from one point of view to another, from the generality of the opening to the particularity of Heyst, and then finally to Lena, who comes to assume a central and pivotal role.

This circling method suits Heyst, for in his incapacity for attachment he himself literally circles: the method and the man are one. Lena, too, is only reached obliquely, and although Conrad writes more directly of her than of Heyst, she is, as well, "circled" and "found out" piece by piece. In the early chapters, Conrad went back into Heyst's past and by means of short narrative portions began to fill in, but as he progressed toward the reader's present, the chapters lengthen considerably and slow up the pace of the novel. There is frequent juxtaposition of two different times in the past or of past with present time; so that Heyst as he was and Heyst as he is, are both simultaneously before the reader. Heyst is reconstructed historically by the omniscient author at the same time Heyst's contemporaries are commenting upon his present activities—all this before we have met him in his own right on the island with Lena. We have Conrad narrating Heyst's past, we have Heyst in relation to his father, we have Schomberg slandering the now departed Heyst; in addition, while we know that Lena and Heyst have already run off together, in the foreground of the novel they have only met. Intensified in six pages (Chapter 3 of Part 2), this story within a story continues with additional sequences and digressions until Part 3 of the novel. By this time, the reader has met Heyst in all his possibilities: as a detached creature of the past caught in a human situation, responsible through his own efforts for a helpless girl who is completely dependent upon him.

The method of the novel, then, posits a conflict between events of the past and those of the present, just as

Heyst's problem—the overt theme of the book—is a personal conflict between dictates of the past and necessities of the present. By catching Heyst in a narrative sequence circling between present and past, Conrad was able to suggest technically the two nodes of Heyst's behavior, and to make narrative method an organic part of the novel's theme. How much more significant the narrative involutions of *Victory* than of *Chance,* with its superficial complexities!

The sympathetic relationship between Heyst and his father is especially important for the novel's social and political theme. The elder Heyst had tried to sustain a form of idealism that constantly ran counter to reality. Unlike Stein, the elder Heyst could not live by means of illusions while tacitly doubting their existence. Axel is a true offspring of that silent advocate of "Look on—make no sound"; long buried with the father is a substantial part of the son. Retreating into himself, Axel tried, like Villiers' Axel, to avoid the compromising contamination of human matter. But unlike Villiers' Axel, he even disbelieves in the efficacy of spiritual perfection; his despair is secular, heaven holds no reward and hell no punishment for his disenchantment. What is not dust is ashes; love is vanity, and attachment is momentary weakness. The pure life, the perfect life, is not for him a positive ordering of virtuous acts, but a complete negation of action.

This spirit of withdrawal should be stressed, particularly that influenced by the elder Heyst, for it extends from the individual to society at large. Thomas Mann once remarked about *The Magic Mountain* what can also be said of *Victory:* that each character in the book is a person and yet symbolically each is more than himself; and that Hans Castorp in his double role as individual and as society must go, Mann says, "through the deep experience of sickness and death to arrive at a higher sanity and health; in just the same way that one must have a knowledge of sin in order to find redemption." So Heyst must be chastened into realization. The narrative of his chastening is the allegory of an age that chose detachment in the face of violence. Heyst realizes, though too late to save himself, that immersion in the realities of life may indeed be melancholy advice, but it is, nevertheless, the only way to survival.

On another level, Heyst's conflict within himself is a dramatization of certain obvious aesthetic ideas—the role every artist faces of a life of social consciousness versus a life of "pure art." Conrad was concerned with the problem of art for itself as early as the Preface to *The Nigger* when he attempted to divorce the serious artist from the ivory tower by demonstrating that devotion to craft transcends any temporary formula of so-called pure art. "In that uneasy solitude," he said, "the supreme cry of Art for Art itself, loses the exciting ring of its apparent immorality." Writing in the summer of 1914, Henry James in *The Ivory Tower,* asked the same question: whether a person of Graham Fielder's sensitivity can survive in the corruption and insensitivity of his day. Fielder's is responsible detachment, we are led to believe, for his achievements are yet to come, no doubt in literary accomplishment. But like Heyst who cannot come to terms with life, Fielder is unable to exist in a predatory and moneyed background; and just as Heyst, realizing his incapacity, destroys himself, so James, recognizing Fielder's bleak future, perhaps "destroyed" the novel by not completing it. Both Fielder and Heyst sensed the bleakness and mercilessness that are behind the great possessions of the world, and unable to abide the world, they chose to leave it. When violence does come to Heyst,

his defenses cannot be changed, and unlike Prospero he
has no magic wand to do his bidding.

The reference to *The Tempest* is not fortuitous. Conrad
had always shown a close awareness of Shakespeare not
only by using epigraphs from three plays,[2] but also by the
repetition of certain cadences and by early experiments
with blank verse prose. It is well known, through Conrad's
own words in *A Personal Record*, that he carried a volume of Shakespeare's plays during his twenty years of sea
voyages; it might be added that Jim brings a copy of
Shakespeare with him into the jungle. We also know that
Conrad read A. C. Bradley's *Shakespearean Tragedy* a
few months before he finished *Victory*. Conrad first became aware of Shakespeare's work as a child in his father's personal library and read at least *The Two Gentlemen
of Verona* in the proofs of his father's translation into
Polish. In the years from 1913 to 1915, the references to
Shakespeare reached their peak. In *Chance*, for example,
Conrad reverted to a Desdemona-Othello-Iago triangle as
background for the trio of Flora-Anthony-de Barral. He
says of Captain Anthony: "With his beard cut to a point,
his swarthy, sunburnt complexion, thin nose and his lean
head there was something African, something Moor-
ish. . . ." And then later, Conrad describes Captain Anthony as: ". . . swarthy as an African, by the side of
Flora whiter than the lilies. . . ."; while menacing all is
de Barral, the Iago of the piece, who tries unsuccessfully
to poison the mind of Flora. The *Othello* references add
another aspect to *Chance* without of course forcing the
similarity.

In the volume after *Victory*, *Within the Tides* (1915),

[2] *Tales of Unrest* (1898): *Henry IV*, Second Part, IV, 5, 213 ff. *Nostromo*
(1904): *King John*, IV, 2, 108. *Within the Tides* (1915): *Hamlet*, III,
2, 43-44.

the epigraph is from *Hamlet*, but without any appreciable application to this volume of stories. The epigraph from *Hamlet* perhaps would have been more appropriate to *Victory*, for Heyst and Hamlet in their common plight have certain similarities that should not, however, be forced. An early reviewer called Heyst a veritable South Seas Hamlet, but essentially a Hamlet of our days, and this remark was later repeated by James Huneker in his appreciative chapter on Conrad in *Ivory Apes and Peacocks*. In the common tensions of Hamlet and Heyst between detachment and involvement, between a destructive idealism and a violent reality, and between the pulls of the past and present which each tries to synthesize, the two figures must face similar problems in a way that eventually proves fatal to both. In the carnage that clears the stages of *Hamlet* and *Victory*, the protagonist of each succumbs to the forces of destruction. The melancholy Swede perhaps speaks for the early twentieth century as much as the melancholy Dane speaks for Elizabethans three hundred years before.

In the relationship between Heyst and Lena, his own sacrificial Ophelia, many critics have seen numerous and diverse implications: the Adam and Eve interpretation by M. C. Bradbrook, in *Joseph Conrad: Poland's English Genius* (1941), in which Heyst and Lena are betrayed by evil but withal dignified by their strength of rectitude and their power of love; the view of Dorothy Hoare, in *Some Studies in the Modern Novel* (1938), that the innocence of Lena and Heyst is both destructive and regenerative; the Faustian interpretation given by Alice Raphael, in *Goethe The Challenger* (1932), who sees in Heyst, Lena, and Jones the Faust, Margaret, and Mephistopheles of the twentieth century.

Continuing, however, in the line of possible Shakespearean influences, there is also a fourth dimension: *Victory,* as Conrad's last major work, has in it many of the qualities of *The Tempest,* an idyll—though not Edenesque— which is suddenly invaded by violence, deceit, and dissembling outer-worlders; as it were, a literary farewell in which peace finally comes after violence. Lacking magic, Heyst must call upon his own resources, which are unable to respond; and so, unlike Prospero, he cannot command the scene. However, while differing in their respective abilities to reach decisions and to carry them out, both the weary Heyst and the aging Prospero possess an emphatic awareness of self. Both see in foreign intrusion a blow at personal equilibrium, and both find their existing worlds too heinous for participation. The result for each is a way of life in which self is supreme, in which important decisions are minimized or postponed, and in which peace can be obtained only by evading action. As Prospero must protect Miranda, so Heyst is responsible for Lena; but while Prospero through magic can hold in abeyance the uncivilized Caliban and the civilized intruders, Heyst is unable to handle either the savage Pedro or his perverse masters. After the violence has ended, Prospero is left to live in peace and quiet, while Heyst, ineffectual and surely a failure, dies, although, it must be recognized, with his dignity intact.

In Heyst, Conrad delineated possibly his most poignant character and his most significant human symbol. When we talk of Conrad's experiments with the novel, we must always take into account his characters, who suggest much in twentieth-century life and literature. Heyst is still attractive, perhaps because of his very ineffectuality and not despite it. As a symbol of anti-power and anti-action, he becomes in his world-weariness a strong reminder of everyman's desire to escape social pressures and to be himself, despite the nagging knowledge that this is impossible of attainment.

III

Much as Heyst dominates the material of *Victory*, he is by no means the sole figure of interest. Conrad was able to move away from Heyst frequently, for example to Jones and Ricardo or to Lena, because each one partakes of a psychological segment of Heyst himself. Technically, Conrad was repeating his use of doubles in *Lord Jim*, *Nostromo*, and *Under Western Eyes*. Through this technique, the principal character hovers over the scene as a spiritual or psychological presence even when physically absent. By means of a carefully worked-out system of character shifting, Conrad maintained the unity of *Victory*.

In the fourth part of *Victory*, the narrative distinctly shifts from Heyst to Lena in the foreground of action. By the time the situation on the island has been fully developed, Lena is the center of the novel, and everyone except her in one way or another is being deluded: (1) Heyst himself is being misled by Lena concerning Ricardo; (2) Jones, duped by his man-servant, Ricardo, does not know of Lena's presence on the island; (3) Ricardo does not know of Lena's double-dealing, that she is using him as part of a scheme to protect Heyst; (4) and Wang, Heyst's servant, believes Lena is betraying his master by secret meetings with Ricardo. Only Lena is in full possession of the truth, and all threads of action emanate from her. Her decisions, then, determine the outcome of the book, for by now it has been fairly well established that Heyst can and will do nothing.

The shift from Heyst to Lena under different conditions

could have been disastrous to the direction of the novel; but here any loss of continuity is not noticed, so subtle and effective are Conrad's devices. This continuity is accomplished through the sustained presentation of character doubles. If, for example, we return to Heyst's relationship to Morrison, the man with the grandiose business ideas, we find a partnership in which the passive Heyst temporarily saves the penniless Morrison. Although Morrison eventually dies a failure, he is infinitely grateful to Heyst, who becomes heir to the Tropical Belt Coal Company. Morrison, now long dead, comes to Lena's mind through Schomberg, who suggests that Heyst killed his partner for gain, hearsay that Lena as Heyst's new partner is prone to believe. In her new situation, she quickly identifies with Morrison and sees the two of them as "representatives of all the past victims of the Great Joke." When Heyst tells of Morrison being cornered, of his needing help and getting down on his knees to beg, she asks, with herself in mind, " 'You didn't make fun of him for that?' " And then shortly later she says, " 'You saved a man for fun—is that what you mean? Just for fun?' " Heyst immediately disclaims any fun, but he regrets that in a moment of inadvertence he had created for himself a responsibility, feeling that " 'he who forms a tie is lost. The germ of corruption has entered into his soul.' " Heyst's short meeting with Morrison, a relationship that in itself is only of importance in passing, is used by Conrad to generate intense feelings in the more important Heyst-Lena relationship. Through Lena's persistent identification with Morrison, one side of her ambivalent feelings toward Heyst is presented tangibly and dramatically.

But Conrad worked laterally as well as vertically. The Morrison-Lena-Heyst relationship broadens as Lena is complemented by the predatory Ricardo and Heyst by the abnormal Jones. Within certain ethical and moral considerations, Lena and Ricardo are evidently dissimilar, but through their particular juxtaposition in the novel, they meet undeniably on psychological grounds. It is Ricardo who recognizes what he thinks is a basic similarity when he says to her: " 'You and I are made to understand each other. Born alike, bred alike, I guess. You are not tame. Same here! You have been chucked out into this rotten world of 'ypocrites. Same here!' " Earlier, he had roused her feelings of insecurity by seizing on Heyst's rumored treatment of Morrison, a recurring presentiment to Lena of what she still fears from Heyst. But Lena with her sharper sense of ethics recognizes in Ricardo the same embodiment of evil and vileness that has always attended her; for without Heyst, she realizes, she would be prey for the likes of Ricardo all her life. In one way, then, if only to disprove any further identification with Ricardo, she is spurred to her fierce defense of Heyst, who thus far is the first to show belief in her worth.

The other doubles—Heyst and Jones—are even more subtly complementary to each other. Their superficial similarities—the emphasis on both as gentlemen, for example—are preceded by their sharp psychological identification, more so perhaps than any other related pair in Conrad. Again, it is Jones, like Ricardo with Lena, who recognizes the similarity; he has said to Heyst: " 'We pursue the same ends . . . only perhaps I pursue them with more openness than you—with more simplicity.' " Though Jones misreads Heyst as a fellow confidence man, he acutely senses a psychological affinity. The same type of psychological condition that existed in *The Secret Agent* between the criminals and police is here reduplicated in the attitudes of Jones and Heyst. Each in his way expects

a certain given world, in Jones' case to permit him to
operate as a confidence man, in Heyst's to allow him detachment without danger of interference. Both presup-
pose a society which will leave them to their own courses
of action. Similarly, each is literally "on his own," insisting on freedom of action, each a rugged individualist
choosing to act or not to act as personal wishes dictate.
Both view the world in a certain light, as a shabby affair
which is best left alone on its own terms. So Heyst and
Jones agree on several common assumptions, as the latter
commented above, although they disagree evidently on the
course of action each chooses for himself.

When they meet they do so as representatives of two
distinct cultures which differ in many essentials while
overlapping in basic psychologies. Jones' constant physical illness, similar in some ways to Wait's in *The Nigger of
the "Narcissus,"* emphasizes his mental perversity; sexually he is incapable of normal intercourse and possibly he
disdains all kinds of sexual contact, although the evidence
for his being homosexual is strongly presented.[3] Albert
Guerard, Jr. astutely compares Jones to Faulkner's Popeye
as two studies in psychological perversity. Surely, Jones'
illness is of a symbolic nature, manifesting a psychological
condition that has festered in society. His illness of mind
and body—made visible by his sick body—complements
the "sick soul" of Heyst, embodied though it is in a broad

[3] Conrad emphasizes that even the mention of women makes Jones ill,
and the sight of a woman is more than he can bear (pp. 102, 117). Ricardo says the girls in Mexico would ask if Jones was "'a monk in disguise, or if he had taken a vow to the *santissima madre* not to speak to a
woman or whether————.'" (p. 160). The missing word by inference is,
of course, homosexual. Conrad stresses Jones' pencilled eyebrows (pp.
111, 384), mentions that he had once picked up a "bare-legged boy" (p.
151), and then has Jones almost identify himself when he says to Heyst,
"'Something has driven you out—the originality of your ideas, perhaps.
Or your tastes.'" (p. 378).

and robust frame. Jones' physical weakness is a counterpart of Heyst's incapacity to act, and his sickness of mind
a complement of Heyst's undeveloped social sense. Each
one is less than a fully developed man, and together they
suggest many of the human ills of pre-World War I
Europe.

Pursuing this scheme of doubles in *Victory*—which
like a network of delicate branches spreads throughout
the novel—we have seen how Conrad worked back and
forth and introduced similar psychological types, those
of Morrison-Lena, Morrison-Heyst, Lena-Ricardo, and
Heyst-Jones.[4] The most important pair of doubles—the
pair that finally permitted Conrad to shift the latter part
of the novel without disturbing the reader—is of course
that of Lena and Heyst. Although Lena feels, while Heyst
can only be sincere, she nevertheless willingly effaces herself to gain her goal, which is to find dignity through love.
Heyst similarly effaces himself to maintain his dignity,
but his goal—psychologically akin to hers—is to lose
himself in shadows. Each becomes selfless, each is influenced by society rather than influencing others. Each
wants to get out of the world, Lena to prevent further
hurts, Heyst to avoid further contacts. Each is apart, pre-
ferring silence to speech, although, paradoxically, Lena's
graceful speaking voice is one of her great assets.

If Heyst has godlike characteristics, as one critic claims,
and like a mythological god is purified by an expiation
ritual, then Lena, too, has a supra-surface role which fits

[4] The third member of the morbid trio that invades the island retreat is
Pedro, an ape-like relic of a pre-civilized age. He is not evil, for evil implies a notion of good, a condition to which Pedro could never attain.
Yet in physical brutality he becomes the island counterpart of the mentally brutal Schomberg on shore; Pedro, uncivilized and brutal, Schomberg, civilized but evil. In their own ways, both operate far below the
level of human intelligence.

the story of redemption. When Heyst asks Lena her name, she says that she is called Alma, also Magdalen, although she does not know why. As her first name, Alma, implies, she manifests certain soul-like qualities—the soul of Heyst is Lena; and as Magdalen she can be saved by Heyst from whoredom. Lena is the living side of Heyst; through her identification with Morrison, there recurs the same vein of helplessness that drew Heyst to his former partner. She comes to represent Heyst's concession to society at large; to "save" her he must ask himself new questions and find new answers. By attaching himself to her, he recognizes a hitherto darkened side of his psychological make-up, an aspect continually discouraged in his father's training. She is, curiously, his ordeal.

Lena, despite her surface weaknesses, can act and react in a way impossible for Heyst. Coming as she does already partially identified through psychological similarities to Morrison, Ricardo, Heyst himself, and even Jones, she can be accepted in the novel as a powerful figure who acts intuitively on what she knows and feels. Her smoothly-worked assumption of the pivotal role—wherein she is the only one to understand the various aspects of the situation—is, then, a technical as well as human achievement.

Through sustained doubling, Conrad conveyed verbally and formally a unity of structure which marks *Victory* perhaps more than any other of his novels. In a novel that appeared ten years later, Virginia Woolf's *Mrs. Dalloway* (1925), we find a broad and sustained psychological doubling between the titular character and the mentally disturbed Septimus, a doubling that unifies the book more than any verbalization. Numerous other modern novelists—notably Joyce—have made wide use of this device which, although not of course beginning with

Conrad, was consciously and deliberately shaped by him into a special technique. Many of Conrad's effective techniques, including psychological doubling, are no more than assiduous application of principles expressed in the Preface to *The Nigger* and worked out in collaboration with Ford. Trying always to get beyond surface realism, Conrad strove to develop techniques which would broaden his longer works. Verbal irony was not enough —although this element was never far from a Conrad novel—if it were not meshed with a technical apparatus that could be, as he said, "the secret spring of responsive emotions."

I V

I mentioned above the book by Alice Raphael, *Goethe The Challenger*, in which she persuasively placed *Victory* as the Faust of our generation. This novel, she says, is as much a criticism of later nineteenth-century life as Goethe's was of late eighteenth. According to her interpretation, the eighteenth century reflected in *Faust* sowed the seeds of its own destruction in the same sense that the nineteenth century, reflected in *Victory,* brought about its own frustrations by refusing to accept the logical consequences of its acts. Through this reasoning, Heyst and Jones are equated with Faust and Mephistopheles, and the innocent Lena and Margaret respectively are sacrificed to their selfishness. Now any extended comparison of the two works would of course prove fruitless; the differences are too numerous: Jones as a *fin-de-siècle* Mephisto surely does not contain the variety of Goethe's creation; obviously his shallowness is too patent; Heyst is early Faust, the diligent student and detached viewer, certainly not the later *bon vivant* who seeks after freedom and pleasure with abandon; and the "sacrificed" Lena is too active and too self-willed for her similarity to Margaret to be more than superficial. Nevertheless, this juxtaposition, despite its recognizable superficiality, does suggest new potentialities in *Victory* and does bring into relation some of the novel's component elements. The comparison with *Faust*, if nothing more, gives greater historical range to Conrad's novel and moves *Victory* from a study of individuals solely to the study of an age.

In his choice of setting, for example, Conrad was evidently attempting to convey an instance of individual struggle that is nonetheless universal. The "paradisiacal" island to which Heyst and Lena retreat is something less than Eden and something closer to a symbol of Heyst's own desiccated spirit. What the pair try to hold onto is simply a place to live, a place which in its darker sides contains an innate ugliness, an innate threat to happiness. From Davidson's point of view, the loneliness and ruined aspect of the island are evident:

> That black jetty, sticking out of the jungle into the empty sea; these roof-ridges of deserted houses peeping dismally above the long grass! Ough! The gigantic and funereal blackboard sign of the Tropical Belt Coal Company, still emerging from a wild growth of bushes like an inscription stuck above a grave figured by the tall heap of unsold coal at the shore end of the wharf, added to the general desolation.

The heap of coal dust, the ghostly rails laid down by the company, and the dirt of abandoned offices and bungalows all visibly detract from an earthly paradise. Long before Jones and Ricardo have arrived on the island, Conrad's description suggests something different from an Eden which is disturbed by intruders. He suggests that the desolation on the island, mixed as it is with the purely idyllic, is a condition of life, and that even without the predatory violence of Jones and Ricardo, existence in itself is full of threatening shadows.

Arriving at human conclusions through natural description was a mainstay of Conrad's method from *Almayer's Folly* through *The Rover* thirty years later. One remarks Conrad's use of storm symbolism, seen before in *Under Western Eyes* and *An Outcast of the Islands*, where he was trying to suggest, however obviously, certain complex emotions through the violence of nature. Frequently his settings are in purpose not unlike the scene on the heath in *King Lear*. In *Victory* itself, as Heyst and Lena go toward dinner with Jones, what is for them literally a last supper, the storm rumbles incessantly, and "pale lightning in waves of cold fire flooded and ran off the island in rapid succession." Similarly, while Jones and Heyst face each other and fence for position, the "muffled thunder resembled the echo of a distant cannonade," and "like the growl of an inarticulate giant muttering fatuously" it is fitting accompaniment for the life and death struggle on the island. Shortly after, the "angry modulation" of the thunder curls its way, ironically, around the framed profile of Heyst's father, a man who had tried to avoid thunder all his life, and who now can only look on severely as his son becomes involved in personal struggle. When Lena's victory is complete and her love has triumphed over death, the thunder ceases to growl, for "the world of material forms shuddered no more under the emerging stars." Admittedly, this type of symbolic accompaniment is superficial; but taken together with the dramatic situation, it realizes the scene. The noise of the thunder is the noise of Heyst's own war, and when it finally rumbles to a halt no one is left to enjoy the clearing skies.

The victory of the title, as Conrad emphasized in the Author's Note, is surely Lena's. Her sacrifice, in this sense like Margaret's in *Faust,* forces Heyst to recognize the inadequacy of his personal philosophy. In his last words to Davidson, he confesses that a man is cursed whose "heart has not learned while young to hope, to love—and to put his trust in life!" In short, to follow Stein's advice in *Lord Jim.* The social significance of his words is plain, for, as William Bancroft comments, Heyst is a living example of Donne's proposition that no man is an island unto himself, and that human solidarity must often take precedence over the individual will. For as Heyst attempts expiation through death by fire, the storm fully subsides, Lena's voice is stilled, Ricardo's knife and Jones' gun are useless, and the growls of the ape-like Pedro have been muted. The stage has been cleared; only the knightly Davidson holds the field, and the rest is truly nothing.

As a small-scale *Faust* for the nineteenth- and twentieth-centuries, *Victory* prophesies that a head-on meeting of the two ages will result in violent destruction for both; but along the way the novel makes clear that moral courage in confronting difficulty is finer than complete withdrawal, and that a satisfactory life for the philosopher, the artist, or even for the man with no pretensions to greatness must include participation and involvement. So Heyst must be chastened into realization, just as Faust had to recognize the depth of his sin before Goethe allowed him to be redeemed.

V

Any extended analysis of *Victory* must eventually come around to a discussion of its aesthetically unsatisfactory ending. If Heyst were an artist finally realizing in his last words to Davidson the necessity of an active life, surely he would have been embarrassed by the dramatization of his conflict as Conrad presented it. Perhaps the ending of *Victory* is no worse than that of *Nostromo, Under Western Eyes,* and *Chance,* but admittedly it suddenly transforms the novel from noble tragedy into trite melodrama. Exactly as *Under Western Eyes* loses its impetus after Razumov's dramatic confession to Miss Haldin, so *Victory* ends its dramatic thrust with Lena's triumphant death. As described in the John Quinn catalogue, the first typed copy of the *Victory* MS is complete to the end of the next to last chapter; a typed line of asterisks indicates that possibly Conrad intended to terminate the story with the death of Lena. What happened, however, between the MS and the completed novel is not known.

After Lena's death, Davidson's five-page summation, while accounting for everybody in a neat package, relates much information that is extraneous. It is true that some of Davidson's commentary is necessary, also that Heyst's last words and tragic end are necessary for the narrative; but even if this is granted, Conrad's specific form of summary destroys the rhythm of a study in feeling while temporarily creating the aura of a thriller, in which what happens becomes more important than how and why it happened.

Conrad had always emphasized the How of a subject, the treatment that invests content with what he called the "potentiality of almost infinite suggestion," as much as he had strongly de-emphasized the What, the facts which he felt were the common property of every writer. He shrewdly recognized that his special skill lay in his power of "infinite suggestion," and his major novels bear him out. Conrad is least significant when the What—the diligent working out of story detail—predominates, when his power of suggestion is secondary to surface action.

Conrad's endings—which stress the working out of surface action—might well have been matters of expediency. Ford himself suggested that Conrad "would abandon some of his aims in order to ease the strain of writing." The ending of *Victory*, with the loyal Davidson straddling the scene, is surely at variance with the complexity and variety of its earlier scenes. Conrad's usual "thickness" of method and his ability to create intricate situations contrast with the thin summary and hasty stage cleaning of his final chapter. Possibly by minimizing method in the novel proper, Conrad might have made his ending seem less frivolous and more organic; but then the novel itself would perhaps have been sacrificed for the sake of consistency.

Despite his marked modernity, Conrad was unable to forgo traditional end-cleaning, that accounting for all characters and that tying together of all situations which marked the Victorian novel. But its flaws notwithstanding, *Victory* remains the last of his major works, a work that even with its melodramatic ending endures dignified and significant. After *Victory*, the surface action of Conrad's novels tended to predominate, as his power of suggestion waned and flickered out.[5]

[5] Conrad's ambivalence in handling Lena—often making her act more masculine than the male characters themselves—fits Moser's theory and is further developed by Dr. Bernard Meyer: that Conrad's inability to confront his own hatred and fear of women can help explain the weakness of his later work, concerned as that is with love, marriage, and sex.

chapter 8

Late Conrad

Why is my verse so barren of new pride,
So far from variation or quick change?
Why with the time do I not glance aside
To new-found methods and to compounds strange?

No, Time, thou shalt not boast that I do change:
Thy pyramids built up with newer might
To me are nothing novel, nothing strange;
They are but dressings of a former sight.

Shakespeare,
Sonnets 76, 123

This book has been concerned to some extent with Conrad's experiments with technique and form as they "created" part of the meanings of his individual works. After 1914, however, Conrad's "technical discovery" slackened considerably, as he returned to the more conservative methods of his early novels. Since technical invention in his work was often allied with aesthetic excellence, his later fiction manifests a thinness of substance that becomes evident when placed beside the fiction of his rich middle period. Nevertheless, granting that the later fiction is indeed a letdown after the profundity of *Victory*, it is still of great importance as a mirror of the established, but exhausted, novelist, who, no longer able to experiment, had to draw upon all his practical skill to produce five more novels.

Many reasons, all speculative, could be advanced for

the directness of Conrad's later style: advancing age that possibly brought with it a clearer vision and an accompanying simplicity of technique; or, a steady loss of conceptual power; or, the desire to appeal to larger audiences on their terms; or, a growing inability to turn waning personal experiences into imaginative fiction. Even when young, Conrad had complained of the thinness of his memories; he frequently remarked that he was fearful of depleting his literary material once his "souvenirs from the past" had slipped away. It is not surprising, therefore, to find in his later work—that of the last ten years of his life—an even heavier reliance than usual on past personal experience. Many of the later novels and long stories—*The Arrow of Gold, The Shadow Line,* and *The Rescue* among others—are either almost direct reproductions of personal experiences or thinly veiled restatements of earlier material and methods. How different this work is from *Nostromo, Victory, Under Western Eyes,* and *The Secret Agent,* all of which were imaginatively created from the merest of suggestions or from the slightest of personal adventures! This is not to say that Conrad could not imaginatively reshape direct personal experience into an art form—"Heart of Darkness" would disprove that theory—but frequently before he could play the verbal alchemist, he needed an elaborate formal method to gain aesthetic distance. The point is that the later work shows a smothering of method owing either to Conrad's refusal or inability to turn personal material into conscious art forms.

By the time of publication of *Within the Tides* in 1915,[1]

---

[1] London: Dent, 1915; New York: Doubleday, 1916. "The Planter of Malata," *Metropolitan,* XL (June-July 1914), written toward the end of 1913; "The Partner," *Harper's Magazine,* CXXIII (November 1911), written in the summer of 1910; "The Inn of Two Witches," *Metropolitan,*

Conrad had found a popular audience with *Chance* and *Victory*. In 1911, he had received a Civil List pension of one hundred pounds through the efforts of Edmund Gosse, William Rothenstein, and John Galsworthy, and this taken together with his new reading public considerably reduced his financial worries. The four stories in *Within the Tides*, with the exception of "The Planter of Malata," were written prior to *Chance* and *Victory*; "The Planter," in fact, was composed toward the end of 1913 during a break from the labors on *Victory*.

The stories comprising this volume are among Conrad's weakest, and we have to go back to the lightweight *A Set of Six* (1908) or look ahead to the posthumous *Tales of Hearsay* (1925) to find their equal. Only "The Planter of Malata" warrants attention, and then solely for its chief character, Renouard, who in certain personal characteristics is akin to Axel Heyst and Decoud. Conrad himself thought rather well of *Within the Tides;* writing to Lady Wedgwood, he said: ". . . but I cherish a particular feeling for that volume as a deliberate attempt on four different methods of telling a story,—an essay in craftsmanship which of course the public won't notice. . . ." [2] The craftsmanship, however, is lost in the slightness of the stories, and Conrad should not have expected his readers and critics to take them seriously as examples of his technical skill.

XXXVIII (May 1913), *Pall Mall*, 1913, written in the winter of 1912; "Because of the Dollars" (appeared as "Laughing Anne"), *Metropolitan*, XL (September 1914), written in the winter of 1912.

[2] Jean-Aubry, II, 168, January, 1915. As to the four methods: "The Planter" is narrated directly by an omniscient observer; "The Inn" is narrated from a MS which contains the story; "The Partner" contains a frame and a flashback within which four personal sources are responsible for the material; and "Because of the Dollars" is related by a narrator who had personally participated in some of the action of the story.

I remarked before that the epigraph from *Hamlet* attached to this volume—". . . go, make you ready."— would have been more appropriate to *Victory* and to Heyst in particular. However, Geoffrey Renouard, the planter of the initial story, has several qualities in common with Heyst. As a detached and isolated person, he finds that his life must follow a course of solitude and resignation. Renouard deliberately cultivates his apartness and his ability to forsake the desires of other men. Looking inward, he can find only self-love until he sees Felicia Moorsom, who "seemed to give a new meaning to life." His detachment manifestly lessens as her indifference becomes steadily more evident. For she, unable to believe in any man, seeks her fiancé Arthur merely as a salve for her own conceit. Her dream, as Renouard suggests, is to influence a human destiny; a man's happiness is not her goal. Recognizing defeat and incapable of drawing on his own depleted resources, Renouard swims out beyond the confines of life.[3]

The relationship between Renouard and Miss Moorsom, especially in its emphasis upon morbid motives, shows that Conrad was well able to explore the byways of the psychoneurotic mind. In Renouard, slight though the execution is in this story, Conrad presented another of his tortured personalities, a man who, while destroying

---

[3] Decoud's feelings for Antonia Avellanos come to mind, but Antonia is admirable and high-minded, while Felicia is egocentric and shallow. Renouard's relationship to Felicia also looks ahead, as Paul Wiley has pointed out, to that of Lingard and Edith Travers in *The Rescue* (1920). In some ways analogous to this is the Willems-Aïssa affair, although Willems, unlike the others, is a disreputable character. Conrad seemed obsessed by certain relationships which undermined a man and made him unable to function, or at best caused him to function below his usual competence. Perhaps Conrad was ever the seaman who looked askance at those land entanglements which are manifest in an attachment to a woman.

belief, also destroys his ability to come to terms with life. Although Renouard rarely attains stature because of the commonplace presentation of the story, we must note that his brooding type of personality, in different settings, has become a commonplace of twentieth-century literature.

II

Just before the outbreak of the World War, Conrad began a long journey (on July 24, 1914) to his native Poland, and only escaped internment for the duration through the intervention of Mr. Frederick C. Penfield, the American ambassador at Vienna. His Polish impressions were subsequently recorded in four articles written for the *Daily Mail* and later included in *Notes on Life and Letters* (1921). Shortly after his return from Poland via Austria and Italy, Conrad began *The Shadow Line*, which he completed by the end of 1915. The book appeared two years later.[4]

Dedicated to his son, Borys, who was serving at the front in the British Army, and written in memory of all youth who had passed the shadow line of maturity through duty, discipline, and fidelity to idea, the book in substance, as Conrad explains in the Author's Note, is very close to his own experience. Originally thought of as "First Command," *The Shadow Line* is a personal reminiscence which becomes a near allegory of man's victory in the face of adversity. The first-page quotation from Baudelaire—". . .—D'autres fois, calme plat, grande mirroir [sic]/ De mon désespoir"—suggests that to cross the shadow line one must first be chastened by subjection to frustration and dejection. The striving of the

[4] London: Dent, 1917; New York: Doubleday, 1917; serialized in *The English Review*, September 1916-March 1917.

young Captain in *The Shadow Line,* like that of his young predecessors in "The Secret Sharer" and "Youth," becomes the struggle of youth everywhere and at every time meeting life and finally mastering it.

While the young Captain is being tested in relation to both man and nature, his frustrations occur in many different ways: in the form of the calm sea which reflects the uselessness of a diseased crew, in the discovery of the worthless medicine, in an unreliable second mate and a helpless chief mate, in a physically weakened cook, and above all, in himself, an unsure Captain amidst his first command. The symbols of *The Shadow Line* are the obvious elements of the Captain's dilemma—the sick crew and the "sick sea." Purely human in its terms, this book, like *Typhoon,* contains few if any abstractions. Despite the superstitious chief mate and the superficial elements of a haunted ship, there are solidity and tangibility in nearly every aspect of the story.

The Shadow Line, then, is a return to an earlier and simpler technique, to "Typhoon," "Youth," and "The Secret Sharer" rather than to "Heart of Darkness," which is more suggestive and connotative. The frame of the story, a simple first person narrative by the omniscient author, takes one-quarter of the book, but it subsequently proves of minor importance compared with the ordeal of the young Captain on his command, the *Melita.* What does matter in this short book, as Conrad emphasized in the Author's Note, is the human relationship between the Captain and the crew of the *Melita.* Carl Benson has developed the theory that *The Shadow Line* is a rewriting, as it were, of "The Secret Sharer" in more human terms. In developing this idea, he sees the earlier story as the beginning of initiation and the later book as fruition, as the test of the Captain after a certain competence has already been attained. Ransome, the sick cook, is to the Captain of *The Shadow Line* what Leggatt was to the Captain of "The Secret Sharer," an agent through whom the Captain becomes aware of his own capabilities. Benson argues persuasively that the simple form of *The Shadow Line* is a result of Conrad's emphasis on the humanity of the situation and a conscious de-emphasis of a symbolic framework. In such terms, this short book is typical of Conrad's later work.

Another critic makes the shrewd point that the invasion of the Captain's privacy by the ghost-ridden chief mate is similar in its shock value to the confrontation of Razumov by Haldin in *Under Western Eyes,* though lacking the dramatic portent of this latter meeting. If Haldin does represent the sublimated fears of Razumov, if he is what I have called a psychological double, then Burns also in his way manifests the Captain's fears and serves to stress the latter's insecure side as much as Ransome bolsters his sense of security. Burns is, so to speak, the living remains of the former Captain whose insanity is recognized as a still important force by the present Captain; but, as the latter suspects, his own sanity depends on putting both Burns and his predecessor psychologically behind him. The Captain's insecurity is further externalized in the physical facts of the stagnant sea and crew, even in the cook, Ransome, whose weak heart shows the frailty of his own existence.

Conrad's symbols here are large, obvious, and traditional. Sickness and health are both mental and physical counters, interdependent in their cause and effect and relevant only in their relation to each other.[5] The symbols

[5] The situational importance of stagnancy reappears later very strongly in *The Rescue,* where Lingard's position literally stands still while he pursues the elegant Edith Travers. The loss of movement, the sense of in-

bring together the two relationships central to Conrad's art: man and nature, man and man. In conveying the young Captain's assumption of mastery in fact as well as name, Conrad wrote a "victory," and showed what Heyst was unable to attain. Perhaps it is only on the sea, Conrad seems to be suggesting, that man can gain victory; for while the shore infects all it touches, the sea eventually cleanses and purifies.

The Shadow Line is in many ways the most satisfying book among Conrad's later works; surely it is the least embarrassing, the least flawed by artistic lapses. It is, nevertheless, a minor work, minor in conception and execution. It partakes of the same frame of mind that created "Youth" and "Typhoon," the lesser creations of a major writer, works that can in part be considered only as preludes to greater things.

M. C. Bradbrook astutely called Conrad's ten years of writing from 1914 to 1924 a period of "Recollections in Tranquillity." This title aptly fits a novel that Conrad published in 1919, *The Arrow of Gold*.[6] A single fact per-

---

activity and dullness as it affects the destinies of Conrad's major characters, could be the subject of a separate essay: *vid*. Decoud on the Great Isabel (*Nostromo*), Heyst on the island (*Victory*), Willems left in isolation with Aïssa (*An Outcast*), Almayer rotting in decline while waiting for fortune to come to him (*Almayer's Folly*), Peyrol trying to live out his years (*The Rover*)—for all of them time stops as they remain suspended and motionless. In *The Shadow Line*, the calmness of water and suspension of activity recall "The Ancient Mariner"; Conrad writes: "With her anchor at the bow and clothed in canvas to her very trucks my command seemed to stand as a model ship set on the gleams and shadows of polished marble." Or later: "When I turned my eyes to the ship, I had a morbid vision of her as a floating grave. Who hasn't heard of ships found drifting, haphazard, with their crews all dead?" Of course, the repeated elements of a haunted ship and ghostly crew further strengthen this comparison with Coleridge's ballad.

[6] London: Dent, 1919; New York: Doubleday, 1919; serialized in *Lloyd's Magazine*, no vol. number (December 1918-February 1920). The novel

sistently emerges as one ponders Conrad's later work; in
the failure of adequate conception and lacking new imaginative material, he wrote bulky resumés of all his major
themes—novels that, paradoxically, are his least distinctive while, at the same time, they are among his most
inclusive. As a personal story, one that harks back to Conrad's youthful experiences (see the essay, "The 'Tremolino,'" in *The Mirror of the Sea*), *The Arrow of Gold* contains most of his popular themes: the awakening of youth
to maturity after trials and anguish; the rescue of the
lady in distress; the necessity of courage in the face of adversity; the struggle between responsible heart and selfishness and expediency; even the aesthetic connotations
of an artistic temperament, like Rita's, trying to impose
itself upon the world. The novel has everything except
dramatic intensity, and this one may claim is a technical
failure, a claim that on the surface would seem contradictory to this closely planned novel. However, technique
here is no more than a manner of presentation; it is not
integral, not organic. Certain Conradian touches are evident, especially in matters of juxtaposition and in use of
symbol, but the novel lacks withal the energy and scope
that made many of his earlier works technical and artistic
achievements.

The substance of *The Arrow of Gold* is, as the subtitle
states, a story between two explanatory notes, and this
mechanism replaces the necessity of a Marlow-like narrator. The story will unfold, the first note tells us, from a
sheath of letters written from a man to a woman friend
as related by an omnipresent narrator who fills in any
lacunae in the letters. Conrad was, once again, as in *Lord
Jim, Nostromo, Chance,* and *Under Western Eyes,* pre-

---

was written from August or September 1917 to June 4, 1918 and was
known in MS as *The Laugh.*

senting the "open structure" of the novel. The story is a first-person narrative that follows what Ford called the impressionistic method of time sequences, in which time shifts are of greater import than direct chronology.

The novel is an attempt to reproduce one of the most active periods in Conrad's youth—when he entered into an agreement to smuggle contraband arms to the Carlist forces hoping to regain control of Spain—and yet the story is concerned almost solely not with action but with personal relationships. Despite complications and variations, the plot is the familiar triangle of hero—Monsieur George; heroine—Rita de Lastaola; and villain—Ortega, completed by the repressed older sister—Therese. The use of these conventional characters is an index to Conrad's loss of imaginative creation, even though certain techniques are used to buttress the commonplace relationships, techniques which admittedly add dimensions to the novel.

The title of the book derives from an arrow worn by Rita as a hair pin, a gold arrow with a jeweled shaft. Much can be made of the arrow as a symbol of art: as a symbol of Rita's transformation in the hands of the artist, Henry Allègre, from a peasant girl into a desirable woman of the world; as a symbol, therefore, of the triumph of the artificial and sterile over the natural; and, finally, as a symbol of the attempts of aestheticism to control a world of meanness and jealousy. Conrad's intent, according to this view, was to treat the world of art through a central symbol with extended ramifications. The arrow, however, fulfills a more traditional function—in its direct use as Cupid's dart which pierces George's heart, the arrow symbolizes chivalrous love mixed with sensual overtones. The arrow comes with Rita, is, in fact, Rita, and when George finally seizes it, he gains her as well; through possession of the arrow he successfully fulfills his quest, self-mastery and maturity. The erotic suggestiveness of this relationship is obvious; the arrow is an apparent object of passion, first as a male sexual symbol and then, upon possession, as a female symbol. George, who literally owns the arrow, finally loses it when he realizes his true mission, and, now free from this diversionary feeling, can return to his first love, the sea. Sensual passion and the sea evidently do not mix. But unlike Tannhaüser—unlike Willems and Lingard (*The Rescue*) as well—George is not unmanned by the fires of passion nor exhausted from the effects of his momentary attachment.

The arrow appears in all key scenes, and symbolizes what really occurs in Rita's heart. With her dart she "pierces" all men who come into contact with her, a diverse group composed of the monstrous Ortega; the artist, Allègre, who had married her; the American knave, Blunt; and the sincere and virtuous George. Even Dominic, the taciturn seaman, is sympathetic toward her and identifies to some degree with her. Only her morbid sister, the pathological Therese, is unimpressed. In that long scene of terror in Rita's room, while Ortega paces outside armed with the assorted trophies of a medieval arsenal, and George inside is bewildered, alternately angry and impassioned, the arrow, symbol of Rita's feelings, lies unclaimed on the marble console. Shaking with cold and dumb with terror, Rita is sexually frigid, no doubt the result of Ortega's assault upon her as a child, while the "arrow of gold sparkled like hoar frost in the light of the one candle." Only when Ortega is finally immobilized, only then can George seize the arrow, and with that Rita gives herself to him. The sexual, if not the artistic, connotation of the arrow was never more apparent.

Therese and Ortega, the personifications of abnormality, are persistent intruders upon the happiness of George and Rita, whose affair represents normal love, touched though it is by other complications. The epigraph to the novel—"Celui qui n'a connu que des hommes polis et raisonnables, on ne connaît pas l'homme, on ne le connait qu'à demi"—suggests that irrational and abnormal passions are central to the book. In the Author's Note, Conrad spoke of the "quality of initiation . . . into the life of passion" as the subject of the novel. This emphasis on the passionate and the abnormal appears in many recurring characters and scenes. It has been remarked that the threatening invasion of Therese and Ortega upon Rita parallels the intrusion of Jones and Ricardo upon Heyst in *Victory*. Perhaps Ortega's irrational lust and Therese's unnatural morbidity seem like those dark passions from melodrama; but we must note that lust and morbidity are recurring qualities in nearly all of Conrad's characters, in Almayer, Willems, Donkin, Brown, Kurtz, de Barral, the anarchists, and others. Whereas, though, these characters make dramatic sense, Ortega and Therese seem foolish counters and grotesque oafs in a novel that never comes to terms with the lights and darks of man's psychology.

Conrad, however, tried to find a rougher surface for George's young love in order to make his romantic attitudes appear less sentimental. There is, for example, the Marseilles carnival scene that George enters at the beginning of the novel, a scene of wild irrationality which recurs exactly twelve months later, after the breakup of the *Tremolino*. The bedlam of the later carnival scene contrasts sharply with George's depression—"I slunk on and on, shivering with cold, through the uproarious streets"— the scene, in fact, becomes a way of demonstrating his tempestuous feelings that lie beneath the depression. At the carnival he meets Ortega, whose aberration fits the bedlam of George's physical surroundings—". . . these yells of festivity suggested agonizing fear, rage of murder, ferocity of lust, and the irremediable joylessness of human condition. . . ." This vivid but grotesque scene joins in the same night with that melodramatic episode in Rita's room in the street of the Consuls; the result is an ordeal for George wherein his own passion meets the insanity of Ortega and the whole of Marseilles. When George and Rita do come together on her bed, it is purportedly the meeting of sanity and normality that both celebrate.

The Arrow of Gold, then, is not lacking in technical devices. In certain symbolical objects and scenes, in the doubling, superficial though it is, of character and situation, in the suggestive paralleling of the internal and physical elements of the story, it is representative of many tendencies in Conrad's books. Nevertheless, as a novel, it is among his lesser works. Rita is too unconvincing to sustain the bewitching power of an Aphrodite or an Athena, George is closer to Telemachus than to Ulysses, to whom he is often compared, and Ortega and Therese are caricatures rather than human beings. The potentialities of the carnival scene, for example, are lost amidst that ridiculous encounter in Rita's house wherein Ortega, wielding medieval arms, stalks his helpless victims. The novel, despite Conrad's attempt to probe psychologically, is too physical, too obvious; George and Rita are not subjects for subtlety, and Ortega and Therese are visible frauds. Conrad was evidently willing to settle for mediocrity by forgoing the dramatic intensity which could have been gained only through a more imaginative conception of his material.

The Rescue[7] is always of interest because, as the result of twenty-three years of intermittent work (from 1896 to 1919), it affords an insight into both the early and late Conrad. Geographically, it fits the Malayan and island backgrounds of *An Outcast, Almayer's Folly,* and *Lord Jim,* but thematically and structurally it provides an excellent resumé of Conrad's entire career. It is, incidentally, Conrad's last lengthy novel, for neither *The Rover* nor the unfinished *Suspense* extends beyond three hundred pages. Nevertheless, despite the effort Conrad put into *The Rescue,* despite the fact that it contains everything good and bad in his work, the book is sluggish and only infrequently engages the mind seriously. The heroic Lingard, or "King Tom" and "Rajah Laut" as he is called, has the emotions of a little boy who succeeds in adventure, but he is too weak emotionally and too headstrong in love to sustain nearly five hundred pages of romantic prose which winds and unwinds around his vacillating activities.

A close reading of *The Rescue* will prove fruitful, for more than any other Conrad work after 1914, it shows him in his later decline; its problems seem to be his problems, and its shortcomings his own. Even though many of its methods are similar to those used before, the structure and theme are nevertheless too slight to bear the weight of the grand design. In short, the center is soft, unsure, even meretricious; Lingard's own inability to select a suitable course of action might be a weak objectification of Conrad's own inability to finish this sprawling novel. He admitted in the Author's Note that the conception of the novel was not clear to him:

[7] London: Dent, 1920; New York: Doubleday, 1920. Published first as a serial in *Land and Water* (England), January 30-July 31, 1919; and in *Romance,* November 1919-May 1920.

I saw the action plainly enough. What I had lost for the moment was the sense of the proper formula of expression, the only formula that would suit. This, of course, weakened my confidence in the intrinsic worth and in the possible interest of the story—that is in my invention.

Gordan's close study of the novel in its gestation demonstrates Conrad's troubles, which were considerable even for him. His letters to Garnett at this time are particularly heavy with despair and disbelief, bemoaning his lack of inspiration and his constant physical illness, an illness which was spurred, in part at least, by his mental indecision. He wrote in one letter:

> To be able to think and unable to express is a fine torture. I am undergoing it—without patience. I don't see the end of it. It's very ridiculous and very awful. Now I've got all my people together I don't know what to do with them. The progressive episodes of the story *will* not emerge from the chaos of my sensations. (June 19, 1896)

And two months later Conrad wrote again to Garnett:

> I am paralyzed by doubt and have just sense enough to feel the agony but am powerless to invent a way out of it. . . . I had bad moments with the Outcast but never anything so ghastly, nothing half so hopeless. When I face that fatal stagnation it seems to me that I have forgotten how to think —worse! how to write. (Aug. 5, 1896)

As this despair and stagnation continued, Conrad turned to other stories and novels; he wrote "The Idiots," "Youth," "Heart of Darkness," and began *Lord Jim*. When he finally put aside "The Rescuer," as it was first called, in February, 1899, somewhere near the beginning of part four, less than half of the novel had been completed. He then devoted himself entirely to *Lord Jim* while "The Rescuer" was to lie unfinished in the drawer until 1916.

The effort that went into *The Rescue* promised richer rewards. Conrad seemed to be dredging up from the recesses of his imagination the one book that would become his masterpiece; and his indecision in the face of the novel's problems would seem to be those waverings which result, finally, in a deep expression of the artist's entire personality. But instead of mastering the materials of *The Rescue,* Conrad perhaps allowed the indecision he experienced in writing the novel to carry over into the chief character, Lingard, and this indecision became the center of the book. Lingard, however, is too frail to sustain a cosmic sense of indecision. The problem Conrad originally posed for himself—the choice one must make between honor and passion—is surely incapable of solution in the form he decided to use. Perhaps only a Faust, not a Lingard, could provide the aesthetic satisfaction suitable to this theme.

The beginning of *The Rescue* came hard upon *An Outcast of the Islands,* and for his major character Conrad went back into the earlier life of the Lingard of that novel —as in *An Outcast* itself he had gone back into the earlier lives of Lingard and Almayer of *Almayer's Folly.* The books, in their characters and overlapping situations, form a special kind of trilogy in reverse chronological order. *An Outcast* and *The Rescue* are connected, however, even more conclusively: in each it is passion leading to neglect of duty that "destroys" Lingard. In the first novel, Willems' infatuation with Aïssa leads to his betrayal of the river route to the Arabs, and this cuts deeply into Lingard's trade with the natives; in the second, it is Lingard's own passion for Edith Travers that makes him neglect his duty to Hassim and Immada, a neglect that loses him the honor and integrity he values highly. Stated differently, the theme of the novel is Lingard's loss of manhood in the face of sensual infatuation; Lingard is a Tannhaüser without the latter's hope of a miraculous forgiveness.

The violent storm of *An Outcast* becomes the violent explosion of *The Rescue*, for both the storm and explosion are symbols of an inner failure manifest in physical chaos. When Jörgenson (*The Rescue*) sets off the powder under his protection, he blows up not only himself and the hopes of Hassim and Immada, but the whole world that Lingard had created for himself, a world in which his followers had implicitly believed. Lingard admits his failure to the loyal Jaffir, admits that he was "deaf, dumb, and robbed of all courage [and that there was] no one to know the greatness of his intentions, the bond of fidelity between him and Hassim and Immada, the depth of his affection for those people, the earnestness of his visions, and the unbounded trust that was his reward." Once again, Conrad perhaps had the contemporary world in mind; for the explosion of powder "destroys" a neglectful and complacent Lingard who, like Heyst, is too preoccupied with personal feelings to take action exactly when action is needed for survival.

Conrad, evidently, approached *The Rescue* with the same care that he had taken with *Lord Jim* and *Nostromo*. The language, the setting, the pace of the novel, the awareness of nature are all close to the latter novel. The opening of *The Rescue* sets the tone with a description similar to the one in *Nostromo* of those tacit and omnipresent natural surroundings which engulfed Sulaco:

Out of the level blue of a shallow sea Carimata raises lofty barrenness of grey and yellow tints, the drab eminence of its arid heights. Separated by a narrow strip of water, Suroeton, to the west, shows a curbed and ridged outline resembling the backbone of a stooping giant. . . . To the south and east the double islands watched silently the double ship that seemed fixed amongst them forever, a hopeless captive of the calm, a helpless prisoner of the shallow sea.

But unlike the compelling mystery of nature in *Nostromo,* the sense of mystery in *The Rescue* is lessened by the quite unmysterious Lingard and by purple passages which denigrate the quality of the novel. That Conrad allowed these passages to stand after the numerous revisions the book underwent, is testimony to his loss of critical power. For illustration, I have purposely chosen sentences that occur within the first hundred pages and are therefore the fruits of both early and late revisions.

(1) *". . . you shades of forgotten adventurers who, in leather jerkins and sweating under steel helmets, attacked with long rapiers the palisades of the strange heathen. . . ."*

(2) *". . . the song of the wind would swell louder amongst the waving spars, with a wild and mournful note."*

(3) *"Men saw her [Lingard's brig] battling with a heavy monsoon in the Bay of Bengal, lying becalmed in the Java Sea, or gliding out suddenly from behind a point of land, graceful and silent in the clear moonlight."*

(4) *"The water in it shone like a patch of polished silver."*

(5) *To Lingard his brig was "precious—like old love; always desirable—like a strange woman; always tender like a mother; always faithful—like a favorite daughter of a man's heart."*

These passages, not the worst of Conrad's writing, but by no means impressive, establish a cheap style for *The*

Rescue, and give it a rhythm and pace that make the reader expect little. Despite Conrad's excoriation of Rider Haggard's work, many passages in *The Rescue* read like the worst of that master of pomp and circumstance. Describing Edith Travers, Conrad wrote:

> She didn't move. In the dim gleam of jewelled clasps, the faint sheen of gold embroideries and the shimmer of silks, she was like a figure in a faded painting. Only her neck appeared dazzlingly white in the smoky redness of the light.

When such overwriting is attached to a self-righteous Lingard, the novel cannot be salvaged. At times, Conrad is embarrassing when he writes directly about human feelings, and Lingard is a frequent source of this embarrassment. The latter speaks of his brig as " 'being an English craft and worthy of it, too.' " When Hassim asks why powerful England does not crush weak Holland, Lingard answers that it " 'is not the custom of white men. We could, of course—but it is not the custom.' " Earlier, Lingard had placed himself with the angels, " 'I am a white man inside and out. . . .' " Conrad describes Lingard as "defenseless as a child before the shadowy impulses of his own heart. . . . No doubt he, like most of us, would be uplifted at times by the awakened lyricism of his heart into regions charming, empty, and dangerous." Surrounding the "unfathomable" qualities of Lingard's feelings is the mystery of night and water, all too mysterious for direct expression. Everything is cloaked in obscure tones and in the mystery of murky shadows, masked by the same kind of impenetrability which some find disturbing in "Heart of Darkness"; but that story contains so much to engage us that it hardly can be classed with *The Rescue.* Even the Part headings of the novel are full of pretentious solemnity: "The Shore of Refuge," "The

Point of Honour and the Point of Passion," "The Claim of Life and the Toll of Death." These overblown phrases, taken together with the tired language, the fanciful descriptive passages, and the bumptious and self-righteous Lingard, simply do not coalesce with the air of mystery that Conrad evidently intended. To say the worst, and this novel calls for such frankness, Lingard is too much an open personality, too much a blowsy character, to convey any sense of the depth or the ambiguity that Conrad tried to impart to the novel. The initial description of Lingard is hardly reassuring; a popular hero, a matinee idol, he is a handsome and simple man of nature to whom vagueness or ambiguity is a contradiction in terms. It is embarrassing whenever Lingard—a Malayan Tarzan—flexes his muscles or someone questions his perfection.

D'Alcacer, that gentleman of detachment who accompanies Mr. and Mrs. Travers on their yacht, is a perfect foil for Lingard. Recognizing the niceties of duty and personal relationships, while retaining a refinement of form, he is a minor character who draws interest away from Lingard: ". . . Mr. d'Alcacer was a civilized man and though he had no illusions about civilization he could not but admit the superiority of its methods." Once again, Lingard suffers in the comparison.

If d'Alcacer contrasts with Lingard, many of the other characters complement him. Conrad's procedure in *The Rescue*, as in his previous novels, was to link characters through recurring incidents and points of view or through the counterpointing of individual interests. By introducing the aged failure Jörgenson—a man who must borrow to eat—as a contrast with the robust and complacent Lingard, Conrad, from the early part of the book, created an omen of Lingard's end. " 'He [Jörgenson] resembled you,' " says Belarab the Arab to Lingard. Similarly, in the

seaman Shaw, Conrad presented the bad seaman, one
who like Donkin knows his rights but not his duties.
Shaw's self-love and refusal to coöperate portend, if only
in part, Lingard's own neglect of duty to the natives
while he pursues Edith Travers. Even in chief Belarab,
who sits in his stockade and refuses to enter into conflict,
we see another side of Lingard, his inability to act at the
right time.

Edith Travers, the bored wife of a rich and snobbish
Englishman, is a sort of weak female Axel Heyst. But her
boredom has so completely sterilized her emotions that
she is unable to realize even sexual passion. Her years of
repression have sublimated all her desires for release. The
overtones of a Lawrence novel—Lady Chatterley and
her lower-class gamekeeper—are implied, but Mrs. Travers is unable to work up any of the enthusiasm of Lawrence's sexy heroine. Her skepticism and detachment
complement d'Alcacer's inability to come to terms with
life; each in turn is a direct antithesis of Lingard's intense emotional involvement. Together with Mr. Travers,
they also provide a solid contrast with the natives, Hassim,
Immada, Jaffir, Wasub, all of whom live and die within
the ideal of dedication to duty; ironically, these are the
people with whom Lingard had identified before meeting
Mrs. Travers.

By trying to become part of what he is constitutionally
and psychologically unable to attain to, Lingard destroys himself and those who believe in him. The social
overtones are obvious, and Conrad's complacency would
seem clear. Conrad, however, is not claiming that Lingard was destroyed solely because of his desire to climb
the social ladder, but, rather, that an awareness of one's
position is the first and most necessary step in self-fulfill-
ment. In Lord Jim, for example, Jim meets destruction

because he tried to make reality out of the stuff of his dreams, and in *The Rescue* Lingard loses his reputation, though not his life, because he moves from the world where he is a professional to the world where he is an amateur. Worse yet, he tries to do so without realizing the gap. With his intelligence blunted by passion, he lacks the self-knowledge that might have possibly spared him from disaster. With this type of awareness, however, Lingard would have been another figure, perhaps a Stein, who could straddle all forms of activity and excel in each. The epigraph from Chaucer's "The Frankeleyn's Tale" is truly remarkable irony: "Allas!" quod she [Dorigen], "that ever this sholde happe!/ For wende I never, by possibilitee,/ That swich a monstre or merveille mighte be!" The unforeseeable happens to both Dorigen and Lingard, but while Conrad wanted high tragedy, Chaucer settled for chivalry.

The Rescue is Conrad's last attempt to say everything: a summation of his life's work and a hodge-podge of his major techniques and themes centering on the fortunes of the failing crusader, Lingard. By design, Lingard, like Decoud, Heyst, Renouard, and Razumov, is only part of a complete man. By creating Lingard divided and incomplete, Conrad recognized that wholeness is particularly difficult of attainment in our or any age; but he stressed, here and elsewhere, that it can be achieved under the demanding terms of physical and mental initiation to life, during which time the "victim" must realize, through self-knowledge, the various ways he can go wrong. Conrad admitted in a letter to J. B. Pinker that the entire tragedy of the book "must depend on the romantic presentation of man's feelings," and it is this presentation, failing as it does in effective language and in an effective chief character, that I have found lacking. Conrad, in the same letter to his literary agent, remarked that the novel "is not fit for juvenile readers, not because it raises any sort of problem but on account of the depth and complexity of the feelings involved in the action. . . ." Conrad was right when he stressed the depth of feelings that he intended to convey; but he was artistically insecure when he tried to disguise through diversionary techniques the frailty of Lingard and his ineffectiveness as a serious character. Conrad had to choose between a hero and a man, and he chose a hero.

Perhaps *The Rescue* should be read only as a document which presents for comparison Conrad's early and late styles and shows his frame of mind a few years before his death.

III

The essays collected in *Notes on Life and Letters*[8] along with those in the posthumous *Last Essays*[9] had been published separately by Conrad beginning in 1905. These essays, taken together with his remarks in *A Personal Record* (1912) and in his personal letters, constitute most of Conrad's literary criticism. Several of the essays from *Notes on Life and Letters* concerning James, de Maupassant, Daudet, France, Turgenev, Marryat, and the three others on Stephen Crane have found their way into my earlier chapters. Many of the later essays, especially those in *Last Essays*, are full of reflections about the sea, touching on the same ideas that Conrad dramatized in his novels and stories. They add factual information to what we already know about the author, but aside from their biographical value they are also of interest for the per-

8 London: Dent, 1921; New York: Doubleday, 1921.
9 New York: Doubleday, 1926, with an introduction by Richard Curle.

sonal feelings that Conrad divulges. The essays show that
he approached the sea with the same awareness that he
brought to art; and that for him, as I have remarked before, all life, whether from the point of view of the sailor
or the writer, was to be treated as art.

Conrad had early recognized the stage possibilities of
his own work and dramatized three of them personally;
the stories, "Tomorrow" [10] and "Because of the Dollars," [11]
and the novel, *The Secret Agent*.[12] "One Day More"
(based on "Tomorrow") is a guileless piece of ironic writing that no doubt was effective on the stage. "Laughing
Anne" (based on "Because of the Dollars") is no better
than the story and need not detain us.

The Secret Agent in its stage version (written in early
1920) shows Conrad's emphasis on the "thriller" aspects
of the novel. In the play, Winnie is strong and sure of herself from the first, and her initial appearance prepares the
spectator for her later self-assertion. Also, the exigencies
of a simple setting make the store more important than in
the novel; all but Act II takes place there. Other points of
difference: Ossipon, the revolutionary, declares himself
to Winnie early, not late, in the play and she immediately
rebuffs him; the cab ride of the novel, its very center-
piece, is eliminated in favor of emphasis on the "detective" qualities of the story and on the evidence that ties

[10] "Tomorrow" was dramatized under the title "One Day More: A Play
in One Act," and published in *The English Review*, XV (August 1913).
It was performed in Paris and London, in the latter place by the Stage
Society on June 25, 1905.

[11] "Because of the Dollars" was dramatized in 1920 under the title of
"Laughing Anne," which is the original name of the story. This play, as
well as "Tomorrow," was published by J. Castle, London, 1924, with an
introduction by John Galsworthy.

[12] *The Secret Agent. Drama in Four Acts*, published in London by T.
Werner, Laurie, Ltd., 1923. The play was performed on November 2,
1922, but was soon withdrawn.

Verloc to the crime; and, finally, the dramatic implications of the novel frequently are lost in the retelling of
important action. As a technical piece of work, the play is
straightforward and realistic, losing both the drive and
range of the novel. Conrad evidently found it impossible
to suggest on the stage that murkiness and grubbiness of
London life which mark the original. Losing the personal
thrust of the novel, the play is obviously reduced in
power.

In *The Rover*,[18] his last completed novel, Conrad returned to the form of the Flaubertian novel that he had
used in *Almayer's Folly* and *An Outcast of the Islands*.
The Rover, a major result of Conrad's continued interest
in the Napoleonic era, has been rightly criticized for its
slightness. Conrad half acknowledged its lack of weight,
and asserted that his next novel, *Suspense*, would be more
serious. That novel, however, is less worthy than *The
Rover*, which is, withal, competent although slim and self-
evident. Conrad called it a "seaman's 'return'" and the
epigraph from Spenser—"Sleep after toyle, port after
stormie seas,/ Ease after warre, death after life, does
greatly please"—became Conrad's own epitaph on his
gravestone at Canterbury. Old, tired, his battles over,
Peyrol, like Prospero-Conrad, is a man who has always
depended on his wits, and who becomes inevitably a symbol of the artist, independent and self-sufficient, now
waiting to die.

Except for a short section of conventional counterpointing two-thirds through the novel, the narrative of

---

[18] New York: Doubleday, 1923. According to Jean-Aubry, the novel was
published on July 28, 1922—obviously an error, since *The Rover* was
only completed in June. In a letter to F. N. Doubleday in 1923, Conrad
said the day was approaching for the publication of *The Rover* and
named January 2, 1924, as the English publication date. This novel, like
so many others of Conrad's, was begun as a short story.

Peyrol's retirement is direct. By the time of *The Rover,* Conrad was no longer trying to understand and depict the world through style. He was now sure of his methods, putting down almost directly the memories of what he knew and understood. Although his early exploratory technique was a way of comprehending his material, a way of ordering and informing his experience, now his experience had set and he was not concerned with radical form. The tried and traditional methods of story-telling were, in his old age, sufficient. Conrad admitted as much in a remarkably candid paragraph to Edward Garnett; he wrote (Dec. 4, 1923, Yale U. Libr.):

> Yes, my dear, I know you will believe me when I tell you that I have a momentary vision of quite a great figure worthy of Peyrol; the notion of a struggle between the two men [Scevola, the pathological revolutionary, and Peyrol]. But I did deliberately shut my eyes to it. It would have required another canvas. No use talking about it. How long would I have had to wait for that moment?—and the mood of the other was there, more in accord with my temperament, more also with my secret desire to achieve a feat of artistic brevity, once at least, before I died. And on those grounds I believe you will forgive me for having rejected probably a greater thing—or perhaps only a different one.

Conrad fully recognized that he had simplified the story and knew that what he called "another canvas" meant a lengthier book, one that he was at the moment unable to project.

Matters of form aside, *The Rover* can engage us, though perhaps only momentarily, with the characters of Peyrol and Scevola. Taking the lesser figure first, one can see Scevola as a logical descendant of those ragged anarchists and revolutionaries in *The Secret Agent* and *Under West-*

ern Eyes. Once again, Conrad was unable to take the revolutionary world seriously; once again, the humanity of the book commands more attention than the political activity. As a child, literally one, of the French Revolution, Scevola's thirst for blood-letting is surely more psycho-pathological than politically expedient. His political activity, like the Professor's in *The Secret Agent,* is only a sham excuse for a deeply-rooted mental disturbance. Grotesque rather than formidable, he is, as Conrad said, a failure because he requires explaining.

In the figure of Peyrol, more than in anyone else, we can see the waning of Conrad's creative powers. While Peyrol is admirable as a person, his creation by Conrad is, nevertheless, a retrogression rather than an advance. He tells us nothing new, nothing that was not already apparent in the creation of MacWhirr, Lingard, and Whalley, in all of whom personal honor and integrity are a moral philosophy. Peyrol is a simplification, a return by Conrad to the past with no further discernment to show for his additional years. The repeated emphasis on exhaustion and on the sailor who has come home to die seems a summary of those former Conradian "heroes" who have bored us with their virtue. Peyrol is, then, among the least interesting of Conrad's creations, certainly among the least exciting intellectually. His mixture of honor, inscrutability, and lassitude mirrors many aspects of the aged Conrad himself, who, in this novel, shows no new sides and conveys no new insights. Conrad seems to have exhausted his resources in characterization; retreating now to figures like Peyrol and Lingard, who are true to their instincts, he has returned to a simple view of life, an admission, in a way, that his imagination is no longer master of his verbal facility.

In this as in his other novels, Conrad seemed compelled to bring together all loose ends. For seventeen pages after Peyrol's death—a death that successfully ends the forward thrust of the novel—we are led, respectively, through Captain Vincent's tribute to Peyrol's patriotism in Vincent's interview with Nelson, the burial of Peyrol in the cuddy of his tartane, the coming together of Lieutenant Real and the much-abused Arlette, their subsequent marriage and frequent discussions of Peyrol's virtues. Their speech praising Peyrol, coming long after the reader has ceased to care, echoes nature's final sentimental tribute:

> . . . and the mulberry tree, the only big tree on the head of the peninsula, standing like a sentinel at the gate of the yard, sighed faintly in a shudder of all its leaves, as if regretting the Brother of the Coast, the man of dark deeds, but of large heart, who often at noonday would lie down to sleep under its shade.

Suspense,[14] according to Ford Madox Ford, was originally intended as a collaboration on the Napoleonic era, a novel which Conrad subsequently wrote alone and left unfinished at his death on August 3, 1924. Begun in 1920, after the publication of *The Rescue* and before *The Rover* was written, *Suspense* gave Conrad much anxiety. He expected a masterpiece once the novel was well along— "I am going now to grapple [he wrote to F. N. Doubleday] with the novel in which those critics that found *The Rover* somewhat slight work will find size and weight enough, I can promise them." A few days earlier he had written along the same lines to Eric Pinker: ". . . *The*

---

[14] New York: Doubleday, 1925, with an introduction by Richard Curle.

Rover must have appeared to some people rather slight. Well, they will find weight and body enough in what's coming. I can safely promise that."

It is quite possible that Conrad's large plan for *Suspense* was a conscious effort to write a vast "war and peace," with Tolstoy's masterpiece perhaps directly in mind. Writing about *Suspense* as early as 1907, Conrad said: "All I want now is to discover the moral pivot—and the thing will be done." He expected to mix intrigue, adventure, history, and morality—a grand design, indeed. Cosmo Latham, the Pierre of *Suspense,* is another of Conrad's youthful initiates to life, but his shallowness of character almost immediately betrays the frivolous nature of the novel. Opening with Napoleon on Elba and the European world in suspense about his next move, the novel suggests a background of peace and a foreground of suspicion and intrigue between wars. Conrad's ground plan, however, was too slight and too inconsequential to allow projection; his ambition was far in excess of his ability and energy at this time. His original design may have been to rival Tolstoy's work, but his superficial working conception resulted in what is perhaps his worst novel. Even the possibility of revision, had the novel been finished, would seem to promise little.

The novel contains an almost straightforward narrative that opens *in medias res* with Cosmo in Genoa. From there, a short flashback presents Cosmo's background in England; by page 43, the action is back in Italy and continues directly to the end of the manuscript. Conrad's formal work was rarely simpler. The dominant themes of the book as they emerge are disillusion, intrigue, corruption, and deception. The characters are a predatory group caught in a world suspended between war and peace in which human values are lost among the expediencies of daily existence. No doubt Conrad had the post World War I scene in mind, but the novel itself reveals little, and whatever ideas were intended never become clear.

Of the four stories collected in the posthumous volume, *Tales of Hearsay*,[15] none except "The Tale" need engage us, and that only for a moment. The stories are minor; the two on Polish themes—"Prince Roman" and "The Warrior's Soul"—are of concern only to the Conrad biographer. "The Tale," however, is of some interest, not as a technical achievement, but as a representation of Conrad's personal philosophy. Duty had forced the narrator of the tale into a decision that he finds morally reprehensible; he had to decide whether or not to send to destruction what he suspected was a contraband cargo ship, perhaps destroying an innocent captain and an innocent crew. In the righteousness of his war feeling, he condemned the ship to the rocks, while recognizing that he would never know the justice or injustice of his act. All he realizes is that the exigencies of immediate action often call for a point of view morally repugnant in times of reflection and peace. The last words of the narrator are, "I shall never know," perhaps the final words for Conrad himself. For in his best work, it is the spirit of "not knowing" and yet acting as if full knowledge were attainable that marks Conrad as an artist.

[15] London: T. Fisher Unwin, Ltd., 1925, with a preface by R. B. Cunninghame Graham. "The Warrior's Soul," written in the early part of 1916; "Prince Roman," *The Metropolitan*, January 1912, under the title of "The Aristocrat," also in the *Oxford and Cambridge Review*, January 1912, under the title of "Prince Roman"; "The Tale," written in the early part of 1916; "The Black Mate," *London Mail*, April 1908. This latter was Conrad's first story, written for a prize competition in *Tit-Bits* in 1886. The version we have here is probably not the original version, of which there is no extant copy.

Despite the slightness of his work in the last ten years of his life, Conrad, in "Heart of Darkness," *Lord Jim, Nostromo, Under Western Eyes,* and *Victory,* perhaps along with *The Secret Agent,* "The Secret Sharer," and *Chance,* added new force to the English novel, a pursuit that he had devoted his life to realize. Through his five or six major works, he stands with Joyce, Lawrence, Mann, Gide, Proust, Kafka, and Faulkner as one of the significant creative novelists of the twentieth century, a writer who brought to the English novel a devotion, intensity, and willingness to experiment that have not since been duplicated.

Bibliography

I. The Writings of Joseph Conrad

Complete Works. 26 vols. Kent Edition. Including, with Ford Madox Ford, *Romance* and *The Inheritors.* New York: Doubleday, 1925.

Conrad to a friend: 150 selected letters from Joseph Conrad to Richard Curle, edited with an introduction and notes by Richard Curle. New York: Crosby Gaige, 1928.

Conrad's Prefaces to his work. With an introductory essay by Edward Garnett. London: Dent, 1937.

Five Letters by Joseph Conrad to Edward Noble in 1895. London: Privately Printed, 1925.

Joseph Conrad's diary of his journey up the valley of the Congo in 1890. Introduction by Richard Curle. London: Privately Printed, 1926.

Joseph Conrad's Letters to his Wife. London: Privately Printed, 1927.

Last Essays. Introduction by Richard Curle. Garden City: Doubleday, 1926.

Laughing Anne and *One Day More.* Introduction by John Galsworthy. London: J. Castle, 1924.

Letters from Joseph Conrad, 1895-1924. Edited with introduction and notes by Edward Garnett. Indianapolis: Bobbs-Merrill, 1928.

Letters of Joseph Conrad to Marguerite Poradowska, 1890-1920. Translated, edited with introduction, notes, and appendix by John A. Gee and Paul J. Sturm. New Haven: Yale University Press, 1940.

Letters to William Blackwood and David S. Meldrum, edited by William Blackburn. Durham, N.C.: Duke University Press, 1958.

Lettres françaises. With introduction and notes by G. Jean-Aubry. Gallimard: Editions de la nouvelle revue française, 1929.

The Nature of a Crime. With Ford Madox Ford. New York: Doubleday, 1924.

The Secret Agent. Drama in Four Acts. London: T. W. Laurie, 1923.

The Sisters. Introduction by Ford Madox Ford. New York: Crosby Gaige, 1928.

II. Books, Essays, and Articles on Conrad

(An asterisk indicates an important work)

Allen, Jerry. *The Sea Years of Joseph Conrad.* New York: Doubleday, 1965.

———. *The Thunder and the Sunshine.* New York: Putnam's, 1958.

*Baines, Jocelyn. *Joseph Conrad.* New York: McGraw-Hill, 1960.

Bradbrook, M. C. *Joseph Conrad: Poland's English Genius.* Cambridge, England: Cambridge University Press, 1941.

Conrad, Jessie [Mrs. Joseph]. *Joseph Conrad and His Circle.* New York: Dutton, 1935.

———. *Joseph Conrad: As I Knew Him.* Garden City: Doubleday, 1926.

Conrad Supplement. *Transatlantic Review,* II, No. 3 (August 1924), 454-465, 570-582, 689-700.

Crankshaw, Edward. *Joseph Conrad: Some Aspects of the Art of the Novel.* London: John Lane, 1936.

Curle, Richard. *Joseph Conrad: A Study.* London: Kegan, Paul, Trench, Trübner, 1914.

Fleishman, Avrom. *Conrad's Politics: Community and Anarchy in the Fiction of Joseph Conrad.* Baltimore: Johns Hopkins Press, 1967.

Ford, Ford Madox. *Joseph Conrad: A Personal Remembrance.* Boston: Little, Brown, 1924.

Gillon, Adam. *The Eternal Solitary: A Study of Joseph Conrad.* New York: Bookman Associates, 1960.

*Gordan, John Dozier. *Joseph Conrad: The Making of a Novelist.* Cambridge, Mass.: Harvard University Press, 1941.

*Guerard, Albert. *Conrad the Novelist.* Cambridge, Mass.: Harvard University Press, 1958.

————. *Joseph Conrad.* New York: New Directions, 1947.

Hay, Eloise Knapp. *The Political Novels of Joseph Conrad.* Chicago: University of Chicago Press, 1963.

Hewitt, Douglas. *Conrad: A Reassessment.* Cambridge, Eng.: Bowes & Bowes, 1952.

Howe, Irving. "Joseph Conrad: The Political Novels," *Kenyon Review,* XV, No. 4 (Autumn 1953), 505-521; XVI, No. 1 (Winter 1954), 1-19. [Reprinted in *Politics and the Novel.*]

*Jean-Aubry, G. *Joseph Conrad: Life and Letters,* 2 vols. Garden City: Doubleday, 1927.

————. *The Sea Dreamer: A Definitive Biography of Joseph Conrad,* trans. by Helen Sebba. New York: Doubleday, 1957. [Translation of *Vie de Conrad,* 1947.]

Leavis, F. R. *The Great Tradition.* London: Chatto and Windus, 1948.

Lohf, Kenneth A. and Sheehy, Eugene P. *Joseph Conrad at Mid-Century, Editions and Studies, 1895-1955.* Minneapolis: University of Minnesota Press, 1957.

The London Magazine, edited by John Lehmann, IV, No. 11 (November 1957), 21-49 (essays on Conrad).

Mégroz, R. L. *Conrad's Mind and Method: A Study of Personality in Art.* London: Faber and Faber, 1931.

*Meyer, Bernard. *Joseph Conrad: A Psychoanalytic Biography.* Princeton: Princeton University Press, 1967.

Modern Fiction Studies, I, No. 1 (February 1955); also X (Spring 1964).

Morf, Gustav. *The Polish Heritage of Joseph Conrad.* London: Sampson, Low, Marston, 1930.

Moser, Thomas. *Joseph Conrad: Achievement and Decline.* Cambridge, Mass.: Harvard University Press, 1957.

Mudrick, Marvin, ed. *Conrad: A Collection of Critical Essays.* Englewood Cliffs, N.J.: Prentice-Hall, 1966.

*Najder, Zdzisław. *Conrad's Polish Background: Letters to and from Polish Friends.* London: Oxford University Press, 1964.

Sherry, Norman. *Conrad's Eastern World.* Cambridge, Eng.: Cambridge University Press, 1966.

Stallman, R. W. *The Art of Joseph Conrad: A Critical Symposium.* East Lansing, Mich.: Michigan State University Press, 1960.

Warren, Robert Penn. Introduction. *Nostromo.* New York: Modern Library, 1951. [Reprinted from *Sewanee Review,* LIX (Summer 1951), 363-391.]

Wiley, Paul L. *Conrad's Measure of Man.* Madison: University of Wisconsin Press, 1954.

Wright, Walter F. *Romance and Tragedy in Joseph Conrad.* Lincoln: University of Nebraska Press, 1949.

Zabel, Morton Dauwen. "Conrad: The Secret Sharer," *New Republic,* CIV, No. 16 (April 21, 1941), 567-574.

———. "Joseph Conrad: Chance and Recognition," *Sewanee Review,* LIII, No. 1 (Winter 1945), 1-22.

Index